Memory and Hope

Interreligious Reflections

Series Editor: Alon Goshen-Gottstein, director, Elijah Interfaith Institute

With the rise of interfaith relations comes the challenge of providing theory and deeper understanding for these relations and the trials that religions face together in an increasingly globalized world. Interreligious Reflections addresses these challenges by offering collaborative volumes that reflect cycles of work undertaken in dialogue between scholars of different religions. The series is dedicated to the academic and theological work of The Elijah Interfaith Institute, a multinational organization dedicated to fostering peace between the world's diverse faith communities through interfaith dialogue, education, research, and dissemination. In carrying out Elijah's principles, these volumes extend beyond the Abrahamic paradigm to include the dharmic traditions. As such, they promise to be a source of continuing inspiration and interest for religious leaders, academics, and community-oriented study groups that seek to deepen their interfaith engagement. All volumes in this series are edited by Elijah's director, Dr. Alon Goshen-Gottstein.

Titles in the Series

The Religious Other: Hostility, Hospitality, and the Hope of Human Flourishing, edited by Alon Goshen-Gottstein

The Crisis of the Holy: Challenges and Transformations in World Religions, edited by Alon Goshen-Gottstein

Friendship across Religions: Theological Perspectives on Interreligious Friendship, edited by Alon Goshen-Gottstein

Memory and Hope: Forgiveness, Healing, and Interfaith Relations, edited by Alon Goshen-Gottstein

Memory and Hope

*Forgiveness, Healing, and
Interfaith Relations*

Edited by
Alon Goshen-Gottstein

WIPF & STOCK · Eugene, Oregon

Foreword

Alon Goshen-Gottstein

Each of the volumes of Interreligious Reflection either tackles a challenge that is common to different religious traditions or that provides theory for on-the-ground relationships between leaders and members of different religious communities. As scholars and world religious leaders, we find ourselves reflecting on those core issues that are the make or break of meaningful interfaith relations. As participants in our meetings testify, this allows us an engagement that is personal, profound, self-critical, and transformative. And as others will testify, working in this theoretical domain in the way we do, is one of the unique aspects of Elijah Interfaith Institute, serving the unique gathering of world religious leaders. The present project tackles the challenge of how memory impacts our interfaith relations. Briefly stated, no matter what efforts we make in cultivating positive relations today, the memories of the past continue to inform our present day relationships. If we are to look to the future together, we must find ways of revisiting, understanding and healing past painful relationships between religious communities. In this project, scholars of six traditions explore what strategies their religion offers for purifying or transforming negative and painful memories, reducing the violence they can generate and setting horizons of hope before all religions. If memory defines our past, hope frames our future. All our traditions must therefore walk the path from memory to hope.

Memory and Hope was the theme of the sixth meeting of the Elijah Board of World Religious Leaders that took place at St. Ottilien Abbey, near Munich, in 2014 and we all maintain a debt of gratitude to the Benedictine community that offered us not only classical Benedictine hospitality at its best but also shared a deep understanding for the theological and practical challenges that were the focus of our meeting. Holding the meeting in Germany was particularly poignant in terms of the challenges of healing memory. The meeting included visits to Dachau and encounters with Carmelite sisters who have devoted their lives to grappling with and healing painful memories through the power of prayer. Elijah's website features reports of this meeting and captures some of the moments lived by the religious leaders.

Thanks are due to all authors of papers, as well as to those who have helped think the process through, without contributing an essay. These include Vanessa Sasson, Awet Andemicael, and Kurt Schreiber. Peta Jones Pellach is a pillar of our organization and has helped the process move forward with grace and acumen. She played a vital role not only in the development of the project but also in the editing of the present publication. Sarah Craig and Carissa Marcelle have seen this book through the process of publication with patience and the highest professional standards. A final word of thanks to the co-chairs, members of the steering committee, and the entire Elijah Board of World Religious Leaders. It is only because they have been our initial audience, that we are able to share our work with broader audiences through Interreligious Reflections.

Chapter One

Memory and Hope

Overview of Papers and Project Synthesis

Alon Goshen-Gottstein

MEMORY AND HOPE—AN INITIAL PROJECT OVERVIEW

Memory occupies an important part in the religious life, because it is an important aspect of our individual and collective selves. In some way, talking about memory is talking about what one considers most important in one's tradition. For religions to share their view of memory and how it operates in their religious lives is a means of sharing fundamental views of the religious life and key strategies and approaches to the spiritual life. This is an important conversation and one that suggests mature sharing between practitioners and seekers of diverse religions.

There is a further dimension to memory. Memory is an asset, in that it recalls what is most important in our spiritual life, but in some contexts it is also a burden, or a problem, or a challenge one must contend with, precisely as one seeks to advance towards the goals of a religious tradition. Our religious traditions are complex entities. They include the highest spiritual and moral teachings; they are also the reservoirs of the memories and imprints of the entire range of human realities that religions, as social realities, have manifested in their histories. This includes, among other things, the history of tension between competing religious groups, the imprint of trauma inflicted in the name of religion and the recollection of the various ways in which religion and violence have been related to one another throughout human religious history.

The present project focuses on memory with awareness of the dual dimensions of memory, but what drives it is the recognition that problematic memory must be confronted in the framework of interreligious engagement.

As heirs to traditions, we receive not only their finest spiritual teachings, but also the residue of resentment, hatred, and negative view of the other, born of the religious hostility of yesteryear. This hostility still festers and to some degree or another, consciously or subconsciously, at surface level or at a deeper and more hidden level, impacts the views of one religious group towards the other. We have witnessed enormous advances in interreligious relations over the past decades. Yet our traditions continue to bear witness to painful memories, at times kept alive by present-day hostility, and these must be dealt with, as we seek to advance relations between different religious communities. Not dealing with memories means we keep something poisonous in our system. Unchecked and untreated, it will either come to the fore at a later point in time or will impact other members of our faith community. Our painful and negative memories, born of situations of religious violence, require treatment, if we are to continue advancing along the path of interreligious friendship and harmony.

John Paul II has coined the term purification of memory. This term suggests that our memories need to be revisited and purified, so that their negative impact is removed. While this notion has broader application, it is particularly relevant to interreligious relations. Recognizing this need, our think tank has attempted to grapple with the problem of difficult memories in the framework of interreligious relations. The problem obviously looks different from the perspective of each religion. The specific memories that are carried, the particular wounds that have been inflicted by a religious other, will vary from one tradition and its particular history to another. But more fundamentally, each tradition configures memory differently. The sources of authority are different, the challenges are different, and the tools that each tradition makes available for dealing with our problem are accordingly different as well. Recognizing a common need and common ground in dealing with these questions, we also recognize there is great diversity and complementarity in how we go about approaching our difficult memories. We need to acknowledge this diversity for two reasons. The first is because we need to consider what is required or possible for each tradition, as a way of gaining better understanding of one another. The second is that we may be able to share strategies, drawing from each other's wisdom, despite differences in how our traditions are configured.

It may be that the two aspects of memory noted above are both relevant to healing or purifying memory. It may be that in order to purify historical memory each tradition must turn to the highest form of memory it recognizes, the memory of its highest values, as a way of balancing and reorienting perspectives that are informed by the vicissitudes and vagaries of politics, history, and social realities. Most of our papers have suggested points of contact between these two dimensions of memory, though the exploration of the former dimension of memory has not been systematically undertaken in all papers. Strategies for purification of memory may be put forward even without appeal to what a tradition considers its highest memorial values.

In an important way this project is about sharing memory, following on the heels of earlier projects that focused on sharing wisdom and sharing friendship. By "sharing memory" I refer to the two senses above—sharing what memory is for each tradition and what obstacles to good interreligious relations memory presents. But there is a third sense as well. As several of our papers suggest, an important strategy for clearing through past and present tension is the sharing of memory itself, or simply put—dialogue. We are in the business of dialogue and we seek to provide theory for how the broader project of interfaith dialogue might advance in meaningful ways. The suggestion of several of our authors is that dialogue should include a dialogue over actual conflicting memories. This comes up in Rambachan's paper, as well as those of Sendor, Keshgegian, and von Brüeck, and is implicit in the presentations of Umar and Gill. Religious communities will always understand their actions in light of what they consider to be noble principles. And yet, where there is religious violence, different communities may view the same events or circumstances in conflicting ways. Sharing each other's perceptions of the same events or realities is itself a process of dialogue. The present project showcases moments of pain in inter-group relations. These moments of pain invite a sharing as part of their healing and as a strategy for addressing memory and the havoc it may continue to wreak in our lives.

Sharing memory itself raises an important issue—the status of truth in relation to memory. Does sharing memory open the way to a truthful retrieval of memory or is the importance of such sharing in making room for pain and trauma, without necessarily revising our view of memories and their truthfulness? This is a question to which we will have to pay attention on a case-by-case basis. It seems that our authors are not of one mind on this issue and the difference may be less a matter of principle than a function of the different situations that each one of them addresses. One thing is certain—sharing involves trust. Sincere dialogue involves trust. And sharing in trust can itself create positive dynamics that offset the negative impact of destructive memories.

Considering the question of truth leads to some fundamental discussions that relate to memory and truth. Several of our authors make us realize that it is wrong to think of memory as something fixed, given, static, that is simply passed on from generation to generation. There is no objective memory, and as one of our authors suggests, it may be better to speak of remembering as an active process, rather than of memory as something fixed and given. If so, past and present mingle in rich and complicated ways. The past is seen and appreciated in terms of the present and its needs. One of the primary needs that memory serves is identity construction. Indeed, memory conflicts often revolve around identitarian needs and sharing memory is therefore a strategy for affirming and legitimating the other in his or her particular identity.

What we remember involves some selection and what is selected and how it is remembered are in accordance with the perspective of the present. This is as much a part of the problem as it is a part of the solution. If we grant that it is impossible to simply speak of memory with full objectivity, this opens up for us the possibility of bringing the present to bear on memory. The various strategies offered in our papers may be seen as ways of doing so. Not least of these is the affirmation of dialogue and sharing of memory as a way of revisiting memory and offering it a new, present-based context. While this does not mean that we can never speak of truthful memory or seek to recapture some events or some historical moments as they were, it does call upon us to be considerate in our quest for truth. Not only may it not always be possible; in a certain sense it may not even be the most important thing we are after.

One of the upshots of this recognition of the fluidity of memory, its malleability in the history of a tradition, is that we may not need to limit reference to memory to past events, relying on their historical accuracy. If memory is important for the dynamic of remembering and for the impact this has on our lives, and if remembering can be subject to dynamic processes of revisiting in a movement of healing and transformation, we might be able to consider a broader range of phenomena as being remembered. What is the status of remembering imaginary realities, that is: realities that exist only by virtue of faith, but with no clear historical correspondent? Our discussion of Buddhism below will make the case that this is also to be included within the range of memory and its operations. Or consider the future. Moving on the axis of time from past to future, what does it mean to remember a future? If there is a promise, a hope, an eschatological expectation, how does it reframe our understanding of the present? In theory, eschatological expectation might heighten interreligious tension, as it affirms the supremacy of one tradition over another. But situating the present in light of the future can also open up resources that help revisit tensions of the present in view of a more harmonious future that is remembered in the present.

All this leads us to hope. Our project has two foci—memory and hope. Truth be told, when announcing the focus on hope we had not anticipated how closely related it could be to the challenges of memory in interreligious relations. As we at Elijah are working on the creation of an interreligious center called the Center of HOPE (acronym for House of Prayer and Education), we thought it would be useful to introduce the theme of hope into our discussions as an introduction to a contemporary project. It turns out that hope and memory are much more closely related. To begin, we note that our project takes us along the axis of past-present-future. If the past is represented by memory, the future is represented by hope. Between the two is the present, comprising forces which balance, compete, and conflict.

Hope has emerged as relevant to our concerns in other ways. If our goal is to liberate memory, to heal and purify it, we are in fact seeking to remove obstacles that exist along the path of interreligious relations. Every such liberation, every such opening, brings hope to situations that seemed to be hopeless. Hope is affirmed in our ability to move beyond trauma, past pain, beyond conflict. Hope is affirmed in the very recognition that our memories are not fixed, but always open to interpretation, to restatement, to new perspectives. Hope is not simply the passive waiting for circumstances to change from the outside, but the hard won efforts of bringing about transformation in our traditions and overcoming those places where they seem to be locked, beyond hope, into negative views of the other. Ultimately, hope is the fulfillment and realization of the higher goals of our tradition. If our collective memory brings to us the higher ideals of our tradition and the pained memories of our tradition's interactions with others, hope lies in fulfilling the higher ideals of our tradition in the very arena that had been given to conflict and disharmony previously. Our higher ideals inspire us and give us hope that they may be realized even in the domain of conflicted memory.

Following this synthesis of what our project is about, I would like to offer a summary of each of the papers, representing six faith traditions. The composite picture above draws from all six papers and describes the project in its entirety, on a theoretical level. None of our papers covers all the aspects described above. All of them explore memory and the challenges of viewing memory in situations of conflict, in most cases—religious conflict. Some ground this in the higher memory that their tradition calls for; some leave the point implicit. Some ground it explicitly in a view of hope; others are implicit on the point. Some focus on the very problematic nature of memory itself; others seek to retrieve truth. In presenting the papers, I shall group them according to two key questions that enable clustering the papers around subthemes. The first theme is the fluidity and malleability of memory—this subject is treated explicitly in the papers by Meir Sendor and Florea Keshgegian. A second cluster explores how a tradition's higher spiritual memory can serve as a resource for revisiting painful and conflicting memories. Here we note the contributions by Anantanand Rambachan and Rahuldeep Singh Gill. It is already noteworthy that the Jewish and Christian contributions approach memory from a theoretical and critical perspective that calls into question its stability, while the Hindu and Sikh contributions approach memory with an eye to concerns of metaphysics and spirituality. This may say something about the traditions, and not only about the authors' preferences. Judaism and Christianity are strongly historical traditions, and therefore revisiting the very nature of memory in a critical way is a means of moving beyond the dead end of pained memories. Hinduism is much less historical in its consciousness (though the same may not hold true for its younger offshoot). Concerns of spirituality are prominent for both traditions. The papers by Muhamad Suheyl Umar and Michael von Brüeck and Maria Reis-Habito occupy a middle ground. Umar combines a vision of memory and spirituality with an attempt to tackle problems of truthful memory. Because his paper assumes retrieval of truthful memory is possible, at least under the circumstances described in his paper, he can integrate concerns of spirituality with a view of addressing memory in one corrective move. Von Brüeck too considers the higher functioning of memory, but does so in a theoretical framework that is aware of the fluidity of memory. Here, a theory of memory combines with a spiritual view of memory (Buddhist), that itself stretches memory beyond the range of conventional discussion. Moving then between the complementary foci of theoretical discussions and spiritual resources, I shall now offer summaries of the papers in the order just presented. After presenting the individual papers, I will not attempt to draw together insights from the papers suggesting common recognitions. The summary above already suggests a good measure of accord, while highlighting some fundamental differences as well. Rather, at the end of this collection I shall offer a common case study, that brings to bear assumptions and strategies that have been learned from the various traditions.

MEIR SENDOR'S THE MALLEABILITY OF COLLECTIVE MEMORY IN JEWISH TRADITION

The title of Meir Sendor's article focuses our attention on the essential contribution of his paper. "The Malleability of Collective Memory in Jewish Tradition" takes for granted that memory is not fixed, nor is it factual in a fundamental positivist sense. Memory is malleable and is transformed in light of the present. If this is true for all memory, this is particularly so for collective memory, the subject of Sendor's presentation, focusing on how Jewish collective memory addresses painful memories and its own view, from the victim's side, of a history of oppression. Reference to "Jewish tradition" also suggests dynamism and the possibility of interpretation, as these take place within tradition. Reference to tradition implicitly points to the present as a link in the chain of tradition and to our task to craft memory in light of the present and its concerns and needs.

Sendor frames his discussion with reference to memory and interreligious hostility. Victimhood can fuel hostility. There is a need to advance interreligious relations. Perhaps more significantly, there is an internal need (which can be justified psychologically or even religiously) to be freed of attitudes of fixation on victimhood and the ensuing attitudes of resentment and exclusion. To attain these ends, Sendor walks us through theoretical discussions of memory and how these shed light on Jewish practices of remembering, which in turn can serve as contemporary resources. Given the centrality of memory in Jewish consciousness, and especially memory of suffering and victimhood ritualized in prayer and key festivals, how does one go about developing a theory of memory that does not keep a Jewish mentality fixed in a mental space of victimhood and isolation?

Sendor's work relies on several theoreticians of memory. The first part of his presentation is a discussion of how collective memory works and the challenges and dynamics of transforming collective memory. Sendor relies on the work of Maurice Halbwachs who teaches us that all memory is a social act. "The past is not preserved but is reconstructed on the basis of the present." This axis of past and present forms the backbone of Sendor's presentation and lays the foundation for his constructive suggestions. The process of remembering is intrinsically related to the process of forgetting. Something is remembered, while something else is forgotten. Memory tells a story and the act of telling the story requires a selection, in light of criteria drawn from contemporary needs, concerns, and values. The problem with constructing memory is that it can come at the expense of truthful remembering. Truthful remembering is needed for countering propaganda, but also for liberation from some of the negative consequences of fixation on negative memory, such as obsession and the desire for revenge.

Truthful remembering is itself a strategy, flagged here by Sendor, though not fully developed by him. He will return to it in his consideration of Israeli-Palestinian relations. This strategy also serves as the basis for Suheyl Umar's presentation in the present collection. Sendor focuses his efforts more on dynamics of balancing memory and of balancing remembering and forgetting. Adjustment of religious collective memory involves authority, as it typically requires addressing the authority of scripture or tradition, that have carried forth memory up to the present. As Halbwachs suggests, authority must balance authority and therefore alternative religious authority from within tradition must be found in order to temper the negative impact of painful memories. Complementing Halbwachs's discussion of transforming negative memory are theoretical discussions by Paul Ricoeur and others that teach us that remembering also involves forgetting and that therefore the "art of memory" is in some ways also the art of forgetting. The selectivity involved in constructing memory therefore of necessity also involves us in forgetting. Balancing memory within tradition and balancing remembering and forgetting are the two major strategies offered by Sendor. Whereas the former features multiple voices from the past, balanced in view of the present, the latter features the very juxtaposition of past and present and the attempt to endow the present with existential and spiritual weight equal to the burden of the past.

The first strategy is that of balancing memory. If memory is selective, we have the possibility of revisiting it with a view to establishing a new equilibrium, based on balancing alternative voices of tradition within our view of memory and its present command. The archetypal subjugation in Egypt is a case in point. Scripture, festivals, and liturgy all impress upon us the memory of our subjugation in Egypt and ensuing liberation. However, the Torah's view of the Egyptians is not exclusively as oppressors, but also as those who gave hospitality to Israel in the first place. Moving along the axis of time, Sendor notes that authoritative voices from later tradition can also temper unequivocal negative collective memories. Thus, Amalek, Israel's biblical arch-enemy whose evil deeds we are commanded to remember, can be redeemed in some way, as we note in later tradition. The rabbis teach us that the grandchildren of Haman, of Amalekite descent, became converts and Torah scholars. Later authorities draw distinctions between individuals and the collective, and above all—mystical resources affirming the power of love offer a vision that ultimately neutralizes the negativity of Amalek, urging those who can rise to such heights to engage in the work of its spiritual upliftment, seen in the light of Divine love. Memory is transmuted, through authoritative practices of interpretation and the application of halachic and spiritual criteria that neutralize the negative view of the other or its practical consequences. Sendor refers to such mechanisms, following Halbwachs, as alternative memories that balance out that original negative memory. Perhaps it is better to term them "recollections." These are in fact not competing memories of different historical moments or of complementary dimensions of the same moment, as in the case of slavery in Egypt, but the recollection of spiritual and legal principles that have their own authority and validation and that balance out the testimony of memory, carried through in history. If so, Sendor's work opens us up to the possibility of memory operating in multiple dimensions. It operates in history—and this is the focus of his presentation. But it also operates in the spiritual domain, bringing to light essential principles that shape memory in the present. (For such applications of memory, see Sendor's note no. 1, as well as the concluding discussion of the Rabbi of Gur.) One might therefore consider some of the instances brought by Sendor as balancing memory of past with an alternative memory of past as further evidence for his second thesis of balancing past with present, when under present we consider the higher spiritual reality and not simply the testimony of the historical present moment.

Before moving on to detailing this strategy further, one notes an important move in Sendor's presentation, that appeals to the eschatological dimension, the future. Part of the shift in how the past is viewed comes from the possibility of reading the past in light of the future. Biblical prophecies that downplay the memory of the past in light of what might be called a future memory allow us to contextualize and relativize the burden of past memory.

In this way hope addresses memory. However, the significance of eschatological memory is only inasmuch as it is lived in the present, which brings us back to Sendor's core strategy—confronting past memory with the present moment.

This strategy has in fact already been applied by some of the sources brought by Sendor, where Amalekites are judged by their present individual status, rather than by their collective affiliation, rooted in the past. The strategy is applied in individual relationships, where the prohibition of taking revenge is in fact an instruction to live in the present and forget the past. Such forgetting is understood by Maimonides as necessary for the well-being of society. Thus, the present and its needs mandate some forms of forgetting. Sendor develops this notion into a broader theory of the present. The idea is applied beyond the context of individual relations within the collective of Israel to inter-group relations, itself a significant move. He grounds it further in the example of Joseph, who deals with his brothers based on where they are "this day." The present view is closely related to processes of repentance. Honest repentance allows one to live in the framework of the present, leading to forgiving. While forgiving may not be forgetting, it does provide the foundation for balancing present and past in a way that creates new balances also between remembering and forgetting. What is active and uppermost in our minds is the present, informed by repentance and redefined relations.

Sendor does not go as far as suggesting that the present and its social needs require letting go, in the name of a better future. Nor does he suggest that there are higher spiritual states that, when made present in our awareness, allow us to transcend all negativity engendered by painful memory. Such a view might arise from the wisdom of other traditions, as we shall shortly see. His view of the present balances the commanding force of memory with the power of transformation and redefining memory in light of the present, as this is mediated through movements of repentance and reconciliation. Repentance allows us to transform the painful memory of the past into a more harmonious present.

Sendor has offered us models for neutralizing what might be termed the tyranny of painful memory. Memory can be liberated because memory is malleable. His exercise allows us to take stock and then to apply those factors that have the power to transform memory and to which we might look as we seek to bring about such transformation. The factors are contained within tradition and its mechanisms, both in how the past is remembered and in how past is related to the present, in the life of the individual, and by extension in relations between collectives.

These foundations allow Sendor to explore how his understanding of memory might be applied to contemporary situations. He first looks at German-Israeli relations, post-holocaust. Normalization of relations is understood as consonant with the positive moderating role of the present and with the rabbinic principles of not over-generalizing past trauma and avoiding collective accusation. It is based on repentance and transformation of behavior, even if it does not assume forgiveness. Rather, normalization creates the space to acknowledge trauma and to work towards reconciliation.

The relationship of past and present is more complicated in relation to the Israeli-Palestinian conflict, where roles of victim and perpetrator are not as well defined. The conflict is still ongoing, and therefore the tensions of present and past do not apply in the same way. There is a further significant complication here. Memory is a means of constructing identity. As Sendor teaches us, the Israeli-Palestinian or Israeli-Arab conflict is not only about land or political rights; it is a struggle for identity. The stakes in memory relate directly to identity construction and recognition. Given the particularities of this situation, Sendor opts for another strategy, alluded to above—seeking truthful memory. This requires making room for one another's narrative, rather than agreeing upon a joint narrative. Recognition that collective memory is never fixed provides the foundation for willingness to make room, and to a certain extent incorporate, the narrative of the other. However, Sendor notes asymmetry in the process, with most of the work along these lines having taken place on the Israeli side. Therefore, he proposes an alternative source of hope—common rituals of reconciliation. There may be enough common ground on other fronts to allow us to move forward by appeal to those rituals. Still, one wonders whether the application of such rituals can fully ignore the need to revisit memory on both sides. Put differently, Sendor considers the Israeli-Arab conflict essentially a political conflict and not a religious one. This is why he holds hope that religion can provide resources for reconcilliation.

Sendor hasn't taken us this far, but we might offer the following insight in light of his work. Sendor lets us know how central memory is in the construction of identity, as witnessed in Jewish ritual and prayer. He also makes us aware of how the battle over memory between Israelis and Palestinians is, in fact, a battle over identity. Perhaps his strategy for shifting balances between past and present finds its greatest relevance precisely in the domain of identity. While appealing to memory is constitutive of identity, it is not the only means of establishing identity. Simply put, one may affirm the other's identity simply because the other is, or the other requires one to recognize him or her in that particular identity. If so, shifting the emphasis from past to present strikes at the nexus of memory and violence precisely because it has the potential to liberate identity from its dependence on memory. Making room for the other in the deepest sense of affirming identity need not require buying into the other's story or memory. If in the case of Israeli-German relations, processes of reconcilliation informed a present that provided a different context for viewing the past, in the case of Israeli-Palestinian relations, processes of peace-making might allow us to focus on the present and, in a different way, to make the memory of the past less relevant.

Let me conclude this summary of Sendor's work by posing the question of where is hope found. We have already noted the eschatological dimension of hope, that reframes memory in light of the future. But it seems to me Sendor is making a more fundamental argument for hope. Hope lies in the liberation of memory. Hope lies in the capacity to reframe and revisit not only memory but our mechanisms of human behavior. Hope lies in our capacity to change. Hope lies in gestures, rituals, and processes of transformation, repentance, and reconciliation. Above all, hope lies in our recognition that we are never locked up in the memory of the past and the roles it casts us in. Rather, the past is always subject to the interpretation of the present and it is the present that opens up new possibilities. Whether we understand the present in mystical terms, in terms of improved human relations, or in terms of reformed human behavior—the present is different than the past. This present, understood in the fullness of its religious significance, is the source of our hope.

FLORA KESHGEGIAN'S MEMORY AND HOPE IN CHRISTIANITY

Flora Keshgegian's "Memory and Hope in Christianity" shares many of the assumptions of Sendor's paper, but she approaches the subject from a different methodological and ideological perspective. Her paper shares the assumption that memory is never fixed but something subject to transitions. This is why Keshgegian prefers to speak of "remembering," rather than memory. Her analogy is to photographs. "Memory" assumes a photograph that is passed on in safety from one generation to the next. "Remembering" refers to a faded photograph, whose meaning is kept alive through the active process of remembering. Remembering is therefore active. Memory is always constituted in the present. Instability and change are fundamental to the process of remembering.

That remembering is an active process means there is no neutral or objective remembering. What is remembered is intrinsically related to the dynamics of the remembering community, and these in turn open up to political dimensions and perspectives of power. Remembering is, ultimately, a political action. Keshgegian offers a very helpful illustration for the changing dynamics of remembering and the significance of locating the perspective from which something is appreciated or remembered. A statue of the virgin Mary in New Mexico carries simultaneously the Spanish title "the Conqueror" and the English title "Our Lady of Peace." The dual titles, clearly not translations of one another, present interesting challenges of how and what is remembered and who does the remembering. The dynamic nature of remembering, overlays, interpretation, and shifting perspectives, all characterize and problematize the process of remembering and the content of memory. This corresponds, in a popular context, to the dynamics that Sendor describes in rabbinic interpretation.

Remembering provides Keshgegian with the opportunity to tell—to re-member—the entire Christian story, from the very vantage point of memory and its relationship to shifting power dynamics. I note that this retelling takes on special meaning in the context of an interfaith conversation. It not only offers members of other faith traditions a condensed view of Christian history. That history is described in relation to some of the core concerns that have impacted Christianity's relations with other religions, as these center on issues of power and its application, often involving abuse of power and inflicting of suffering to others.

Remembering the Christian story allows Keshgegian to revisit core tensions that touch upon Christianity's positioning between Hebrew and Hellenic thought. The dynamic, narrative quality of Hebrew thought gives way to metaphysical thought, typical of Greek philosophy. How does this alter the content of memory? Memory largely gave way to the deposit of truth, the correct formulation of an eternal metaphysical reality. In the process, little remained of the historical Jesus, save for those points of contact with his person, required for the new metaphysical statement of truth.

Related to this new emphasis on what is remembered is also the question of who it is that does the remembering. Recognition that for most of its history the Church has been associated with empire is crucial to a recognition that the Church's memory is largely that of the conqueror, the colonialist, the one who has power and who applies that power at the expense of others. In the process, other voices have been written out of history. This includes voices of forms of Christianity that did not conform to a "proper" theological or metaphysical view, as well as voices of various religious traditions that were taken over by conquering Christianity. Thus, Christian memory dominates the memory of others. Forms of Christianity that are dismissed as folk religion, or expressions of Christianity that relate to local cultures, should be re-owned as Christian remembering extends beyond the boundaries and control of power and authority structures. Recognizing power dynamics in the shaping of memory is an invitation to bring back to the theological table voices of the oppressed or powerless that may have previously not been given adequate hearing.

The work of purifying and retrieving memory is very particular in the case of Christianity. Keshgegian brings to our project the awareness that in considering dynamics of memory and their transitions, we cannot divorce these from issues of power and empowerment. Accordingly, the problem of dealing with painful memories will look very different from the side of the powerful or the disempowered, the conqueror and the conquered, and ultimately—from the side of the victim or the perpetrator. These dynamics must be owned if we are to consider memory a meaningful category and if we seek to apply it to inter-group relations. It is not simply that we must clear obstacles to contemporary relations that are posed by the accumulations of difficult memories. Rather, we must incorporate in our remembering an awareness of power considerations that allow both sides to acknowledge how power has been used. This reminder is especially necessary for Christianity which for most of its history has been associated with power. Keshgegian does not hesitate to refer to the painful and bloody history of Christianity and to bring into the conversation the Crusades, the Inquisition, and other aspects of Christian history that should be owned, especially in the framework of an interreligious conversation. Highlighting the relations of memory and power brings to our discussions an important dimension that invites all authors to take stock of how perspectives on memory in their tradition are impacted by considerations of power relations.

The dual themes of memory and hope come together in the second part of Keshgegian's paper. Keshgegian invites us to consider what trauma is. For Christians, the archetypal trauma is the crucifixion. But the structure of her argument suggests that Christians too have inflicted trauma on others. How can trauma be incorporated within the framework of memory? The problem is that trauma takes us beyond the realm of a narrative we can make sense of. There is something inherently disruptive in trauma that cannot be accounted for in terms of meaning, logic, and reasoning. Considering the fundamental Christian trauma, Keshgegian argues for the problematic attempt to simply make sense of the crucifixion in terms of a theory of sin and redemption. This scheme, all too often practiced in the history of Christianity and all too current in many forms of contemporary Christianity, domesticates the cross, and ultimately leads to a personalized and individualized form of salvation that is at great remove from the original collective vision of Christian redemption. Moreover, it obscures fundamental aspects of the life of Jesus and of his story—the incarnation, his mission and even the resurrection. These are often eclipsed by an exclusive focus on what is in and of itself beyond sense. Furthermore, this emphasis contributes to a view of reconciliation and forgiveness that often does injustice to the victim. Making sense of the trauma of the crucifixion has been coupled with an emphasis on sin. This emphasis ignores the difference between victim and perpetrator. All senseless and traumatic suffering has been seen through the dynamic of sin and forgiveness, creating unjustified pressure on the victim to offer forgiveness. One might add to Keshgegian's presentation that also in interreligious situations, seeing the victimization of others as a consequence of sin can often provide a facile way out of deep acknowledgment of the pain inflicted on others.

Keshgegian offers an alternative approach. In part, it is an approach that, drawing on prior work of Metz and Moltmann, does not see Jesus on the cross as suffering *for* us, but rather as suffering *with* us. But in order to fully appreciate the dimension of suffering in the non-sensical situation of trauma, suffering and sin must be decoupled. Christians must find alternative ways of approaching suffering and trauma than through the paradigm of sin and forgiveness. Only thus can the difference between victim and perpetrator—taking us back to the earlier considerations of power relations—be respected.

Keshgegian points to ritual as the domain that will allow us to address painful memory, traumatic memory. But the rituals she recommends are not the conventional rituals of forgiveness, that place the burden on the victim. New rituals need to be developed. The practice of lament, an ancient biblical practice, is suggested as one possibility. Lament allows to name suffering, to cry out in anguish, even to express anger, without being forced into forgiveness. At the same time, the perpetrator, especially the institutional perpetrator, has to deeply own the violence committed. Mourning and acknowledgment lead to a process. They allow the pain and trauma to be held. Such holding opens up to the power of life and moving on. Herein lies hope. Hope is not the ultimate historical vindication described by the theologians she discusses. Rather, for Keshgegian hope consists in the capacity to resume life despite trauma. Going on with life (one assumes with a measure of meaning, even if meaning has not been given to the trauma itself) is Keshgegian's definition of hope.

For Christianity this would be a humbling definition. It undercuts the kind of triumphalism associated with the cross and captured in formulae of truth that make Christianity more true, and more power-full than other religions. Instead, Christianity is viewed in light of its formative trauma, and it is a sign of hope (only) inasmuch as it has shown the ability to keep on going with life, despite the trauma it has endured. This view of Christianity forces it to humbly acknowledge the suffering and trauma it has wrought through its use of power. But, I may add, it might also provide a new witness to Christian reality, in that it points to a deeper spiritual power that allows it to function despite its own trauma. Properly understood, this trauma, rather than being a source of inflicting trauma upon others, is a witness to the depth of spiritual life that allows one to continue despite traumas that have been endured. It is a testimony of faith, humble faith. Christianity may not be unique in this respect, especially given that others have suffered traumas. Though, if one may speculate based upon Keshgegian's foundations, it may be the only religion founded upon trauma, or for which trauma plays such a central role in its fundamental story, in what it remembers. If so, Christianity, understood in this light, has a story to share, a memory that, precisely because of the particularity of later Christian history and its relation to other religions, can also offer a teaching or a testimony to others.

ANANTANAND RAMBACHAN'S "HOPE IS GREATER THAN MEMORY"

Anant Rambachan begins his presentation of memory in Hinduism by introducing the broader context within which memory functions. Memory has a crucial role in Hinduism and many of its key practices hinge on memory. This includes recitation of scripture, personal piety revolving around chanting of a personalized mantra, a constant memorial of Divine presence, the celebration of festivals and more. The outward expressions of practices of memory should be understood in light of the deeper meaning of memory and how it orients life in general and the spiritual life in particular.

Rambachan suggests that various practices of memorialization and especially five daily memorial obligations are centered around one core principal—recognizing our indebtedness to others and cultivating gratitude and generosity to share with others. This is true for the memory of the teacher and the fact that we have been recipients of wisdom as well as for attitudes in the family and for how the individual is positioned in relation to society and nature. Awareness of being receivers is the foundation for giving to others.

Memory also provides the deep logic for the spiritual quest itself. Memory of the Self and the lost truth of its unity with the Divine is the purpose of spiritual practice and the key to spiritual liberation. In this sense, then, the entire spiritual life, ranging from practices to the ultimate purpose of the spiritual life, may be presented in terms of memory.

If indeed the spiritual life is read through the prism of memory, this suggests that memory is also at the heart of the battle for spiritual evolution. Whereas for other traditions featured in our collection it was group memory of the enemy or of painful historical moments that had to be overcome for the sake of peace, reconciliation, and group relations. In the case of Hinduism, discourse begins with the individual and memory relates to subtle examinations of how the individual is metaphysically positioned. Memory lies at the root of one of the most fundamental spiritual challenges—going beyond likes and dislikes and the negative attitudes, such as possessiveness, anger, or jealousy, that they generate. Memory of things we like and dislike is at the source of loss of identity. The quest for ultimate identity, the identity of the Self and its union with the Divine, informs the spiritual life as presented here.

If historical memory, in the case of other religions, was related to group identity, in the case of Hinduism, personal memory, viewed along the axis of attachment and liberation, is foundational to recovery of true and ultimate identity. It is worth pausing for a moment on this contrast. Let us compare this view with the reality brought about by Jewish memory-management, as described by Sendor, and shared by Singh Gill and other authors in our project. For Rambachan, instilled attitudes based on collective memories become fuel for our prejudice, stereotyping, and demonizing of others. These get in the way of our true spiritual identity, which affirms unity of all. That these memories are spiritually unwanted is proven by the negative qualities they engender. Contrast this with the alternative view of identity, where memory of past injury sustains identity and generates hostile attitudes to others. With Rambachan's shift in what constitutes identity, we also focus on alternative spiritual goals, leading to a consideration of harmful attitudes engendered by group memory. This perspective provides a serious critique for the alternative view. It challenges it to account for why particular identity is important, what attitudes it can or should sustain and what are the moral yardsticks by which it is maintained. The history of interpretation that Sendor shares with us suggests that these are issues that traditions struggle with from within, leading to transformed understanding. Nevertheless, an interreligious conversation allows us to highlight these questions, possibly pushing us to recover higher meanings and applications of memory within a tradition.

Returning to Rambachan, memory requires purification. Wisdom is the means of purification. Wisdom involves true cognition of reality. It provides a framework that allows us to loosen the grip of memory upon us, and in some cases even to liberate ourselves from it completely. The core of wisdom is recognition of a unitive view of life, affirming our unity with the Divine and the ultimate unity of all. If one can see all as one, and see the Self in all, the negative qualities that are the outcome of negative memories are overcome. If one recognizes ignorance as the root cause of all problems, rather than malice and intentionality, then a compassionate and understanding view ensues, that helps us rise above the attitudes born of ignorance and attachment.

This world-view is grounded in a view of the individual in relation to God. However, it also provides the foundations for a view of society and for solving social issues. To begin, unity of existence is fundamental to this worldview. This can be readily translated to the social dimension. Rambachan makes the conscious effort of extending the teachings of the tradition concerning the individual to the realm of inter-group relations. The same factors that govern personal relations—the attitude generated will be mirrored back, the need for practice of compassion and a variety of other lessons that grow from this spiritual view, are relevant also to how one relates to larger social units. Consequently, dealing with painful memories in intergroup relations should also proceed in light of wisdom principles provided by the tradition, as suggested at the end of his presentation.

Moving from the individual to the collective domain is necessitated by an examination of the kinds of memories that form attitudes that require purification and liberation. Negative attitudes do not come to us simply as a consequence of our own doing. They are often inherited, transmitted across generations, part of our collective self. Recognition of the unity of life allows Rambachan to identify patterns of connectedness even where the tradition does not emphasize such patterns. Accordingly, Rambachan is able to relate to larger units than the individual, units that transmit attitudes, that carry memories and that struggle under the burden of such memories. It is important to recognize that this application is an important constructive step that Rambachan is taking in the context of the present group exercise. Rambachan applies the foundations of a unitive view of life, coupled with an extension of personal dynamics to larger group dynamics—across groups and across generations—to unpack the broader social implications of the religious worldview he expounds. We, the readers, are viewing a certain brand of Hindu theology in the making, as it seeks to address contemporary social challenges, within Hinduism (especially with reference to social problems related to the caste system) and potentially in the relationship between various groups beyond Hinduism. One of the expressions, in the social realm, of spiritual attainment, associated with recollection of true wisdom and going beyond limiting memories is the attitude to others. This is expressed in compassion. It also manifests in an attitude of benevolence and, more broadly speaking, in a disposition to reconciliation, which takes us again to the realm of group relations.

As observers, we might say this is all a sign of hope. Extending the tradition creatively to address novel challenges is a sign of hope. Moreover, the very message of the religious vision offered by Rambachan is one of hope—hope of liberation, of going beyond the negative imprint of harmful memories, of increasing wisdom, of growing reconciliation, and social harmony. But before putting these to the test, Rambachan himself offers us one more important factor by means of which hope is made possible. Rambachan tackles a common view of Hindu tradition as locked into a passivity with reference to social action and transformation, on account of the doctrine of *karma*. Rambachan offers us an analysis of this doctrine, and suggests that the common passive sense is only one of its meanings. Another sense highlights the importance of constructive action and its capacity to bring about transformation. Such transformation pertains also to the realm of overcoming the imprint of memories and of advancing group relations constructively. One might say that the application of the traditional insights to the social realm actually require a theory of dynamic and positive transformation, which Rambachan identifies in the theory of karma.

With all these elements in place, we can now turn to the final part of his paper, where Rambachan devotes extensive attention to inter-group relations and to how conflicts over memory are a dividing point between different religious groups. This conflict is related to the deep and ongoing social problem of the caste system and touch upon contemporary India's most burning interreligious problem—the problem of conversion. Hindus and Christians have radically different views of conversion. For Christians, it is liberation from caste oppression. For Hindus, it is a form of religious violence, whose violent fruits can barely be contained. The views on the issue are completely polarized. Rambachan suggests dialogue as the way forward. Dialogue is memory shared. Rambachan offers us a strategy that seeks to implement the spiritual insights of the tradition, spelled out above, into a social program that can bring about healing in social relations. Dialogue is the method.

Dialogue revolves around listening, and listening involves the sharing of memory. Dialogue also challenges us to apply the wisdom of our tradition to the situation. Thus, we must see ourselves in the other and practice dialogue in that light. Dialogue must be informed by compassion and its purpose is ultimately similar to that of the spiritual life itself—going beyond painful memories to the higher spiritual vision of unity. Awareness of unity thus provides, from the Hindu perspective, the metaphysical ground for dialogue.

But dialogue also involves the quest for truthful memory and here Rambachan echoes concerns that appear in the papers by Umar and Sendor. Sharing must be done in a search for truthful memory, even if one recognizes that one may not reach an agreed upon memory. Nevertheless, the process of sharing requires trust and through trust a shared humanity is discovered. Thus, truthful memory is the goal that may never be reached, but one that opens us up to sharing memory, which in turn allows us to recover the highest of truths, our deeper unity, our common humanity.

RAHULDEEP SINGH GILL'S MEMORY AS BENEVOLENCE: TOWARD A SIKH ETHICS OF LIBERATION

Rahuldeep Singh Gill's essay offers what may be considered an integrated theory of memory, that provides a means of transcending the inbuilt limitations of memory, thereby holding the key to transformation and purification of memory. For Gill, memory operates on two planes or in two dimensions. This dual function of memory addresses two complementary dimensions of the religious life. One dimension concerns the memory of the community and its history. Memory has a role in constructing identity and it is particularly painful memory, the memory of martyrdom and persecutions, that helps a group solidify its memory. This is as true of Sikhs in their homeland of India as it is of Sikhs in the Diaspora. In fact, the memory of persecution and martyrdom functions for Sikhs in the Diaspora as a means of establishing deeper ties to the Sikh tradition as such. A second dimension of memory touches upon the recollection of fundamental truths of spiritual reality. Two aspects are noted here. The first is the memory of death, which conditions our awareness of life. The second is our memory of God, which is the focus of spiritual intention and of practice. The practice of *simran* focuses one's awareness in God's presence, and holding God's name in one's mind (*nam simran*) is a means for attuning the person into God's presence.

The two dimensions of memory come together in a constitutive prayer, recited on various occasions, called the *Ardas*. The Ardas begins with a recollection of the various historical identitarian dimensions of memory. After a long recitation it makes an interesting transition to a completely different aspect of memory, that shifts the focus of the praying community from its history to God Himself. The human act of remembering joins up with Divine remembering, understood as caring. God's caring for His creation is a constant form of remembering. Ultimately, in remembering God, we are called to join our own power of memory with that of the Divine, transforming our attention from our community and its history to God and His provision for all of humanity and all of creation. This shift in awareness is ultimately founded upon the human capacity to unite or to find its common ground or foundation in the Divine. By turning to God, one assumes Divine qualities. Therefore, by recollecting God, one takes on God's capacity of memory. Praying to God in the framework of memory ultimately involves a transcending of human or communal memory and an entry into the all-caring, beneficent Divine memory.

The two aspects of memory point to two dimensions of our identity—a more limited particularistic view and a broader universal view. The two must be integrated and harmonized. The means for their harmonization is ultimately God Himself, who chooses a community for a purpose. The purpose of the Sikh community is understood through service, where it becomes an instrument for Divine caring.

The same structure may be considered not only in terms of caring but also in terms of justice. One form of caring is to seek justice. Seeking justice may be thought of as a means of legitimating or affirming a particular history. But seen from the higher Divine perspective, seeking justice is a form of caring for all, for the perpetrator as well as for the victim. Justice is a concrete expression of caring.

The Sikh attitude of caring, made manifest through recollection of the Divine, is a training and conditioning of hearts and attitudes. It is the source and strength of Sikh practice as this has come into expression in repeated situations of violence and persecution throughout history. Stretching from responses to the execution of the fifth guru, Arjan, to contemporary Sikh responses to the shooting of Sikhs at the Wisconsin Gurudwara, Sikhs have shown themselves able to rise above instinctive responses, by successfully applying the ethos of service and caring at the very moment that might have otherwise occasioned the violent response grounded in concerns for identity and self.

And yet, Sikhs too are human and one cannot present all Sikhs as successfully implementing this complex transformative approach to memory and its transmutation. This is noted in particular with reference to the charged events of 1984, where the Sikh holy sites were stormed and where thousands lost their lives. It is clear that much work needs to be done to attune popular Sikh reaction to these traumatic events to the high ideals that the Sikh tradition offers. This is educational work, but it is also work that requires establishing a view of Sikh tradition in a broader framework.

Throughout the essay, Gill lets us know how deeply implicated Sikh tradition is with an interfaith perspective. We know that the gurus and the Sikh Scripture itself are open in unique ways to the spiritual testimony of different traditions and spiritual sources. The ideals of the Sikh tradition are themselves best lived in an interfaith awareness. Caring for others can be practiced through the engagement with others and practical collaboration in service with members of other traditions. More fundamentally, it is by gaining a broader perspective, through interfaith engagement, that we can find the appropriate balance between our particularistic identity and the broader universal vision and mission that it is called to serve. But at the same time, Gill also makes us aware that not all Sikhs share this perspective, even if it is correct that there are fundamental ways in which the Sikh tradition is interreligious. Those Sikhs who find no value in appreciating their tradition within and through a broader spiritual context are also those who have the hardest time channeling their pain beyond the negativity engendered by painful memories. Put differently, interfaith engagement is itself a means of self-transformation and a way of helping Sikhs balance out complementary, and at times competing, aspects of their spiritual tradition. Perhaps one could add that it is often in the framework of interfaith engagement that one is invited to take up the higher aspects of one's tradition, where remaining exclusively within one's own tradition might cause one to lose sight of those aspects. Thus, if memory by rote is contrasted, as does Gill, with memory of the heart, interfaith engagement could ultimately be conducive to cultivating memory of the heart.

Gill suggests a method for transforming painful memory. Service is ultimately a means of purifying memory. Going beyond the memory of one's wounds and persecution is made possible by service. This method is more than catharsis or channeling one's negative emotions to a good end. It relies on a broader view of service as grounded in Divine caring, and on the sharing of memory that brings humans and the Divine into alignment. Therefore, in service we rise above all that is limited in our particularity, including our pain, and review the source of our pain from the perspective of the Divine. Service, then, is the ultimate form of *simran*, remembrance of the Divine.

Herein lies hope as well. What keeps hope out of our horizons is the narrow perspective that we see through when we see only our own limited reality, nourished as it is by the pains inflicted by others. Hope is liberation. As Gill demonstrates, memory of God is a means of liberation. Carrying this core insight of Guru Nanak further, Gill suggests that not only the memory of God, but sharing in how God remembers us is also a means of hope and breaking past the confines of narrow memory. When our horizons open, in caring, in service, in the quest for justice, to God's own view of reality, and as we are united to God and attuned to His being through higher spiritual memory, we are liberated from the pains of the past, and find hope in the one eternal reality and in its caring expressions towards humanity.

MUHAMMAD SUHEYL UMAR'S MEMORY, HOPE, AND SYSTEMS OF REPAIR IN ISLAM

Muhammad Suheyl Umar's paper "Memory, Hope, and Systems of Repair in Islam," tackles the problems of memory and hope by reversing the order of discussion. Rather than laying the emphasis on theory and seeking to illustrate it with a case study, Umar examines in depth two case studies, and reflects on the principles that inform these case studies. For purposes of this summary, I shall reverse the emphasis and highlight the more theoretical dimensions of Umar's paper. The problem tackled by Umar is the problem of corrupted memory. Memory occupies a high position in the framework of transmission of Islamic knowledge. Mechanisms of transmission suppose accuracy and truthfulness, as religious tradition is handed down. Nevertheless, tradition itself is aware of how it can become corrupted in the process of transmission. Theoretical high regard for memory is contrasted with how memory interacts with history, with politics, and with the corrupting effect of a reception history that introduces change into what should be a stable and reliable body of knowledge. The recognition that informed Sendor and Keshgegian's theoretical presentations is presented here in terms of the reality of Muslim memory-keeping.

Changed memory can be the source of religiously motivated violence. Facing the challenge of altered memory, Umar suggests there is a way of retrieving lost memory. Such retrieval can function as a means for reducing religious violence. While Sendor, Keshgegian and, as we shall see, von Brüeck would likely consider that retrieving an original memory may no longer be possible, with regard to Umar's case studies there is ample evidence of a long-standing tradition that was altered at a given point in time (in one case, fairly recently). Recalling historical truth, despite contemporary political pressures, enables the retrieval of lost memory, leading to significant attitudinal changes between members of diverse religious communities.

The quest for correct memory is itself a religious quest. It is founded upon a spiritual vision and an eschatological perspective, wherein truth will ultimately reign, and that truth includes how we shall be judged for our own truthful practice. Retrieval of corrupted memory involves two stages. On the technical or outward level, it requires mastery of tradition and a constructive dialogue with it, in which forgotten sources are brought to light and a process of interpretation or reinterpretation takes place. This is the process of *ijtihad*. However, in order to apply such principles, there must be spiritual motivation. It is only when higher spiritual memory encounters concrete historical memory that such motivation is fully present. Higher memory is memory of God Himself, leading to reintegration of the soul in the Divine, with peace as its fruit. It is only by attaining such inner peace that one can revisit the various outward points of tension that dot the landscape of lives of religious communities. Thus, inner peace ultimately leads to outer peace. However, the movement, in this construct, is not one of simple translation from one realm to the other. Rather, the inner dimension motivates a revisiting of tradition and a reestablishment of memory. One may say that parallel to the reestablishment of higher memory is the reestablishment of true historical memory, lost to contemporary sight but still available to those who study the tradition with honesty, free from political pressures and other corrupting influences. The ultimate impact of inner peace is the liberating knowledge of correct memory, which in turns has a calming effect on situations of tension, reducing the potential for religious violence. Umar thus ties together the two conceptual strands of our project—higher memory and historical memory and the critique of memory and its changes through time. His presentation supposes that the former issue provides the motivation and the religious framework within which the latter issue can be worked out.

With this theoretical framework in place, we are equipped to appreciate Umar's presentation of two case studies, where he describes work that has taken place along these lines. One relates to internal Muslim relations, the other to Jewish-Muslim relations. The latter takes up the larger part of his presentation. The Jewish-Muslim issue concerns the status of the Temple Mount/Haram al Sharif and more broadly speaking the Holy Land. This has been the subject of a lively debate in the Pakistani context, from which he comes and which he reports. Suheyl Umar's presentation is founded upon recognition of different geographical centers of one common religion (Islam) having diverse perspectives on common issues. Thus, how one is situated will impact one's ability to perceive reality, and one may require the aid of a complementary perspective to balance one's own position. Serious scholarly debate, which has had impact on public discourse, school curricula, and media, has taken place in Pakistan. This debate has focused on Muslim claims for possession of the Haram al Sharif. A long-standing tradition of Muslim authorities, especially in the Indian subcontinent, affirmed the Muslims as temporary custodians of the Temple Mount, due to the sins of the Jewish people, until such time that the Jewish people are able to reclaim or re-own it. Thirteen centuries of custodianship have impacted the Muslim psyche so that a sense of rightful possession has settled in, leading not only to denial of the Jewish right to the Temple Mount, but even effacing the historical memory of Jewish presence on the Temple Mount. Umar's paper points to the corrupting effects of power over memory. Thirteen centuries of empowerment have corrupted Muslim memory. The retrieval of memory is therefore linked to decoupling truthful memory from sources of power. One notes how contemporary tensions between Jews and Arabs have further impacted this view, leading to a change in what is considered a proper Muslim view even in countries not directly implicated by the political struggle, such as Pakistan or India.

Umar's paper makes a fundamental claim concerning the diffusion of memory and the agents of its transmission. It suggests that public perception, propaganda, and media can have a distorting effect on how we perceive our traditions and that it is the role of faithful scholarship to balance such public perception. The public debate that took place sought to reestablish truthful memory and to remind Muslim teachers, students, and the broader public that Muslim claims are not claims to rightful possession, but are limited to temporary custody, all the while maintaining sight of the fundamental rights of the Jewish people. This debate, as Umar describes it, was largely successful in educational and religious terms, even though it did not translate into the diplomatic arena of Israeli-Pakistani relations. For Umar, and the recovered Muslim voices that emerged during this debate, the Israeli-Muslim problem is not beyond solution and this includes also the most contested of issues, the status of the Temple Mount. In an appendix, Umar proposes a solution to the question of the Temple Mount that is very much at odds with contemporary Palestinian sensibilities, but which nevertheless draws out the implications of correctly reconstructed historical memory.

A second case study concerns internal relations between Shi'a and Sunna. Umar shares with us efforts that have taken place in Yemen, Iraq, Iran, and India to revisit the relations between these two conflicted Muslim communities. At the core of their divide are divergent approaches to what counts most in the spiritual life—Truth (teaching, memory) or Presence (continuity of the Prophet's presence). Putting the matter in these terms already suggests that what is required is a balance between two complementary, and legitimate, forms of the spiritual life, rather than choosing one over the other. Reaching such a balance requires dialogue, and the recovery of the truths of the tradition. The efforts described involved a give and take between both schools, in which the status of religious teaching was shifted, in order to make room for the other, based on the realization that both perspectives have validity. Mutual theological accommodation has led to significant improvement in relations on the ground between members of both communities. While here it is not a matter of recovering a lost historical truth, this case study is similar to the first one in that religious teachings need to be understood in terms of their broader context and the place of any given teaching or position within the broader economy of religious teaching. Muslims have a right to the Haram, but it must be appreciated within a broader view of history, or better yet—within a broader view of the religious history of humanity, in which Muslims are but a part. Similarly, both Sunni and Shi'i perspectives must be appreciated truthfully from a perspective that offers balance and a larger picture, allowing for mutual accommodations.

Returning to the core strategy suggested above, it seems that the work of retrieval of correct memory is ultimately a process of finding balance between conflicting realities. Umar does not suggest dialogue as a means of such retrieval, though the processes he describes by means of which these issues were worked out are indeed processes of dialogue, even if between competing groups of scholars, rather than between members of different religious groups. In any event, the balancing of conflicting realities ultimately relies on balancing the human perspective with the Divine. Only with the recollection of higher truths, mystical, spiritual, and eschatological, do we gain the needed perspective for revisiting statements of a historical nature, especially as these concern inter-group relations. From this higher vantage point, a harmonizing or balancing vision can be found that recognizes multiple and conflicting claims and finds truth or validity in multiple perspectives. It offers a vision of ultimate peace, grounded in the higher spiritual peace, translated into the traditional mechanisms that allow a shifting of perspective in concrete historical relationships.

Umar's view is a religious view full of hope and the path he offers is one of regaining hope. True memory has become mired in human reality, but there is a way of reclaiming it. Whether it is regaining of the higher spiritual memory or the retrieval of lost historical memory, we need not be limited by contemporary political circumstances. There is a way forward, beyond present limitations. The liberation of memory and the liberating power of higher memory provide us with what is needed most in our complicated human reality—hope.

MICHAEL VON BRÜECK AND MARIA REIS HABITO'S MEMORY IN BUDDHISM

The final essay in our collection is Michael von Brüeck and Maria Reis Habito's "Memory in Buddhism." I have left this essay for last because it ties together the two main strands of the project, but also because it introduces new ways of looking at things that in some way redefine our approach to the subject. The first part offers theoretical reflections on memory. Here the role of memory in constructing identities is stated most clearly. This function is true for both individuals and collectives. The identity-constructing function of memory is closely related to memory's dynamism. Memory seems fixed, but in fact it is not. It is ever changing. This recognition has come up in Sendor and Keshgegian, but here it has a different valence, because it reflects not only a "neutral" descriptive view of memory but also carries forth a particular Buddhist sensibility of the impermanence and transience of all things. If all things are refracted through memory, then memory itself is a mirror of their impermanence.

This impermanence, however, is encountered, paradoxically, through moments of illusory fixity, required for the sake of stability of identity. Therefore, there is something inherently paradoxical about memory, that delivers to us stability and transience, folded into one complicated moment. Complicating that moment further and breaking beyond the illusory stability is the goal of Buddhist practice. Buddhism, thus understood, may be seen as in some way organized around dealing with memory. As a method of teaching, it requires stability of tradition, practice, ritual. It locates itself in the past, and carries forth a tradition—itself a time related construct—all of which requires faithful memorizing. But there is something fundamentally subversive about the Buddhist approach. All that is constructed in terms of stability of identity and religious institutions is, in fact, only the ground laid for undermining this very stability. A dynamic of constructing and destroying, forming identity and transcending it, characterizes the Buddhist approach to memory.

In order to understand this better, we must return to the time axis and how a tradition can be posited in terms of past, present, and future. Our entire project is situated along this axis, and so how we negotiate both memory and hope is really how we negotiate time. Buddhist teachings offer us particular ways of doing so. From von Brüeck's presentation we come to understand that the particularity of negotiating these time dimensions is closely linked to broader application of memory. If we had assumed that memory lies in the past and that memorizing is the process of making the past present, von Brüeck and Reis Habito's presentation teaches us that memory should be understood in broader terms. Rather than memory, we might, in a manner analogous to Keshgegian, speak of memorizing. The distinction is in part due to the recognition, highlighted by Keshgegian, of the fluid nature of memory and the active role of the one engaged in remembering. But this article suggests a no less important distinction. By memory we refer not only to the recall of past events. Memory includes all things in relation to which we can apply processes of memorialization. Memorialization here is bringing to awareness, making present, cultivating mindfulness. Thus all that is recalled, taken in, integrated, by way of religious teaching, made present to our consciousness, is here treated as a form of memory. Memory, understood so broadly, is in fact a process of making present. In ways that are similar to Sendor's emphasis on making present, the Buddhist tradition tackles the challenge of identity and transcending it, of the relative order of fixed and conventional meanings and going beyond it to discover the higher ground of nirvanic being, to a large extent by means of the present. Making something present to our awareness allows us to transcend the boundaries of identity that are ego-related and that require going beyond.

There are various expressions of this core strategy of mindfulness and presence as means of transcending constructed identity and its indebtedness to past memory, where conventional religious memory is a lead up to going beyond memory and uncovering an open present. The Buddha's founding illumination is captured in terms of past experiences and past lives. However, the purpose of this realization is to appreciate the interdependence and the connections that exist between all that is. This realization referred to in terms of past is actually a realization of the present. Monastic rituals of memorizing, focusing as they do on faithful representation of the past, are in fact means of bringing attention to mindfulness. Zen tradition is an elaborate tradition that celebrates its authenticity by appeal to a chain of tradition, yet its core teaching cultivates an attitude of going beyond past and memory into an experience, grounded in the present. The past is viewed as limiting, the present as fully open. While memory provides psychological and social stability, the present must not be limited by the view of the past, but be open to an appreciation of its open ended perspectives, far broader than the constraints of the past.

Ultimately, the liberating memory is insight into the true nature of things. In this, the Buddhist tradition is very similar to the Hindu tradition. The liberating memory here is the recognition of the appropriate place of our relative nature and perception, and the concomitant realization that this limited nature is identical with ultimate reality, however it be understood. Wisdom is, once again, the key to liberation from memory.

Making the past present is particularly pronounced in Mahāyāna Buddhism, that enlarges the narrative of the Buddha's tales. More is remembered, and I would add that it matters little what the historical status is of that which is remembered. It is memorizing as an act that counts, and the purpose of such memorizing is to make present that which is memorized. Memory is a dynamic that bridges past and present in faith. Faith in the validity of the content of memory not only gives it meaning for the present, but makes it effective for the present, allowing the individual to identify with the spiritual steps taken by the Buddha and to apply them in the aspirant's life. Pure Land Buddhism makes this process even more obvious. Faith is required to believe in Amitābha's vow. The content of the vow is Amitābha's memory of us and our memory of his vow and their soteriological power. While driven by faith, memory provides the bridge. And yet, what counts most is the way memorizing makes this vow present in the life of the believer, opening her up to the saving presence of Buddha Amitābha. If the present requires relinquishing and letting go of the ego, then the test of memory well performed is its ego-releasing quality. Memory that focuses on identity, while hardening the boundaries of individual and collective ego, is memory performing poorly.

Because memorizing is so central to making the past present, a variety of means are invoked. Memory is ultimately instilled not only into our minds but into our entire beings. Memory is embodied. Memorizing scripture, seeing sacred images, absorbing a presence through pilgrimage, these and more are the strategies that tradition offers for assuming and integrating memory and making it fully present, even in our bodily existence. Because memory is understood as evoking deep awareness, memory well-practiced, through these means of recollection, reaches the entirety of our being. And because it does so, it also allows us to transcend the limitations of our ego, entering fully into trans-egoic presence.

The time axis is not limited to past becoming present. The future too is evoked and made present. In Mahāyāna we learn not only of predecessors to the Buddha but also of successors in time to come. The future Buddha too needs to be remembered, that is—brought into our present consciousness. This provides encouragement and the promise of progress. Memory opens the practitioner up to a grace, grounded in the future, made present through faith. Because time is ultimately an illusion, it can be employed in all its modes—past, present, and future in order to bring about the deeper recognition of the Absolute Present. Thus, all possible worlds, all possible mental formations, can be used to realize the Oneness of Reality, beyond time and space.

What does all this say for a notion of hope? If we consider hope along the lines of past, present and future, we note that hope is not a central concept. Hope for Buddhists does not reside in a future. However, if we consider the process of transcending the negative impact of memory that is attached to ego and opening up to the Oneness of Reality and to the Absolute Present, this is itself a message of great hope, a hope of liberation from the fetters of memory and its limitations. It might be appropriate to refer to some views of Buddhism as a pessimistic religion. Seen in the present context, Buddhism is full of hope, a hope that one can go beyond the limitations of memory and open up to Absolute Present.

One notes that some forms of Buddhism do offer hope, grounded in the future. This is the case for the Pure Land tradition. This tradition is based on the promise of a future rebirth in the Pure Land and as such offers an eschatological view that is inherently hopeful. Similarly, the coming of the Buddha Maitreya can be appreciated in terms of hope for salvation.

The final part of the paper explores the application of these insights to a situation of conflict. The tensions between China and Tibet are viewed in terms of dynamics of memory. Von Brüeck informs us of the complexity of memory and how partial and selective its application is. Accordingly, there is no correct way to tell the story and every telling is partial and offers some interested perspective. Resolution of the conflict must be informed by awareness of the problematic nature of claims based on memory. This in turn leads us to dialogue and to making room for the other. The strategy is the same as that proposed by Rambachan and Sendor. In essence, appeal to memory gives way to appeal to the present. Both sides have legitimate interests. These are grounded on their being humans, who have the right to live in dignity, individually and collectively. Thus, a dialogue of mutual recognition must replace competing memory claims. This practical recommendation is based on Buddhist teaching. Von Brüeck and Habito make explicit appeal to spiritual cognitions of the Buddhist tradition that provide value to all. Loving the enemy is a way of humanizing him. Remembering that in the cycle of rebirths all beings have been mothers and fathers to each other is a way of cultivating compassion, which is ultimately a way of humanizing and validating the other. But perhaps the thrust of von Brüeck's argument in this paper is even more relevant. If the goal of Buddhist practice is to transform memory into openness to the present, this should impact how we dialogue in situations of conflict. Appeal to disputed memory may not hold the key to a breakthrough. Such a breakthrough must be founded on openness to the present, and therefore assumes the unconditional value and right of the other.

The Dalai Lama's practice is offered as an exercise in cultivating this attitude. If the Dalai Lama is typically seen as a model for peacemaking, it may be because of the unique characteristics of the Buddhism he practices that provides him with key tools to engage in dialogue and in peacemaking. The stability of institutions and ensuing identity is ultimately transitory, leading to much greater flexibility and possibility of compromise. The insistence on being right is softened in a practice that seeks to overcome ego boundaries. And the impact of memories is much diluted in a practice that seeks to make the present and full awareness of it, in the effort of alleviating suffering, the core spiritual drive. While the dynamics of past, present, and future may echo those found in other traditions, the key approach to memory and how it impacts identity-construction is different. If other traditions require an external critical view to relinquish some of the trappings of power, as Keshgegian has offered us, and if the practical applications of memory are subject to the hardening effects of political processes, as Umar teaches us, Buddhism may represent an alternative paradigm. Buddhism is a tradition that appeals to memory only to undo it, that constructs identity only to overcome it. It might therefore have built into it the internal spiritual resources that justify the common view of Buddhism as more favorable to causes of peacemaking and reconcilliation.

Chapter Two

The Malleability of Collective Memory in Jewish Tradition

Meir Sendor

Collective remembrance is an essential modality of religious consciousness. Preservative and conservative, the rehearsal of collective memory holds a religious community to a set of ideas and to a framework, a tradition that maintains cohesion and continuity. It is not uncommon for the world's religious traditions to preserve an origins narrative of their rise from a prior antagonistic religious society, culture, or environment, and use such narratives to define their unique principles and commitments. It is also not uncommon for religious groups to record historical experiences of persecution and oppression and find meaning in these experiences in terms of their spiritual destiny. Such canonical memories of victimhood and past trauma at the hands of other national or religious groups may also stoke or ignite interreligious hostility, however, or at least discourage religious communities from reaching beyond their boundaries in relationship with the religious other. Is there an art of memory that would allow a religious community to honor its difficult past, yet remain free of fixations on victimhood and attitudes of resentment and exclusion? Is there an art of memory that would not hinder, and might even help facilitate, interreligious reconciliation?

Collective remembrance is fundamental to Judaism. Traditional Jewish religious and legal thought intentionally processes the present and its options in terms of the remembered precedents, behavior patterns, and values of the past. An inveterate community reaching back over three and a half millennia, Judaism regards history itself as a field of Divine revelation and religious meaning, but much of its political history is a long trail of oppression, persecution, and victimization. Certain commandments of the Torah are framed explicitly as imperatives of memory, including commemorations of past affliction: to remember the Exodus from Egyptian enslavement; to remember to destroy the tribe of Amalek, first of the Canaanite tribes to attack the nascent Israelite nation.[1] The Sabbath and the holy days of the calendar are characterized in part as commemorations of the Exodus from Egypt. Certain central devotional practices reinforce communal remembrance of the core narratives of the Jewish people such as the Exodus from slavery rehearsed during the Passover festival, the salvation from threatened genocide celebrated in the Purim holiday, and the destruction of the First and Second Temples mournfully commemorated over an intensive three week period framed by two fast days and by other fasts throughout the year. These devotional occasions in particular are memorials of victimhood that define Jewish identity over against the hostility of ancient empires: Egypt, Persia, Babylonia, and Rome, respectively. Do such commemorations lock the Jewish community into resentfulness and antagonism towards certain religious or national groups, or does the Jewish tradition have strategies for tempering such negativity?

THE PHENOMENOLOGY OF RELIGIOUS MEMORY

What religious tradition calls us to remember is not something we experienced personally. It is collective memory, and even for those born and raised in the tradition, it is adopted as one's own through training, education, and acculturation. These collective memories are not raw traces of the events themselves, but extensively edited accounts, selectively shaped over generations. Maurice Halbwachs notes that all memory, even personal memory, is ultimately a social act: "it is in society that people normally acquire their memories. It is in society that they recall, recognize and localize their memories."[2] The impact of social norms on collective memory is all the more direct and decisive. According to Halbwachs, in collective memory "the past is not preserved but is reconstructed on the basis of the present," and "collective frameworks are . . . the instruments used by the collective memory to reconstruct an image of the past which is in accord, in each epoch, with the predominant thoughts of the society."[3] As such, all remembrance is subject to construction and reconstruction in accommodation to contemporary social values and viewpoints. In collective memory, especially of the religious variety, societal influence is not subliminal, it is intentional and consensual. On one hand, religious memory is an epitomized history that follows the contours of a society's past: "each religion . . . reproduces in more or less symbolic form the history of migrations and fusions of races and tribes, of great events, wars, establishments, discoveries and reforms that we can find at the origin of the societies that practice them."[4] On the other hand, that history is filtered through a contemporary lens: "society projects into its past conceptions that were recently elaborated."[5]

The constructed aspect of memory is intrinsic to its nature. The process itself of forming memory by consensus and rehearsing it through word, text or ritual, employs what Paul Ricouer calls "the unavoidably selective nature of narrative."[6] As Ricouer shows, what is recounted in remembrance, whether individual or collective, is in the form of a narrative thread that highlights certain details of past experience and ignores or forgets others. A certain element of forgetting is integral to the process of constructing and contextualizing remembrance, emphasizing the significant and downplaying the trivial, without which memory becomes obsessively literal and ultimately meaningless.[7] Ricouer reminds us of the Borges short story "Funes el memorioso" as an example *ad absurdum* of the tyranny of memory not tempered by forgetting, and medical literature actually records cases of such neurological conditions that are regarded as pathologies.[8] Halbwachs describes memories as assemblages of multiple events, an abbreviated, highly edited summary.[9] In this way, collective memory preserves a concise and conveyable message, but it is also subject to adjustment or manipulation through ideology: "society, in each period, rearranges its recollections in such a way as to adjust them to the variable conditions of its equilibrium."[10] This malleability can be dangerous to truthful remembrance, as in the case of propaganda or politically motivated revisionism. But careful revision can also redeem remembrance from pathological fixation, obsession, and revenge and help re-attune memory to truth.

Halbwachs flags a particular challenge when it comes to religious memory: it is regarded as more fixed and more difficult to adjust than other forms of collective memory. Contemporary adjustments to generic social memory can be justified as corrective and even progressive, since the memory is of temporal events subject to temporal critique. By contrast, "religious memory . . . tends to close off, retreat, establish canonical traditions."[11] This closing off is accomplished by a temporal shift: religious memories are viewed as detached from time. Even if they are understood to involve events that occurred in a specific time and place, they tend to be viewed as of timeless significance: "the totality of religious remembrances subsists in a state of isolation and is all the more separated from other social remembrances to the degree that the epoch in which they were formed is more remote . . . the memory of religious groups claims to be fixed once and for all."[12] Adjustments to religious recollection, when they occur, therefore employ a different strategy. Halbwachs suggests that "if the ideas of today are capable of being opposed to recollections and of prevailing over them to the extent of transforming them, this is because such ideas correspond to a collective experience, if not as ancient, at least much larger." He observes that "what a group opposes to its past is not its present; it is rather the past . . . of other groups with whom it tends to identify."[13] His point is that, when it comes to collective religious memory, authority of the past, in some form, is required to transform a principle based on the authority of the past. Sometimes it is just a question of shifting emphasis within existing traditional sources, or highlighting another neglected aspect of the tradition. Nonetheless, while the tactic employed pits past against past, the motivation for invoking another authority or tradition derives from the present, from contemporary pressure to square religious principles of the past with current needs and attitudes.

The selectivity of remembrance means it already incorporates forms of forgetting from the start. Ricouer suggests, on the basis of studies by Harald Weinrich, that an "art of forgetting" could be developed alongside an "art of memory," to ameliorate some of the more toxic and pathological aspects of remembrance and forgetfulness, especially fixations in the remembrance of trauma and, conversely, irresponsible forgetting of guilt. As a French citizen, Ricouer had in mind what he considered French evasion of responsibility for complicity in the Shoah in the decade following the war.[14] He analyzes the roles that both remembering and forgetting might play in the possibility of an authentic forgiveness, and what the requirements for such forgiveness might be. While appreciating the groundbreaking work of "truth and reconciliation commissions" convened by the late Nelson Mandela and presided over by Bishop Desmond Tutu to help South African society reconcile after the Apartheid period, a model employed for post-conflict healing in other African societies as well, Ricouer was concerned that the amnesty granted by such commissions to facilitate the process represents a caricature of forgiveness, amounting to an institutionalized forgetting.[15]

Ricouer sides with those thinkers, such as Levinas, Derrida, and Jankelevitch, who hold that true forgiveness requires a full exchange, a transaction between victim and perpetrator. Jankelevitch, in his penetrating analysis of the possibility of authentic forgiveness, also sets standards for the victim. He insists that if the actions of the injuring party are merely forgotten, or the passage of time used to diminish the feeling of pain, or the injured party wants to be gracious in order to unburden himself or herself of the poison of resentment for emotional or spiritual reasons, such motivations undercut the possibility of genuine and meaningful forgiveness. Rather, true forgiveness must be hard-won, and, rather than the result of a guaranteed therapeutic process or inevitable legal logic, it must be "miraculous, ineffable, and extrajuridical."[16] Similarly, while Ricouer appreciates the practical political virtue of institutionalized reconciliation and amnesty to restore normalcy to society, in terms of the ideal he approves Derrida's assessment that:

> Each time that forgiveness is in the service of a finality, be it noble and spiritual (repurchase or redemption, reconciliation, salvation), each time that it tends to reestablish a normalcy (social, national, political, psychological)

> through a work of mourning, through some therapy or ecology of memory, then "forgiveness" is not pure—nor is its concept. Forgiveness is not, and it should not be, either normal, or normative, or normalizing. It should remain exceptional and extraordinary, standing the test of the impossible: as if it interrupted the ordinary course of historical temporality.

Derrida's high bar for forgiveness is not so removed as to be irrelevant to the politics of reconciliation. It can stand as a valuable reminder to all participants to keep conscience awake, and that all results are provisional. On the practical level, Ricouer resigns himself to positing a balance between forgetting and forgiving, and suggests "an eschatology of forgetting . . . balancing forgetting through the effacement of traces against the forgetting kept in reserve."[17]

JEWISH MEMORY

We can find examples of such strategies of remembering and forgetting in the Jewish tradition, with some unique and characteristic differences. For instance, the memory of Egyptian servitude is part of the core narrative of the Jewish people. The Torah dwells on the conditions of the enslavement in great detail, with emphasis on the cruelty of the Egyptian leaders and taskmasters.[18] The rabbinic midrashic tradition magnifies this cruelty and the complicity of the Egyptian populace.[19] Accounts of the Egyptian servitude and the salvation of the Exodus are recollected, recited and re-enacted ritually in the Passover Seder every year, even in minimally observant Jewish homes. Generation after generation of children are trained to remember the harsh details of Egyptian treatment of Jews. Multiple references to the suffering in Egypt occur in the daily liturgy. Though the events took place over three thousand five hundred years ago, their frequent recollection in Jewish ritual keeps their memory alive. Such accounts, enshrined in Scripture, might be expected to generate and reinforce attitudes of resentment and antagonism against present-day Egypt and Egyptians. Yet the Torah itself contains an instructive antidote against just this possibility. In context of the laws of conversion to Judaism, it warns: "Do not abhor an Egyptian, for you were a stranger in his land. Children born to them in the third generation shall enter the congregation of the Lord (Dt. 23:8, 9)." Though the Torah recounts the victimization of the Jewish people at the hands of Egyptians at great length, it turns around and warns Jews not to hate Egyptians, and rather reminds us to focus on positive memory that is also recorded in the biblical narrative: the hospitality that Egypt extended to the Jewish people when we were strangers in a time of need. Rabbenu Asher ben Yechiel, rabbinic leader of the late thirteenth-early fourteenth century, comments "even though they enslaved you in the end, do not hate them, for you were a stranger in their land and they benefitted you at first, so you should draw them close" in conversion.[20] The victimization is not forgotten or ignored: in biblical law it is represented in the fact that an Egyptian convert to Judaism cannot immediately marry a Jew. He or she may marry another convert, and their grandchildren may fully marry into the Jewish people. Converts to Judaism from most other ethnic groups are granted full prerogatives of citizenship immediately. It should be remarked, however, that the warning not to abhor the Egyptian applies immediately, and not only to converts but to all Egyptians.

The Jewish biblical tradition here is steering a complex moral course. On the one hand, victimhood is acknowledged in the limitation placed on a prospective convert. There is an element of collective blame in this biblical law: the individual Egyptian, even of later generations, is judged as part of his or her national group. On the other hand, the Torah itself warns Jews not to fixate emotionally on injury and resentment and overgeneralize the victimhood, but rather to remember that the Jewish experience in Egypt also included initially generous Egyptian hospitality. Even the limited disadvantage with respect to marriage is only a legal stricture. It is not to be practiced in a spirit of vengeance but with neutral or even reluctant emotional valence: the law at issue deals with someone who wishes to convert to Judaism, after all, and there is also a biblical commandment to love the convert.[21] This is an example of a collective memory tempered by another collective memory from the same authoritative source. It should be noted that by the second century of the common era, if not well before, the rabbinic tradition effectively nullified the marriage restriction on Egyptian converts, citing the reality of the time: that after the seventh century BCE Assyrian conquest of the Middle East, and their policy of forcibly integrating national and ethnic populations to prevent nationalist uprisings, it is no longer possible to identify descendants of particular nations from earlier periods.[22] This is an example of Halbwach's principle that another authoritative group, in this case the rabbinic leadership, invoking another authoritative memory, can overrule or limit the consequences of an earlier authoritative collective memory.

A reevaluation of the remembrance of the Exodus from Egyptian enslavement also occurs in the later prophetic tradition. Jeremiah proclaims: "Therefore behold, the days are coming, says the Lord, when they shall no more say 'as the Lord lives, Who brought up the children of Israel out of the land of Egypt,' but 'as the Lord lives, who brought up and who led the seed of the house of Israel out of the north country, and from all countries into which I have driven them, and they shall dwell in their own land (Jer. 23:7–8).'" Jeremiah confirms that in his time commemoration of the Exodus from Egypt is the core narrative of the Jewish relationship with God, but he expresses hope for the future in terms of the supplanting of this memory by a later, ultimate salvation.

The rabbinic tradition picks up on this shift in value based on hope for the future. Ben Zoma questions whether the Egyptian Exodus will be commemorated in the messianic age. The other rabbis suggest that the Egyptian Exodus will not be forgotten, rather, the ultimate future redemption will become the essential commemoration, and the Exodus secondary to it. They characterize this shift with a passage from the prophet Isaiah: "Remember not the former things, neither consider the things of old. Behold, I will do a new thing, now it shall spring forth (Is. 43:18–19)." In the Talmud tractate *Berakhot* Rav Yosef interprets this verse as a reference to salvation from the intensified oppression expected to precede the messianic age. In the Talmud a parable is offered to explain the dynamic of supplanting a core memory with hope for a prophetically predicted future event:

> What does this resemble? A man was walking on the road and was attacked by a wolf and was saved from it. He would then talk about the incident with the wolf as he traveled. A lion attacked him and he was saved from it. He would then talk about the incident with the lion. A snake attacked him and he was saved from it. He forgot both prior incidents and would talk about the incident with the snake. So, too, for Israel, the later sufferings cause them to forget the earlier sufferings.[23]

The various predators from which the man in the parable is saved represent the succession of world-conquering powers of the ancient period, each of which the Jewish nation survived or are expected to survive in some way. Each of these interpretations, prophetic and rabbinic, is playing with the presumed centrality of the Egyptian enslavement and Exodus as the standard model for Jewish religious and national identity, and uses hope for the future to provide a new perspective that downplays the significance of the Exodus.

Other examples of Halbwach's principle that a collective memory from one authoritative source can be amended by a collective memory of different but also respected sources can be found in the Jewish legal approach to the tribe of Amalek and its descendants, including the arch-enemy of the Jews of Persia, Haman. It is a Torah commandment to eradicate the entire tribe of Amalek because of its attacks on the Jewish people during the vulnerable period of their wandering in the desert, shortly after the Exodus. Not only does the Torah oblige an eschatological military campaign, but also a standing obligation of memory for the individual:

> Remember what Amalek did to you on the way, when you came out of Egypt: how he met you on the way and attacked your rear, all those who were weakened behind you, and you were faint and weary, and he did not fear God. Therefore it shall be, when the Lord your God has given you rest from all your enemies round about, in the land which the Lord your God gives you for an inheritance to possess it, erase the remembrance of Amalek from under heaven, you shall not forget (Dt. 25:17–19).

In the Talmud the Amora Rava rules that the negative commandment not to forget is fulfilled mentally, while the positive commandment to remember is fulfilled by vocal recitation of the biblical passage.[24] Commentators note the unusual emphasis on remembrance in this passage, and the unusual Divine antipathy against this tribe, observing that other enemies of Israel are not targeted so relentlessly. Some suggest that it is the cruelty of their unprovoked attack on a weakened and vulnerable nation, and the abiding flaw in collective moral character it demonstrates, that draws such sustained Divine wrath.[25] The *Mekhilta*, a halakhic midrash, concludes that descendants of the tribe of Amalek may not be accepted as converts.[26] Even so, R. Avraham Karelitz, a twentieth century authority, limits the applicability of this restriction, on the grounds that the descendants of Amalek did not perpetrate the crimes of their ancient ancestors, and the tribe is no longer identifiable, having mixed into other Middle Eastern populations.[27] R. Avraham Yitzhak Ha-Kohen Kook goes further, finding a nuance within this biblical text that calls for transcending the negativity of the memory mandated by the text itself:

> The degree of love in the soul of the righteous embraces all creatures, excluding no people and no ethnicity. Even the name of the wicked Amalek is to be erased by biblical command only "from under heaven." Through cleansing, however, he may be raised to the source of the good, which is above heaven, and included in higher love. A person needs great strength, however, and a high state of purity for this exalted kind of unification.[28]

R. Kook sees a tension within the biblical command. On the normative level, "under heaven," the tribe of Amalek should be destroyed. The text alludes, however, to a supererogatory level, "above heaven," that calls the spiritually advanced individual to a higher love. This love is not merely a shift in attitude. It mandates work to salvage this tribe morally and spiritually, to raise its members to their higher good, their higher humanity, to be reintegrated into the human family. In context, R. Kook takes this injunction as a model for the spiritual ideal of universal love, applied not only in the specific case of Amalek, but in all confrontations with evil and the memory of evil.

The notorious descendent of Amalek, Haman, is the focus of fierce antipathy expressed during the holiday of Purim. According to the *Megillat Esther*, ostensibly recounting events that occurred in Persia of the fifth century BCE, Haman tried to annihilate the entire Jewish people. The genocide was narrowly averted, and the salvation celebrated annually on Purim, during which the events are recalled in detail through public readings of the *Megillah*. So detested is Haman that by widespread popular custom every mention of his name in the public reading, and there are over two dozen such mentions, evokes loud and wild noisemaking by the congregation, symbolizing the erasure of his name and his memory. It is a ritualized memorialization of hatred for an enemy. Yet in the Talmud *Sanhedrin* there is a remarkable statement with regard to Haman and other historical archenemies of the Jewish people:

> Nevuzradan was a righteous convert. Some of the descendants of Sisera learned Torah in Jerusalem. Some of the descendants of Sennacheriv taught Torah in public, and who are they? Shamayah and Avtalyon. Some of the descendants of Haman learned Torah in Bnei Berak.[29]

Nevuzradan was the general under Babylonian king Nevuchadnezzar responsible for the destruction of the First Temple. Sisera was a field commander for a hostile Canaanite king whose downfall is recounted in the Book of Judges. Sennacheriv was king of Assyria and Babylonia from 705–681 BCE, and chief foe of the revered Jewish king Hezekiah. The overall point of this passage is that even the worst enemies or their descendants can change for the good and should never be written off as hopelessly evil. In fact, this rabbinic dictum conveys an even stronger lesson: it is not just that good can come from enemies, but they can actually become participating and contributing members of the rabbinic elite, among the Torah scholars of the preeminent rabbinic centers of Jerusalem and Bnei Barak. As the late Sefardic rabbinic authority Ovadiah Yosef commented in a responsum relating to this dictum: "even from the descendants of the wicked Amalek, may his name and memory be erased, may come holy offspring."[30]

Several strategies for recalibrating and revaluing religious collective memory are in evidence in these examples. The Torah's own warning not to hate the Egyptian and to appreciate Egyptian hospitality in spite of Egyptian oppression is a recognition of the fullness and complexity of actual experience that constitutes the basis for more narrowly selective memory. Recognizing that memory is constructed from the start by highlighting certain events and ignoring or forgetting others, it is legitimate and appropriate to recall and emphasize other events and aspects of the original experience that are liable to be overlooked. The avoidance of overgeneralization of traumatic memory and the limiting of its scope, the imperative to focus on positive memory of kindness and the awareness that experience can be multifaceted and even contradictory, all demonstrate an emotional and moral maturity to which each Jew is called by Torah law. Hope in the future can also be used to relativize an original remembrance and open it to re-evaluation. The recognition that social and political circumstances in the world have changed since biblical times, and that people can change, or their descendants can change, permits a concomitant change in the application of religious laws, and a seasoned and mature religious tradition has ways of accommodating such changes while honoring its sources and precedents. This is an example of the impact of present reality and contemporary moral development on the interpretation and adjustment of memory. Halbwachs noted that "social beliefs, whatever their origin, have a double characteristic. They are collective traditions or recollections, but they are also ideas of conventions that result from a knowledge of the present."[31] He had observed that religious traditions do not merely overrule the past on the basis of the present, but find a traditional group memory that is more attuned to contemporary mores to pit against another group memory that they regard as outmoded. Nonetheless, the impetus for this strategy comes from a clear sense of present reality and present social need.

The present does not serve merely as a timeframe in which social and political pressures conspire to prompt revision of memory, however. The experience of the present also serves as a basis in itself for release from the hold of the past when remembrance becomes maladaptive. For instance, revenge, a pathology of memory, is prohibited by Torah law: "You shall not take revenge and not be vengeful against your fellow citizen, you shall love your neighbor as yourself, I am the Lord" (Lev. 19:18). Maimonides, the twelfth century legal authority, in his discussion of the biblical prohibition against revenge, explains that

> as long as a person retains and remembers an injury, he may come to take revenge for it. Therefore the Torah is strict against vengeance, to the point that one should erase the injury from one's heart and not remember it at all. This is the correct attitude by which it is possible to support society and people's dealings with each other.[32]

According to Maimonides, based on Talmudic principle, the normalization of present relationships is not an evasion of responsibility: it is a consideration that can help disengagement from bondage to past memory of hurt. The ground for the possibility of meaningful change, in action and in attitude, and the ground for the possibility of forgiveness, is the continually refreshed buoyancy of the present itself. To allow this sense of the present to help detach memory of hurt from negative effects of victimization and vengeance is not necessarily a forgetting or a betrayal of the past.

The replenishing fullness of the present is an essential aspect of the basis for forgiveness, also a central Torah value. In Jewish law, true forgiveness requires a full exchange, a multi-level transaction between victim and perpetrator. To earn authentic forgiveness the offending party must honor the pain of the victim, requiring full consciousness and acceptance of responsibility, including compensation where relevant.[33] Maimonides, in his authoritative code of religious law, explains that there are three dimensions to the process of *Tshuvah*, repentance on the part of a perpetrator, that are necessary prerequisites for forgiveness: regret for the offense, resolve not to repeat the offense, verbal confession of the offense.[34] Forgiving is not forgetting. Quite the contrary, the most sincere forgiveness requires the most honest remembrance by both parties, even if that remembrance is ultimately to be archived as dormant once the process is complete. The existential basis for forgiveness, however, rests on the buoyancy of the present. In one of the classic biblical accounts of forgiveness, Joseph explains to his brothers, who had sold him into slavery but are now fully contrite, why he has now forgiven them: "You intended evil against me, but God calculated it for good, in order to bring it to pass at this day, that many people be kept alive" (Gen. 50:20). Two factors prompt and support forgiveness: that God has guided events, even harmful events, for the best; and that the fullness of the present, "this day," allows emotional pain from the past to be released. R. Moshe Alsheikh, sixteenth century bible commentator, says that Joseph's forgiveness was based on the present moral condition of his brothers "this day": that they were now righteous, having gone through a rigorous process of repentance; and that, because of this righteousness, the Divine Presence was with them.[35] Joseph has not forgotten the past. Rather, because his brothers have faced the past and come to terms with it responsibly, they are changed in the present, and traumatic memory does not drag down the divinely refreshed buoyancy of the present.

CONTEMPORARY CHALLENGES

Jewish cultural resources and attitudes to memory of the past are put to the test in the way Jewish society approaches more contemporary challenges, such as relations between Jews and Germans after the Shoah, or between Israelis and Palestinians and Jews and Muslims today. While religious principles do not explicitly or intentionally guide political policy, these principles and attitudes are part of the cultural repertoire of Israeli and Jewish society and can be found to infuse Jewish sensibilities.

The reconciliation process between Jews and Germans after the Shoah has been complicated, as might be expected. Y. Auerbach sums up the range of assessments, with Israel representing the collective Jewish position:

> Today, relations between Germany and Israel can be termed normal. Some analysts go as far as calling them "special," implying that the two countries have given each other more than what each of them gives any other country. Others see the relations as a zig-zag path whose course between friendliness and mutual criticism has been to a large extent influenced by the personalities of the leaders of the two countries ... I would like to suggest that even though the relations are normal, maybe even "special," there is still no *full* reconciliation between Israel and Germany.[36]

Some analysts point to a disjunction in the early process of rapprochement between Jews and Germans. According to Auerbach, "when forgiveness was dearly needed (1940s and 1950s) it was not possible; when forgiveness became possible (1970s and after) it was, apparently, not needed any more."[37] In the years immediately after the Holocaust the surviving victims were not ready to forgive and the perpetrators were just coming to terms with their deeds. Auerbach notes that a process of political normalization took place between Israel and Germany in the decade following the war, and seemed to render a full process of forgiveness unnecessary, or at least not a priority. Some analysts have observed a "dis-synchronism" in Israeli-German relations that continued into the next generation: "whereas Israeli Jews and others view the Germans from the perspective of the German past . . . the Germans view themselves from the perspective of the present and future."[38]

Yet in many respects the process of reconciliation between Israeli Jews and Germans has been significant and meaningful. The establishment of reparations and normalization of political relations over time has facilitated a significant improvement in relations between Israelis and Germans, individually and nationally. On the leadership level, early avoidance of responsibility and apology, such as Adenauer's 1951 speech to the Bundestag,[39] was followed by more sincere expressions, such as Willy Brandt falling to his knees at a commemoration of the Warsaw Ghetto in 1970. Even at that poignant moment, however, Brandt did not explicitly ask forgiveness. As one commentator noted, this may have been tactful and honest: "certainly there was no explicit request for forgiveness, and had there been it is doubtful that Jewish representatives could ever have extended it."[40] It may be that, in the case of trauma of such magnitude, avoidance of direct verbal apology and forgiveness is not necessarily a denial, but can be a way of honoring the depth of pain and the responsibility. Remembrance need not always be explicitly articulated to be powerfully present and impactful. The healing process can occur on levels that may not be fully expressed in words, but can nonetheless be real and important. Dan Bar-On reports on his observations of a series of group reconciliation sessions between Israeli Jews and Germans who were descendants of Holocaust victims and perpetrators. He summarizes the results:

> Through the group experience, it became clear that the outcome of the process was not to forget or be done with the past, but to find new ways to *live with it,* perhaps ways that were more conscious but also less threatening and self-destructive. In working through such massive trauma one does not end it or let go of it; the Holocaust will always be there, will always be a presence. However, its negative impact on the lives of both descendants of Holocaust survivors and descendants of Nazi perpetrators can be reduced through such conscious working-through processes, by groups as well as individuals. In a sense these issues were the group's main "product," which could be presented as its way

of working through forgiveness and conciliation rather than talking about them.[41]

The process of "living with" traumatic memory that remains in the background calls attention to a subtle and deep mode of remembrance that implicitly acknowledges a certain quality of present experience that should be taken into account in assessments of truthful memory and forgiveness. Derrida had rejected a forgiveness in the service of normalization of relations as inauthentic. Bar-On is pointing out, however, that here normalization is not merely a primary political purpose that short-circuits full forgiveness. Rather, normalization serves to establish a context of relationship that can allow the painful process of reconciliation to proceed in an emotionally safe manner. In relations between Israeli Jews and Germans, the will to normalize in the present can be therapeutic for both sides, like sutures binding the surface tissue of a deep wound that can facilitate healing over time. This is consonant with the positive moderating role of the present accepted by Jewish tradition in shaping approaches to the reevaluation of collective memory. Such normalization is in accord with the rabbinic principles of not over-generalizing past trauma and avoiding collective accusation by recognizing that individuals and societies can change their attitudes and behavior over time. This is also in line with Maimonides's explanation for the biblical and rabbinic prohibition of revenge: "the Torah is strict against vengeance, to the point that one should erase the injury from one's heart and not remember it at all. This is the correct attitude by which it is possible to support society and people's dealings with each other."[42]

With respect to the Israeli-Palestinian conflict, M. H. Ross questions whether the German-Israeli reconciliation process can serve as a model. Several factors made the German-Israeli experience unique. First, there was a nearly universal consensus on who was the perpetrator and who was the victim. Second, while German leadership after the war acknowledged German responsibility, they did not regard themselves as having been personally complicit. Third, Germany's desire for political and economic normalization was a strong incentive. Fourth, many Germans felt a moral obligation to seek reconciliation.[43] The Israeli Palestinian conflict has a very different dynamic, and is not only over past trauma, but remains an urgent, ongoing, complex existential struggle over land and nationhood.

Memory plays a central role in the conflict. Though memories of past violence fuel animosity on both sides, the core memory that motivates both Jewish Israelis and Palestinians is not collective memory of hatred, but a collective memory of love. Jews have loved the Land of Israel for over three thousand five hundred years. It is their beloved homeland, the land God promised and delivered to the Israelite people, the land of generation after generation of their ancestors. It is the land they cultivated and that cultivated them as a nation. It is the land lost in exile due to conquest by the Babylonians, regained as a nation in the Second Jewish Commonwealth, lost again due to occupation and conquest by the Romans, and recently regained as the State of Israel. It is a land, the love of which suffuses Jewish Scripture and rabbinic tradition, reinforced in the home and in the school. An observant Jew prays at least three times a day, and typically more often, for the return of the Jewish people and his and her own return to the Land of Israel. Among the repercussions of the ancient Roman policy of national exile is the challenging reality that when the Jewish people would once again return to their homeland, it would have been settled by others in the meantime: Romans, Byzantines, Arabian Muslims, and other Middle Eastern tribes. These others also learned to love the Land. Even if their love is of more recent vintage, it is also fervent and deep, a land of their own ancestors, generation after generation, a land they call home. The core conflict between Israelis and Palestinians is a conflict of love before it became a conflict of hatred.

Both sides frame historical narratives tendentiously, in the service of their political aims. Whereas the conflict is primarily political, parties on both sides invoke religious collective memories as an overall context conditioning understandings and expectations of their own national destiny and their attitude to the other. The fixity of religious memory in general, noted by Halbwachs, has contributed to the intractability of the struggle. M. Benvenisti notes "nothing seems to change and no resolution is in sight. Issues raised twenty, forty years ago seem valid forever . . . The struggle goes beyond the apparent physical survival of the people involved and encompasses basic issues of identity and integrity."[44] The question is whether, short of resolving the conflict militarily, each side has the cultural resources, religious and political, and the will to employ those resources to make adjustments to its understanding of its history and its hopes for the future, that can accommodate the other in some way.

H. C. Kelman has analyzed the Israel-Palestinian conflict in terms of issues of identity. He notes that "mutual denial of the other's identity has been a central feature of the conflict over the decades."[45] This revolves around the way historical narrative and collective memory is used to define identity and justify rights. Kelman argues that

> Confronting history and coming to terms with the truth is an essential component of any reconciliation effort. The reexamination of historical narratives and the reevaluation of national myths—on both sides of a conflict—are valuable contributions to such an effort . . . I maintain that it is unrealistic to aim for the establishment of a single, objective truth and that one has to accept the need to negotiate historical truth to a certain degree. I want to avoid the simple relativistic stance that each side has its own truth and that their conflicting narratives are therefore equally valid. But we have to recognize that different narratives of different groups reflect different historical experiences—occa-

sioned by the same facts and figures—and that, therefore, their experienced truths can in fact not be identical. Reconciliation, in my view, does not require writing a joint consensual history, but it does require admitting the other's truth into one's own narrative.⁴⁶

Original Zionist narrative tends to devalue prior Palestinian presence on the Land, regarding Palestinians as politically unorganized or poorly organized remnants of the Jordanian population left in place after the wars of 1948 and 1967, without a real and distinctive national identity.⁴⁷ Jewish culture, even its religious component, admits a certain degree of flexibility in interpreting its collective memory, however, and some Israelis, including some political, religious and intellectual leaders and academics, have shown some degree of willingness to review assumptions and narratives and revise thinking about the past and hopes for the future. This process has been taken to an extreme by groups like the "New Historians," a controversial, ideology-driven movement underway for several decades in some sectors of Israeli academia, that has explicitly leveraged the constructed and therefore malleable nature of collective memory to attempt to offer alternative historical narratives of the conflict, in the hope that such self-criticism might facilitate rapprochement.⁴⁸

Whether Palestinian intellectual society will have the interest or political courage to reciprocate and openly mirror such a self-critical movement remains to be seen. Currently, among Palestinians and Muslims in general there is a popular propagandistic wave of denial of ancient or continuous Jewish presence in Jerusalem and the Land of Israel, despite abundant incontrovertible historical proof of their presence. Added to the falsehood of denial are attempts to actively destroy Jewish archeological treasures in sensitive areas such as the Temple Mount to try to erase evidence of Jewish presence. Archeological remains are another form of memory. There are, however, some Muslim thinkers offering alternative historical accounts that confirm the longstanding Jewish connection to the Land of Israel without finding such accounts necessarily threatening to Palestinian interests.⁴⁹

Any prospect for rapprochement must address cultural as well as political divides. Ross comments: "a core hypothesis in my work is that settling ethnic conflicts is not simply a matter of finding a clever, interest-based constitutional formula or way to split a limited pie. To develop both institutions and practices that help people at odds live together, solutions must also address basic threats to identity and the intense sense of victimization expressed in cultural, and not just political, acts."⁵⁰ The reference is to the delegitimization of the core narratives and historical self-understanding of the other that has been a characteristic feature of the Israeli-Palestinian conflict. According to Ross "truth and reconciliation matter because they validate the emotional core of individual and group memory in settings where the absence of validation was a central fact of social existence. What is addressed is the deep fear that opponents are engaged in efforts not only to threaten a group physically but also deny their past."[51] Ross suggests methods of working toward mutual validation

> through inclusive rituals that link different communities or the redefinition of older rituals so that they are no longer exclusive. This is not easy where group identity and group celebrations are often defined in opposition to another community. However, legitimating divergent identities in ways that are non- (or less) threatening is an important part of the reconciliation process.[52]

While religion has been used by both sides to incite mutual alienation, Ross holds out the hope that commonalities in Judaism and Islam could also help facilitate mutual respect, understanding, and peacemaking, and cites precedents from other ethnic and religious conflicts around the world.[53] As an example, the religious laws of both Jews and Muslims officially validate the religious other, making room for the presence of the other in their midst. The Jewish legal concept of the *ger toshav*, the resident alien, extends tolerance and protection to non-Jews who seek to reside in the Land of Israel, on condition that they abide by certain basic civil and religious laws. Similarly, the Muslim status of *dhimmi* extends tolerance and civil protection to non-Muslim residents belonging to a religion with a sanctioned scripture, on condition that they pay a tax and comport themselves with deference to Muslims. While both the *ger toshav* and *dhimmi* concepts are usually regarded as demeaning by those they are intended to protect, they are nonetheless a religious starting point for a policy of mutual tolerance and affirmation.

Auerbach has noted another specific area of hope for the prospect of reconciliation: a parallelism between the process of forgiveness in Judaism, which informs Israeli culture, and in Islam, which informs Palestinian culture.

In Islam . . . *Tawba* (repentance), like its Jewish equivalent *Tshuvah*, is a demanding process consisting of three phases identical to those requested by Jewish law and considered a necessary condition for *ghufran*—forgiveness granted by God to the repenting sinner. The rituals of *sulha* (settlement) and *musalaha* (reconciliation), usually performed within a communal framework, are meant to end conflicts among believers and establish peace through acknowledgment of and forgiveness for the injuries between individuals and groups.[54]

The similarities between Jewish and Muslim approaches to earning forgiveness do not guarantee a successful outcome. Both approaches are demanding. Both approaches are usually practiced within the community of the faithful, rather than with the religious other. Both approaches rest upon a change of attitude in the present that has not yet coalesced in either society. If the parties are able to make some headway in building trust, however, there could be hope that both approaches to forgiveness share an honesty and sense of responsibility in relation to the past, to remembrance, and a commitment to transformation in the present, that may permit them to honor each other's collective memories and work sincerely towards reconciliation.

Part of the Oslo process was to include some degree of normalization between Israel and the Palestinian Authority in areas of trade and security cooperation. Cooperation in business served a therapeutic function in helping improve Israeli-German relations, allowing relations in the present to heal memories of the past, in the spirit of Maimonides's explanation of the biblical command prohibiting revenge as designed "to support society and people's dealings with each other." This could have provided the context for building trust between Israelis and Palestinians that might allow some degree of reconciliation, but here , too, progress has been halting.

While religious principles have been used to reinforce intransigence in this conflict, religious vision that calls both sides to a higher consciousness could be used for healing as well. Harald Weinrich's call for an "art of forgetting" alongside an "art of remembering" is reflected in Jewish religious tradition explicitly. Rabbi Yehudah Aryeh Leib of Gur, in a sermon from 1901, notes that while Judaism calls Jews to remember essential spiritual principles, it also calls Jews to forget those things that are inessential or even inimical to true and healthy spiritual life, the "vanities of the world" and the vicissitudes of nature and politics.[55] It is the role of enlightened religious vision to help adherents rise above the pettiness of political power struggles and recognize the essential values of human life and spirit shared by all enlightened religions and their communities. Perhaps we can hope that in this difficult conflict the best spiritual principles of Judaism and Islam can help Israelis and Palestinians forget toxic hatreds and remember their essential shared humanity and shared love of their common land.

NOTES

1. Dt. 16:3, 25:17. Other commandments of remembrance include: not to forget the revelation at Sinai (Dt. 4:9), to remember the mistakes made during the desert wandering (Dt. 9:7), remember the punishment of Miriam for gossip (Dt. 24:9), to remember the Sabbath (Ex. 20:8).
2. M. Halbwachs, *On Collective Memory*, trans. L.A. Coser (Chicago, 1992) 38.
3. Ibid., 40.
4. Ibid., 84.
5. Ibid., 86.
6. P. Ricouer, *Memory, History, Forgetting*, trans. K. Blamey and D. Pellauer (Chicago, 2004) 448.
7. Ibid., 413.
8. Ibid., 400. J. L. Borges, *Labyrinths*, ed. D. A. Yates and J. E. Irby (New York, 1964) 59–66. Treffert, Darold, MD. "Hyperthymestic Syndrome: Extraordinary Memory for Daily Life Events. Do we all possess a continuous tape of our lives?" Wisconsin Medical Society, (2010).
9. Halbwachs, 60.

10. Ibid., 183.
11. Ibid., 98.
12. Ibid., 91–92.
13. Ibid., 184.
14. Ricouer, *Memory*, 412–14, 448–52.
15. Ibid., 466–86, 488.
16. V. Jankelevitch, *Forgiveness*, trans. and intr. A. Kelley, (Chicago, 2005) xxi, 13–56.
17. Ibid., 501.
18. E.g., Ex. 1:11–22; 5:4–20.
19. E.g., *Midrash Shemot Rabbah*, 1:14–34; 5:25. *Sotah* 11b.
20. R. Asher b. Yechiel, *Perush al ha-Torah*, Dt. 23:8.
21. Dt. 10:19.
22. *Tosefta Kiddushin*, ch. 5. Maimonides, *Mishneh Torah, H. Issurei Biah*, 12:25.
23. *Berakhot* 12b–13a.
24. *Megillah* 18a.
25. E.g., R. Moshe Alsheikh, *Torat Moshe*, vol. 5 (Jerusalem, 1990) 268–70 (*loc. cit.*)
26. *Mekhilta de-R. Shimon bar Yohai, Be-shallah*, 17:16.
27. R. Avraham Karelitz, *Hazon Ish, Y.D.* 157:5.
28. R. Avraham Yitzhak Ha-Kohen Kook, *Mussar Avikha u-Middot Ha-Re'iyah*, (Jerusalem, 1971) Ahavah, sec. 6.
29. Sanhedrin 96b.
30. R. Ovadiah Yosef, *Yabia Omer*, vol. 8, *H.M.* 10.
31. Halbwachs, 188.
32. Maimonides, *Mishneh Torah, Hilkhot De'ot*, 7:8.
33. *Yuma* 85b–87b.
34. Maimonides, *Mishneh Torah, Hilkhot Tshuvah*, 1:1; 2:2.
35. R. Moshe Alsheikh, Torat Moshe, vol. 1 (Jerusalem, 1990) 444 (on Gen. 50:20).
36. Y. Auerbach, "The Role of Forgiveness in Reconciliation" in *From Conflict Resolution to Reconciliation*, ed. Y. Bar-Siman-Tov, (Oxford, 2004) 167.
37. Ibid., 173.
38. M. Wolffsohn, *Eternal Guilt?* (New York, 1993) 66.
39. Y. Auerbach, 166.
40. R. Cohen, "Apology and Reconciliation in International Relations, in *From Conflict Resolution to Reconciliation*, ed. Y. Bar-Siman-Tov, (Oxford, 2004) 187–88.
41. D. Bar-On, "Will the Parties Conciliate or Refuse?" *From Conflict Resolution to Reconciliation*, ed. Y. Bar-Siman-Tov, (Oxford, 2004) 250.
42. Maimonides, *Mishneh Torah, Hilkhot De'ot*, 7:8.
43. M. H. Ross, "Ritual and the Politics of Reconciliation," *From Conflict Resolution to Reconciliation*, ed. Y. Bar-Siman-Tov, (Oxford, 2004) 203.
44. M. Benvenisti, "The Peace Process and Intercommunal Strife" in *The Elusive Search for Peace: South Africa, Israel, Northern Ireland*, eds. H. Giliomee and J. Gagiano (Cape Town, 1990) 117, 121.
45. H. C. Kelman, "Reconciliation as Identity Change," *From Conflict Resolution to Reconciliation*, ed. Y. Bar-Siman-Tov, (Oxford, 2004) 119.
46. Ibid., 123.
47. See, e.g., the critique of early Zionist views of the Arab population of Palestine in A. Shavit, *My Promised Land* (New York, 2013) 1–132, 313–324.
48. E.g., *The War for Palestine: Rewriting the History of 1948*. Rogan. Eugene L. and Shlaim, Avi, eds, (Cambridge, 2001). For a more temperate and popular example of historical revision by a journalist, see A. Shavit, *My Promised Land*, (New York, 2013).
49. E.g., Muhammad Suheyl Umar, "Memory, Hope, and Systems of Repair in Islam," in the present volume.
50. M. H. Ross, "Ritual," 198.
51. Ibid., 210.
52. Ibid., 214.
53. Ibid., 219–20.

54. Y. Auerbach, 159.
55. R. Yehudah Aryeh Leib, "Alter of Gur," *Sefat Emet,* vol. 2 (Jerusalem, 1971) 54d–55a.

Chapter Three

Memory and Hope in Christianity

Flora A. Keshgegian

Memory and hope are constitutive of Christianity. The very nature and process of salvation history in Christianity can be read as an ongoing dynamic of memory and hope and, as such, it has a narrative structure and form. In other words, at the center of Christianity is a story, that of Jesus Christ and of God's actions in creating, sustaining, and redeeming the universe through Christ. That story, including how it is told, establishes and shapes Christian identity, directs Christian action, and determines the relationships of groups within Christianity, as well as relationships with others. This essay explores, explicated and complicates this claim through considerations of truth, tradition, and time as loci of Christian memory. It examines the what, why, and how of memory, or more precisely of remembering, in Christianity.

INITIAL CONSIDERATIONS AND ORIENTATION

I prefer the word. "remembering" to "memory." Remembering is an activity, a verb form. In that sense, it is ongoing. Memory, as a noun, is more static and even suggests a sense of capture, such as a photograph taken in a moment in time, that is then frozen, presumably with the intent of holding on to it in a particular way. Memory, however, remains inherently unstable. Only the activity of remembering keeps memory vibrant and alive, although its instability is a given. In that way, remembering as an active process is always also re-membering. There is no memory frozen in time or remembering that does not change. Rather remembering is a constantly moving stream, which is affected by its environment and by any intrusions, obstacles, twists and turns along the way.

This dynamic gestures to a major problematic at the core of any considerations of memory or remembering, especially in relation to tradition: that which is intended to preserve and conserve cannot do so. The idea that memory contains something that is past and that can be known in the present as it was in the past is an illusion. The only way in which memory can be useful is to acknowledge and embrace its changing character and inevitable instability. Remembering always happens in the present.

Additionally, Christianity is not singular. It is much more accurate to speak of Christianities. There is, therefore, no one memory or memory stream. So to claim to represent Christianity (though all too many have done it) is problematic at best. I make no such claim. As a theologian, what Christianity is and what it means is my vocation and work, but I engage in that work from a given location and with a set of interests. My theological voice is located and perspectival. In particular, my Christian practice and theological work are informed by my denominational affiliation as an Episcopalian and as an ordained priest; by my ethnic background, which is as an Armenian American, who is the child of genocide survivors and immigrants, and as such is haunted by a traumatic past; by my political commitments as a feminist striving for a more just world; and by my theological conviction that truth is historical and political. Theology is not simply faith seeking understanding, but is knowledge subject to critique and with a practical intent. Faith seeks to enact and effect what it holds to be true. In other words, I do not acknowledge a division between theology and practice. In relation to memory, ultimately the transformative potential of remembering is measured by what remembering makes possible and what it occludes and excludes. Remembering is a political action.

Christianity and Memory, Authority and Power

Most obviously, Christian memory is carried by tradition. Tradition includes, and claims to be rooted, in the core Christian narrative. This observation, in turn, leads to questions not only about the content of Christian tradition, but also about how the authority of tradition is determined and understood and whose voices are included in it. What is the relationship of tradition and truth? Who gets to determine what is true? And by what authority?

Within these questions are contained still further ones that add nuance and complexity. Is Scripture, which may be understood as foundational memory, part of Tradition or does it have its own status? In other words, what is the relationship of Scripture and Tradition? On the most general and institutional level, Roman Catholics and Protestants would have very different answers to such questions. Not only would their answers differ, but how they understand the authority of each, Scripture and Tradition, and by what authority they make that determination would also vary, with Protestants privileging Scripture and Roman Catholics privileging Tradition. Despite numerous ecumenical efforts and attempts at joint declarations, there is no consensus in theory or practice on such questions. But it is not enough to say there is disagreement, when in reality there is active contestation. In the past, wars have even been fought, ostensibly over such questions. So perhaps a more fundamental question to ask is what is at stake and for whom in these contestations.

Thus, any consideration of Christian memory needs to proceed in recognition not only of the plural and changing nature of remembering in Christianity, but that any particular narrative, any particular point of view, any claim to truth, is politically charged and has a political intent.

A particular symbol illustrates these dynamics for me and also adds further complexity to them by gesturing to the role of what is often referred to as "popular religion" in Christian remembering. In an old chapel in the Roman Catholic Basilica in Santa Fe, New Mexico, there is an early seventeenth century statue of Mary, with the title, *La Conquistadora* (the female conqueror). Below that title, the Spanish has been rendered in English as Our Lady of Peace. Ever since I saw this statue, years ago, I have been haunted by this juxtaposition and the possible meanings to attach to this act of translation, which is also an act of remembering in a particular way. Is the intent to declare that conquest brings/brought peace and so there is no contradiction between the titles? Is the translation an attempt to reclaim Mary in a different way, to change or perhaps cover over the history? An America tourist in the church, which is what I was the day I was there, might not notice the Spanish or know what it meant, so they would only take in the title, Our Lady of Peace. Mexican visitors, however, who do not know English might have the opposite experience. What would the title, *La Conquistadora*, connote to them today?

For me, the statue and its titles indicate that, in practice, Christian remembering and its uses cannot be separated from power and its uses. Ever since Christianity and empire joined forces, Christian remembering has served the uses of empire, although not without challenge or alternatives voices. Claiming to be fulfilling a Divine command, to be acting for the sake of salvation, the Church accompanied the forces of conquest and colonization throughout the world. Christian "truth" was imposed, resisted, adapted, hybridized, etc. Whether and how Christian "truth" is understood as saving memory depends then on social and political location and perspective, as well as on how it is understood and used.

Further, given that memory is collective, the dynamics of power are played out socially and politically in an ongoing cultural and historical process. In that sense there is no given truth or deposit of revelation. What has been understood to be Divine revelation, communicated as encoded knowledge, contained in scripture, doctrine, and teaching is actually communal memory, the recalling, expressing and communicating of the community's encounter with and experience of the Divine, albeit such memory is also the ground for ongoing dynamics of power and control.

Since the process of remembering is ongoing, what is remembered and by whom and why all become important considerations. How the Christian story is narrated and what points of view are included help shape whether, how and for whom it functions as a redeeming story. With such considerations in mind, I offer in the next section a narrative of the history of Christianity, a remembering the Christian story in a way that recognizes these dynamics, attends to the political positioning of any particular expression of Christianity, and maintains awareness of voices and viewpoints that may have been masked or disregarded. I do not presume that this narrative is comprehensive or an adequate account of Christian history. Rather it points to certain moments and directions in order to highlight the dynamics of power and positioning of Christianity in the world.

Remembering the Christian Story

In the ancient Roman occupied lands of the Hebrews, there appeared a prophet, teacher and healer, named Jesus. He had followers and disciples who accompanied him in his itinerant ministry to the people of Israel. His preaching centered on the coming reign of God, which was focused on justice and right relationship, in ways that could challenge the social, religious, and political order. He claimed to act and heal by the power of God. This Jesus was arrested, tried, and crucified on a cross, a common form of state execution used by the occupying Romans. His followers seemed to flee in fear when Jesus was arrested and crucified. However, soon after Jesus' death his followers claimed that Jesus had risen from the dead. They began to proclaim this as good news of salvation, a defeat of death and the powers of the world by the forces of life.

Jews at the time knew about prophets and martyrs who spoke out and even gave their lives to do the work God had given them to do. Their religion also lived in anticipation of the Messiah, who would come at the end of time, as a conquering hero to establish and complete God's reign. Jesus' Jewish followers tried to make sense of Jesus and his ministry through these traditions and ideas they knew. But these did not seem to fit easily. If Jesus was the Messiah, why had he been crucified? He did not act like a conquering hero. If he was a prophet and martyr, what did it mean to follow him now, after his death?

And yet, they also knew, his death did not end things. They experienced a new power in and among themselves that made them want to live differently, continue to follow Jesus, and even proclaim him as Lord. At the same time, they lived under occupation and the vagaries of the Roman Empire. They were a conquered, oppressed peoples with little power in the world's terms. Their power came from their faith, their fellowship, and their sense of the presence of God, including Jesus' own presence, among them.

Others, who were not among those who had not known Jesus in his lifetime, joined them. Notable among these "converts" was Paul, who was zealous about his newfound faith and tireless in his efforts to make it known. Due in good measure to Paul's missions, the proclamation of Jesus was carried to those outside the Jewish community. Tensions arouse as to what it meant to follow Jesus and how to understand Jesus' message in relation to Judaism.

After the destruction of the Jewish temple by Rome and the forced dispersion of Jews from Jerusalem, Christianity's connection with Judaism no longer had a formal and material connection. As Christianity spread among the non-Jewish population, the way in which its central narrative was told and understood changed. More and more, the early Christian movement adopted and adapted the prevailing thought forms of the Hellenistic world in which it continued to grow. It remained, however, a marginalized and minority movement, which endured persecutions under Roman rule, struggled to define and differentiate itself in relation to Judaism, and needed to find its place in the pluralistic Hellenistic world.

Two significant trajectories have roots in this milieu and have influenced Christianity: most notably, how it understands itself and functions in the world. One impacts Christian theology and doctrine significantly; the other has to do with Christianity and the political order.

As already noted, Christianity began as a reform movement within Judaism. Judaism defines itself by its relationship with God as narrated in the history of the Jewish people. The God of Judaism acts and is known in and through history. Jewish identity is constituted in many ways by a collective, narrative remembrance. Although such a characterization of Judaism is overly generalized and simplistic, the central point—that narrative and memory are key to Jewish identity—is accurate. Jews also identify themselves through practices, the keeping of the law as given in the Covenant and as that which what identifies them as God's chosen, covenanted people.

As Christianity struggled with its own identity in relation to Judaism, it contended with both these central dimensions of Jewish identity. What was the status of the law? Were Christians obliged to keep and fulfill the Jewish commandments? And where did Jesus fit into the Jewish narrative? A variety of answers were proposed, including seeing Jesus as the fulfillment or replacement of the law. Hebrew Scripture was also read as foreshadowing and predicting the coming of Jesus. In such ways, Christianity appropriated Hebrew Scripture and history.

At the same time, as Christianity sought to give form and expression to its central affirmations, its theologians looked to Greek metaphysical thought for language and concepts. Greek thought, especially Greek philosophical thought, is very different from Hebraic thought. For Greek metaphysics, what is true, good and beautiful is eternal, ideal, singular, and unchanging.

In the early centuries of Christian history as the process of theological development continued, early Christian theologians, who had been schooled in Greek metaphysics, drew on it more and more to express and define their understandings of Christian faith. Christian "truth" became less historical and narrative and more and more propositional. The creedal statements of the early church councils are illustrative of this process. For example, the narrative of Jesus is reduced in the Nicene creed to: "came down from heaven, and was incarnate by the Holy Spirit of the virgin Mary, and was made man; and was crucified also for us under Pontius Pilate; He suffered and was buried; and the third day He rose again, according to the Scriptures; and ascended into heaven, and sits on the right hand of the Father; and He shall come again, with glory, to judge the quick and the dead; whose kingdom shall have no end." The closest this "narrative" comes to historical specificity is "under Pontius Pilate" which affords Jesus' life a time and a location. What was important for theological orthodoxy was that Jesus truly existed, that the incarnation of the Divine, the Son of God, happened in a flesh and blood human being, and that a human person was crucified and died. The narrative of Jesus' life, his teaching and ministry, were not necessary for this purpose, nor was its historical context.

The differences in language and approach between Hebrew historical thought and Greek philosophical thought have complicated Christian truth as contained in tradition and theology for centuries, as has the creedal tradition intent on encapsulating and eternalizing truth in a way that results in a masking of the cultural specificity of its language and ideas. In this way, Christian memory was understood to be Divine revelation as contained and communicated in Christian doctrine. Such revelation, being of its Divine origin, was unchanging and by definition, non-historical as well as universal. It was deposit more than memory: something given that had to be protected and preserved. Thus the dynamic nature of tradition was denied, or perhaps more accurately, overridden and hidden. If there was debate about what was being handed down, the focus was on coherence and continuity: making sure that eternal truth remained as such.

More recent debates have acknowledged problems with such views, especially given the diversity of Christianity, denominationally and culturally, in the world. As noted above, there is no shared understanding or consensus about the meaning of Christian tradition. Theologically, a primary strategy for dealing with the diversity and differences is to distinguish between "TRADITION" and "traditions" with much of the subsequent argument being about what falls into which category. "Traditions" may reflect and contain differences and are subject to change. They represent localized memory and practice. TRADITION, as communicating God's revelation, remains singular and unchanging, a depository of truth. However, increasingly, in some circles, there is more recognition of pluralism as challenge to any notion of a singular tradition or TRADITION, as well as awareness of knowledge as ideological. There is also more acknowledgment of the central role of communities or institutions in determining what is deemed to be true, as well as more attention to the dynamics of power at play. But with all these shifts and changes, the criteria of coherence and continuity remain central and critical, as does the insistence that there is one, unchanging truth as contained in Scripture or Tradition, that is communicated, preserved and protected by the church (which, in turn suggests a claim to a singular Church rather than churches).

The other historical trajectory of Christianity, namely, Christianity's relationship with the political and social order, cannot be separated from Christian teachings about Divine revelation and truth, but it has its own storyline, so to speak. We might call this trajectory "the history of the Christian church as an institution operating in the world." As noted, in its early centuries, Christianity was primarily a minority, marginalized and sometimes persecuted movement within the Roman Empire which over its first few centuries increasingly ordered and established itself as it developed structures, including rites, rules, procedures, and modes of leadership. These were localized expressions, so even though there were recognizable connections, there was no one structural order or one set of shared practices. Christianity operated in plural forms from its origins.

The growth and establishment, as well as consolidation, of the church changed significantly with the "conversion" of Constantine and the adoption of Christianity as the religion of the empire. This wedding of Christianity and empire, which began in the fourth century, has been key and critical to Christianity's relationship to established power ever since. So the history of Christianity, and its practices of remembering, cannot be separated from the history of empire, nationalism, conquest, and colonialism throughout the world. Even in those parts of the world, outside of the Roman Empire, to which the early Christians found their way, such as India, it is the Christianity of the colonizing western powers that primarily determined the nature of Christianity in those locations.

Any discussion of Christianity's relationship with other religions needs to pay attention to this history. Nor can any productive discussion of relationships between groups within Christianity take place without such attention. In the early centuries of Christian empire, Christianity was imposed in a particular way on those whose own practices of Christianity, albeit ancient, were deemed wrong, out of bounds or heretical, including Arians, Celts, and Nestorians. And it was imposed on those who practiced other religions by means of conquest or conversion of heads of state.

All of this makes for a long, painful and bloody story of Christianity, beginning in the Near East, Europe and Northern Africa, but then spreading throughout the world. Whether Christianity was the religion of those leading the assault or being assaulted or both, as in the case of the Reformation wars, force has often been a factor in the assertion, spread, and establishment of Christianity. Here I will point out only a few "moments" that may be particularly important, especially in any present day encounter with other religious traditions.

The Crusades are a key event in Christianity's historical relationship with Islam and the eternally fought over Holy Land of Jerusalem, as well as areas such as Spain and North Africa that have passed from one to the other and back again. In the Crusades to the Holy Land, western Christianity waged war against Muslims and their occupation of lands, which had once been ruled by Christians (as well as others, including Romans). The Church declared its actions to be motivated not by aggression, but by a crusade for truth and for recapture of its Holy Land. In the process, Muslims were rendered infidels and the rhetoric of holy war was used.

Throughout the centuries before and after the Crusades, discrimination against and persecution of Jews continued, albeit in various ways, times, and places. A particularly pernicious example is the Inquisition, which functioned as a holy war within Christianity and against any who would not embrace Christianity, as determined by Rome. One of the outcomes of the Inquisition was the expulsion of Jews from Spain.[1]

With the beginnings of the modern era and the development of nations and national powers, the dynamics of empire shifted. As the lands that lay west, south, and east of Europe became increasingly available for conquest and colonization, western nations sought to establish empires. The power of state and of church joined together to impose Western rule and its Christian religion on peoples all over the world. The spread of missions accompanied the conquerors and colonizers, beginning in the sixteenth century. The religions that indigenous peoples practiced or adhered to prior to the arrival of missionaries were deemed backward or inadequate.

Missionary activities focused not only on converting the indigenous populations to Christianity, but also on imposing what was deemed civilization on those who were considered uncivilized or inferior. This was done in the name of salvation and a superior form of religion. In that way, the missionaries "preached" not only Christianity, but western civilization as well, in the name of salvation. The history of missions is a tangled web of imposed power, of the marriage of Christianity and conquest, salvation and civilization. But it is not simply that. There were missionaries who came to understand their project and their relationships to the peoples they were sent to convert and civilize differently. Some endorsed solidarity over subjugation and realized the value and importance of culture and context. Often these missionaries were then reprimanded and rejected by their own missionary boards, orders, and churches.

The history of missions needs to be much more fully explored for there to be fruitful encounter between Christianity and the peoples upon which it was imposed. Although this is not, and cannot be, my task here, I would point to and explore briefly a couple of important dynamics and outcomes of this history that I understand to be vitally important to any interfaith encounters or any attempts at healing of memories.

As I have already argued, Christianity cannot claim its truth to be innocent. There is no innocent Christian knowledge. When looking at Christianity across the globe and especially in postcolonial societies, the particular wedding of Christianity and power and how it has functioned in those contexts needs to be acknowledged and accounted for.

At the same time, the question of what constitutes Christian knowledge and identity needs to be left open in a way that allows new and different voices to emerge and be heard. The colonized were not empty vessels into which Christianity was poured. Rather they were actively engaged in a dynamic process of incorporating their own practices and beliefs into whatever forms of Christianity were imposed. These diverse and localized expressions of Christianity have much to teach about Christian memory, especially how it is transmitted and engaged with in different cultures. These Christianities can also point to possibilities for active engagement with other religions, especially "on the ground." Their practices and memorative narratives often connect with and incorporate other religious traditions in creative ways and so may offer valuable perspectives for interfaith, as well as intrafaith, encounters.

These localized Christianities can be illustrative of the category of "subjugated knowledges" (Michel Foucault) that emerge from those Gayatri Spivak identified as "subalterns," those whose voices have not been recognized or heard, who have been considered backward and ignorant, and who have been rendered silent by the dominant discourses. These voices have not counted, nor had a seat at the table. Perhaps they themselves did not know they had something to say, especially theologically. If and when these religious expressions have been recognized or paid attention to at all, it has been as popular religion or folk practices that may be of interest to an anthropologist or those who study ritual and folk customs, but not to theologians or even church historians. In that way, too, these forms of Christianity are generally left out of theological conversations.

This omission has been identified and challenged in recent years as Christians from a wide range of cultural contexts are not only claiming a place in theological conversations, but also doing so from their particular locations with all their cultural and political complexities. In this process, these Christians are revealing the contextual and political character of all theological discourses. These emerging theologies are thus not only broadening and adding complexity to theology but also offering rich resources for different understandings of truth, especially as truth is enacted and practiced, and for learning about how multiple traditions are quilted and held together. They are thus demonstrating the dynamic, contextual, and plural nature of tradition and Christian remembering.

If attended to, such remembering may result in re-membering Christianity, including recognizing such re-membering as an ongoing task and practice. There has been considerable discussion in recent years about global Christianity and the vitality of Christianity in the global South and other locations outside Europe and North America. These are also postcolonial contexts that are seeking to define themselves and their place in the world on their own terms, even as they struggle to identify, name and claim those terms.

Because they are postcolonial contexts, any remembering of the past necessarily includes narratives of violence, victimization, and oppression. Any re-membering in the present and any hope for the future needs to attend to such violence and its accompanying trauma, as well as the traumatic injuries produced. Remembering in these contexts thus has to engage with traumatic memory, which adds even more complicating layers.

REMEMBERING SUFFERING: MEMORY AND TRAUMA

In this section, I will discuss the nature and character of traumatic memory and then apply that to a consideration of Christian memory. This will lead into a consideration of Christian approaches to suffering and hope.

Traumatic events are life shattering, for persons and communities. By definition, they overwhelm and rupture lives. They cannot be taken in and processed by the normal functioning processes of the brain, including the way it processes memory. Therefore, it can be said that traumatic events are not fully experienced as they are happening. The extent to which these events result in traumatic injury and the impact of that injury are in some measure determined by the resources, internal and external, available to deal with their aftermath.

However, whatever life after the trauma is like, there is a way in which the rupture remains. As philosopher Susan Brison writes in *Aftermath*, her account of the rape and brutal beating she endured and her life thereafter, trauma disrupts continuity and "normality":

> [Trauma] introduces a "surd"—a nonsensical entry—into the series of events in one's life, making it impossible to carry on with the series. This account of the nature of trauma draws on both senses of surd—the mathematical sense ... of an irrational number or quantity, not expressible by an ordinary fraction, but

only by an infinite series, and the linguistic sense of a voiceless sound or a sound dampened or deadened by a mute."[2]

Which is not to say that life does not continue, but the series, the sequence, the presumed linearity is gone. And she goes on to write: "Not only is it now impossible to carry on with the series, but whatever sense had been made of it in the past has been destroyed."[3] Writing about the political, Jenny Edkins, in *Trauma and the Memory of Politics*, notes: "Trauma time is inherent in and destabilizes any production of linearity. Trauma has to be excluded for linearity to be convincing, but it cannot be successfully put to one side: it always intrudes, it cannot be completely forgotten."[4] Her image for how to deal with the relationship is one of "surrounding" or "encircling" the trauma, "encircling the event, marking its place without narrating it as part of a linear story."[5]

Thus, a trauma narrative, that seeks to witness to the trauma, to the event, is not able to provide continuity or coherence. Its witness must be not only to the injury, pain, and loss endured, but also to the rupture and what remains untellable and unintelligible. It does not make sense. Its witness is to non-sense.

Given the non-sense of trauma, traumatic memory is often more problem than resource. On the one hand, to the extent that the trauma is not experienced or processed, traumatic memory, remembering the trauma itself, remains inaccessible and unavailable. A traumatic event may be recalled and communicated as we might another type of event, which is to say that someone can narrate the events that occurred: for example, on such and such a day, a man grabbed me from behind, forced me to the ground, then raped and beat me. However, such a narration does not communicate the trauma itself or its effects and to the extent there a coherent narrative is maintained, the trauma is occluded. Thus, trauma can be referenced, pointed to, named and even narrated, but not in a way that really connects to the actual experience of trauma.

As a result, traumatic memory functions differently. It remains incoherent, intrusive, and other. It is undigested, so to speak. When it manifests, such as in flashbacks, it is often as an unwelcome intruder and a reminder of rupture and enduring non-sense.

Christianity's beginnings include a traumatic event: the crucifixion of Jesus. This act of violence caused Jesus' death and left his followers fearful and confused. As the Christian movement struggled with this event and its memory, it began proclaiming it as an act of redemption, along with the resurrection. A traumatic event was transformed into a saving action. A memory of violence was rendered as grounds for hope. Over time, the emphasis shifted more and more to the crucifixion and focused less and less on the resurrection (let alone on the incarnation or Jesus' life and ministry) as the moment of salvation. The proclamation that "Jesus died for our sins" named a trauma that could not be justified as an act of justification. A violent act was rendered a redemptive one. Thus, the trauma of the cross became a different story: Jesus' death on the cross was remedy for sin, a purposeful act, and a Divine action.

Even though the Church has tended not to make any particular understanding of the cross as saving action official doctrine, the claim that Jesus' death was salvific and that Jesus died for the forgiveness of sins is for many the heart of Christianity, across most of its expressions. It is at the center of a redemption narrative that developed in relation to it in order to fill out the story with a beginning and an ending. In skeletal form, the basic Christian redemption narrative tells this story: God created the world and humankind as without sin, which presumably exempted human beings from suffering and violence and even death. Humankind fell, by its own actions, from this original innocent state into a state of sin to which it was then captive. As a result, human beings and all of creation were subject to violence, suffering of all kinds, and death, without the ability or means to change their situation. Jesus' death thus functions as remedy for the sin and subsequent captivity of humankind. However that remedy is understood (among common "metaphors" for it are ransom, sacrifice, payment, substitution, satisfaction, and atonement), it is Jesus' death that saves humankind and allows Christians to live in the hope of redemption.

Again, there are and have been many theological articulations of the nature, shape, and scope of that redemption, including where, when, and how it occurs, as well as what it means and to whom it applies. These range from declarations of the universal salvation of all, already accomplished, to limited atonement for those whom God has chosen or designated, which is not to be revealed until the end of time or which is to be determined at a final judgment. There have also been all sorts of variations in between which sometimes identified the promise redemption with a particular expression or form of Christianity or, in its millennial expressions, sought to fix the time of consummation. Given the strong influence of Greek metaphysics and the political interests of empire, the where and when of redemption was moved out of history and understood to be beyond time (eternity) and space (heaven). Despite Christianity's affirmation of the resurrection of the body, redemption focused on the soul and its status in an afterlife in heaven (or hell). Even though the locus of redemption is ultimately outside of time, this narrative remains within a linear understanding of time: moving from a beginning, creation, and origins, including of sin—the "problem"—through the "solution" of the cross to the final outcome at the end of time. Jesus may have been manifest in the fullness of time (*kairos*) and his death may already have accomplished redemption and inaugurated the eschaton, but the eschaton is not realized in time. Fulfillment remains at the end and outside of time.

This rendering of the Christian narrative, however, ultimately devalues history as the arena of God's actions and along with it, an understanding of the corporate nature of redemptive action. With the Enlightenment emphasis on the individual and capitalism's exaltation of individualism, the corporate and collective dimensions of the Christian narrative faded even further. Hope was reduced to a desire for individual redemption, to what happened to each person and his or her soul. Piety became overly personal and replete with expressions of Jesus dying for me and Jesus being my Lord or my savior. Such emphases on the individual self not only devalued corporate and social perspectives on redemption, but also tended to reduce suffering to personal distress. The needs of the poor, the marginalized, the oppressed, and the violated as social and political conditions had little place in such piety. Concern for the oppressed and victimized was manifest as charity, not as political actions. There have been challenges to this Christian narrative, most notably in recent decades from liberation, political, and contextual theologians.

German political theologians, Johann Baptist Metz (Roman Catholic) and Jürgen Moltmann (Protestant) are among those who have offered a counter discourse to these developments. Because Metz has been such a key voice on memory and Moltmann on hope, I focus on their work here in considering memory and hope in Christianity.

Metz's project has been to reawaken what he has called the "dangerous memory" of Jesus Christ, which for him continues to manifest itself among those who suffer in the world, the poor and the oppressed. In that way, he has sought to provide a western European counterpart to the liberation theologies that began to emerge from the colonized regions of Christianity in the 1960s. These theologies still focused on the cross as redemptive, but in a way that honored the suffering of the oppressed. Jesus' suffering was not so much "for" as "with" them. It was not simply a remedy for sin, but a stance of solidarity with all who suffer in the world, an act of compassion. Because Jesus' own suffering was effective for redemption, there was meaning and value in the lives of those whose suffering is due to the sins of others.

For Metz, the memory of Jesus' suffering is dangerous because it recalls God as redeemer of the oppressed and because it evokes hope. Only if the historical process remains open, can such hope be real for the oppressed. Thus Metz seeks to interrupt the Christian narrative by recalling promises outstanding. He argues that salvation history remains open; we cannot presume the outcome. The memory of Jesus, especially of Jesus' passion and suffering, is dangerous precisely because it challenges complacency, nurtures responsibility and stirs to action. For Metz, the memory of suffering is grounds for hope.

Metz draws on an old folktale, but interprets it differently, to make his point about history: the tale of the hedgehog and the hare. In the story, a hare challenges a hedgehog to a race. The hedgehog has a wife who looks just like him so he positions his wife, similarly attired, near the end of the course. Once the race begins the hedgehog drops out and his wife takes her place at the course's end. When the hare arrives at the finish, he finds the hedgehog already there. So the hedgehog "wins" the race without ever running it. In folklore, the hedgehog is the hero of the story because he outwits the speedier hare. For Metz, however, the fact that the hedgehog never runs the race and that the outcome is given before the race has even begun is problematic. The "race" of Christian history needs to be run and so the outcome cannot be predetermined. Hope lies in an open future.

One can argue that Metz's project is to save Christianity—and Christian memory—from the ways in which it has been distorted in modernity and postmodernity, especially by what Metz calls bourgeois religion. Remembering is itself a redemptive action. The memories that Metz deems redemptive are of suffering. Remembering those who have suffered and mourning the losses are signs of our humanity.

But can such an emphasis on remembering suffering be effective for those who continue to suffer? What might be more effective ways of remembering by the victimized? Are not the victimized and oppressed in the world more likely to cheer for the hedgehog who is able to find a way to outsmart the hare who has the advantage in the situation? In the end, Metz's approach may not go far enough in helping those who suffer the most from oppression and violence to engage in effective action; and it may well overlook the ways in which they already might.

Metz's definition of religion is "interruption." Although Metz's project is to take history as the arena of redemption seriously, the linear and progressive view of time that is so dominant in Western modes of thought, especially in modernity, as well as the timelessness, which he sees as characterizing postmodernity, are both problematic. As remedy, he draws on apocalyptic and its emphasis on intervention and a sense of emergency as grounding hope. However, apocalyptic views of time render power as ultimately outside of history. Metz's view of time thus undercuts his own project to keep focus on history as the arena of redemption. In apocalyptic, the power to save comes from outside to disrupt historical continuity; it breaks in and interrupts historical time.[6]

Jürgen Moltmann is also concerned to address suffering in history and to highlight hope. He proceeds by focusing on the future as the locus of God's action. Hope is in the coming of God who is positioned at the end of time. Hope in restoration and completion as promised by God, but not realized or realizable in history. In that sense, nothing that God has initiated is yet completed. Hope is in knowing that God will make it so, so that present sufferings are not final or definitive.

Moltmann prefers the term "advent" to eschaton and "conversion" to interruption. As he states: "Conversion and the rebirth to a new life change time and the experience of time, for they make-present the ultimate in the penultimate, and the future of time in the midst of time. . . . The future-made-present creates new conditions for possibilities in history. Mere interruption just disturbs; conversion creates new life."[7] Nor does the future follow upon or develop from the past. Without negating or forgetting the past, God's future comes and makes present hope in a new creation.

For Moltmann redemption is ultimately the restoration of all things in God's time, in eternity. Such restoration is a re-membering and a recapitulation of sorts. This hope is rooted for Moltmann in the cross and Christ's descent into hell "that is the ground for the confidence that nothing will be lost but that everything will be brought back again and gathered into the eternal kingdom of God."[8] For Moltmann, the Last Judgment functions to set aright all the horrors of history in anticipation of the new life in God's kingdom. Ultimately, nothing and no one is lost; all are redeemed. A final judgment and subsequent restoration of all things is good news to those who suffer violence and other wrongs in history, because it means the power of their tormentors does ultimately prevail. Oppressors and all who do wrong will themselves be transformed. Universal restoration is sign of God's power and glory.

It is also the consummation of time. The eschaton does not simply end time and inaugurate eternity, but is the moment of God's "de-restriction" and indwelling of the new creation.[9] It is a transformation into glory, which effects completion and fulfillment. God cannot be God without such fulfillment and bringing of all into glory, which, for Moltmann, is ultimately better apprehended by an aesthetic, rather than ethical, sensibility.

I have argued in my book, *Time for Hope*, that such understandings of hope and eschatology do not fully account for trauma and suffering. They are shaped too much by a comedic sense of life and history.[10] This seemingly relentless comedic nature of the Christian narrative, in its various forms, excludes the tragic. The narrative intent remains on God's power to right all wrongs and restore all that has been lost. Theologians such as Metz and Moltmann, who are attentive enough to the uses of power in the world and even the complicity of the churches and Christianity in the misuse of such power, are careful about the claims they make and are reluctant to identify any movement in history as reflection or manifestation of God's purposes. They maintain what has been referred to as the "eschatological proviso," but, as a result, they ultimately locate redemption outside of history.

In seeking to tell a coherent story whose end is a culmination and fulfillment, these theologians do not address sufficiently the rupturing and nonsense of traumatic injury and suffering. For those whose suffering is in history, and for whom any remembering of that suffering is more problem than source of hope, there needs to be a different saving story.

The dominant narrative of creation, fall, and redemption that makes sin universal fault and cause of suffering, leaves little room for the sinned against, those who suffering is not the result of their fault, but the fault of others or even of powers and forces that cannot be easily identified or located in human actions (what can be understood as evil). This story of sin and redemption tends not to differentiate sufficiently between perpetrators and victims, oppressors and those harmed by oppression. It applies a "one size fits all" category of sin and the need for forgiveness and reconciliation to all forms of rupture, injury, and suffering. Nor does it attend to the point of view of the "sinned against" and their experience of loss and injury.

Theologians of the oppressed—liberation theologians, Black theologians, feminist theologians, and others those writing from the viewpoint of colonized and exploited peoples—attend not only to issues of power, but also to the dynamics of victimization. What effects have years of suffering and exploitation produced, they ask? What are the legacies of centuries of slavery, injustice and oppression? What would need to change in the lives of the victimized in order for them to become more whole, to experience freedom, reconciliation, and redemption?[11]

Such questions lead to challenging one size fits all ideas of sin and salvation, as well as unreflected views of forgiveness and reconciliation. Because victims are so often told to forgive those who sin against them, because the burden of reconciliation has so often been put upon those already burdened by injury and injustice, and because empowerment is so critical when victimization has involved coercion, it is important to pay very careful attention to what is asked of those who are sinned against and to question the dynamics of reconciliation. What does reconciliation and redemption look like to them? Do they need forgiveness, and for what? What does forgiving others mean to them, is it important and why?

To begin to respond to such questions, churches need to develop different and multiple ways of understanding and responding to suffering, including rituals and rites of reconciliation, especially ones that recognize the need for reconciliation in relation to suffering and not only in relation to sin. Suffering and sin need to be clearly differentiated so that not all suffering is viewed as the result of sin. More attention needs to be paid to the difference between sin that causes the suffering of others (and oneself) and suffering that is caused by the sin of others.

Those who suffer at the hands of others often feel depths of pain, trauma, alienation, and even despair that leaves them wounded and their lives broken, seemingly beyond repair. They need to experience reconciliation, not because of what they have done so much as what has been done to them. They need hope; they thirst for renewal of life.

In this process and for the sake of this process, the Christian story needs to be remembered differently. Jesus' suffering on the cross continues to be a meaningful symbol, not because Jesus suffered *for us*, taking on our sin and its effects, but because Jesus suffers *with us*, in solidarity with and compassion for all those who experience pain, injury, and abandonment. Jesus knows what it is to suffer at the hands of others, to be betrayed and undergo torture and be killed mercilessly. Jesus' suffering does not take away our own suffering but provides the assurance that those who are persecuted and sinned against do not suffer alone. God knows their pain and suffers with them.

The cross, however, is only a part of Jesus' solidarity, of Jesus being with and for us. In and through his person and ministry, Jesus deployed power to heal and to transform. He recognized the life force in others and called forth the power of those with whom he engaged. The saving action of God in Christ needs similarly to be about empowerment for life. The Christian redemption narrative needs to expand beyond the cross to include such emphases.

PROCESSES OF RECONCILIATION AND TRANSFORMATION

The churches need to develop ways to support the agency and desire for life of those who have been victimized as well as holding victimizers accountable and calling for repentance. This calls for different processes and strategies for the victimized and for victimizers.

Those who have been violated need contexts in which to express their anguish. A helpful resource for doing so may be found in the practice of lament. Many of the Psalms are laments in which the psalmist speaks from the depths of pain and abasement. The lament form allows the sinned against to name their experiences of suffering, to cry out in anguish, even to express anger and accusation and so to begin to let go of silence, shame, and submission. Lament, including its anger, can be directed toward God.

The expression of lament allows for a release of feeling and does not lead to forgiveness so much as to mourning and acknowledgment, and maybe even acceptance, of loss. Those who hear and attempt to respond to lament offer neither explanation nor judgment, but a receiving and holding of the pain expressed. The victimized need to know that their experiences can be heard and their anguish tolerated. Such holding does not presume any easy healing or resolution. It does, however, contribute to a process of transformation and, reconciliation. At this point, however, reconciliation is promise more than fulfillment. Only over time and the slow rebuilding of trust and connection may such promise move toward realization, including a healing of memories and reconciliation. Lament is one step in that process, but one that needs to be given adequate space and time for expression.

For those responsible for the sin and injury, the process of reconciliation is necessarily different. It begins in acknowledgment of fault, acceptance of responsibility, attempts to make amends, to the extent that is possible, and commitment to amendment of life and to change. The traditional practice of confession is one avenue for such a process of reconciliation, especially if more emphasis is put on amendment of life, including making amends to those whom one has injured.

Both the process of lament and of confession can be practiced corporately. For the victimized the solidarity of corporate lament might well be salutatory. For those who have perpetrated violence and injury, especially if the violence and harm were initiated and carried out by institutions or states, it is vitally important to acknowledge the source of the violence and the forms and layers of complicity. Since these situations are rarely ones in which right and wrong are clearly distinguishable and attributable, discerning complicity can be a very complex and difficult process.

A concrete example of such attempts at reconciliation may be found in a liturgy offered by the Anglican bishops of Japan at the 1998 Lambeth Conference, a meeting of all the bishops of the worldwide Anglican Communion held every ten years at Lambeth, in England. As has been the case in the last several decades, this gathering was characterized by contentiousness over the ordination of women and the church's stance on homosexuality, as well as struggles between the North America and European churches and those of the former British colonies, especially in Africa. The bishops of Nippon Sei Ko Kai in Japan were responsible for the liturgy of the day on August 6, which is both the feast of the Transfiguration in the Christian liturgical calendar and the date of the bombing of Hiroshima during World War II. These bishops faced choices about what to remember and how. They could have simply focused on the liturgical calendar and remembered and marked the Transfiguration, a story that highlights Jesus as chosen by God and glorified. They could have called attention to the trauma and victimization of the Japanese people as a result of the American bombing of Hiroshima. Instead, the bishops chose to highlight and remember atrocities committed by the Japanese during World War II, to take responsibility for those actions and to ask for forgiveness for the complicity of the churches during those atrocities. A statement to that effect was handed to each person as she or he arrived for the liturgy. The daughter of the bishop of Singapore, who had been tortured by the Japanese army, preached and was literally given the pulpit in the service. The congregational responses to the prayers of the people were in Korean, the language of another group systematically persecuted by the Japanese. The liturgy was intended to remember the history of that time in a way that acknowledged the misuses of power. It sought to move toward reconciliation by acknowledging, giving voice to, and empowering those who had been persecuted. In that way, it offered what I term "empowering hospitality." The bishops used their power and position to offer acknowledgment, space, and voice to others.[12]

The truth and reconciliation commissions that have populated the landscape of post-violent societies and states in recent decades are also attempts at processes of accountability and making amends. Their varying effectiveness speaks to the complexities and complications of corporate responsibility. Not only is it difficult to distinguish who is responsible and for what wrongs and to deal with the webs of personal responsibility in relation to institutions and structures involved, but the situations are complicated even further by the multiple discourses that may be at play: legal, ethical, religious, therapeutic—to name a few.

All of this complicates any process of remembering and reconciliation. But regardless of these complications, the decoupling of the linkage of suffering and sin, that has been such a hallmark of Christianity, would help in the process of dealing with them, especially in developing different paths of healing for the victimizers and the victimized. Such a decoupling would lead to remembering Christianity—and especially the cross—differently. An important beginning in that process, and one which I have been arguing for, for some time, is to decenter the cross as the site of redemption and to reground it in its historic roots, as an act of state execution, not Divine command, and to acknowledge it as traumatic for the followers of Jesus. There are no grounds here for Christian triumphalism, even with the experience of resurrection. The resurrection is witness to going on with life, despite the defeat of death. That is my definition of hope: life ongoing. Life goes on, at the same time that it lives with the non-sense of the cross and its trauma.

The temptation to try and make sense of the cross and imbue it with meaning is always present, just as trauma survivors try to make sense of what happened to them. Such sense making inevitably turns to available narrative forms and plot lines and in so doing, ends up imposing structure and meaning as possible within those forms. But in doing so it tends to distort and even distances the trauma further, making it more inaccessible. If then we are to remember the cross as trauma, we need to prescind from making it fit our need for meaning and sense making. Rather we need to let it remain, undigested and lacking coherence, at the same time as we maintain it as memory.

Such is the power of the cross. It is memory that erupts again and again to disrupt our assumed sense making, including trying to find purpose in suffering. I would propose that there may well be a connection between acknowledging this non-sense and lack of justification and giving full place in Christianity to emerging voices, who speak not for the victors, but for those who have been victimized again and again in history, including by Christianity itself. This requires attention—honest attention—to the dynamics of power in any and every historical and social context. If *La Conquistadora* is to be

Our Lady of Peace, the voices of all must be included in any conversations and actions.

IN DIALOGUE

Based on what I have written and argued above, the particular contribution of Christianity to an interfaith dialogue about memory is to recognize the dynamics of power, especially in regards to what is remembered, by whom, how, and for what purpose. As I have argued and other contributors to this conversation have as well, remembering is always a process, unstable and changing. I add to that perspective an emphasis on the political dynamics of that process. This is easier to see and assert when religious memory is understood as rooted in history and rendered in narrative, but I think it applies whatever the nature and role of memory. Even a process of forgetting, or letting go of memory, has political implications.

Further, if we are going to talk about healing of memories, there is a presumption of injury or pain and, therefore, suffering. Again, it is important to consider whose suffering is attended to, how and for what purpose. Because Christianity has too often linked suffering with redemption, its memorative practices have not sufficiently supported resistance to suffering or even judgment on suffering. What can Christianity learn from other religions when it comes to how suffering is viewed and dealt with?

All religions must, in some way, deal with tradition and their religious heritage: that is, the status and authority of the past, especially how the foundations of the religion are viewed and understood and what is transmitted and held as sacred. Often, disagreements and contention within religions are related to questions of tradition, both its content—what is fundamental and needs to be preserved and handed down—and by what authority such judgments are made. Since tradition and memory are inherently connected, a focus on tradition and authority would be an important focus of dialogue. Included in such dialogue might well be a consideration of which voices are included in the conversation. As I have pointed out, an important dynamic in recent decades within Christianity has been the emergence of voices from historically marginalized, excluded or disregarded groups, such as women and indigenous peoples, and along with that emergence, attention to expressions of Christianity, often as found in popular religious practices, that not only call into question the "dominant" tradition, but offer alternative ways of practicing and understanding Christianity. What happens to how memory and tradition are viewed if such voices and expressions are attended to, not only in Christianity, but in other religions as well? What resources might they offer? What problems might they pose? How do these voices affect the question of religious authority?

Finally, a key question in considerations of hope is whether and to what extent hope is viewed as historical or not. As I have indicated, Christianity has tended to de-historicize hope in ways that may undercut resistance to suffering and struggle against violence. How does this dynamic function in other religions? What resources might be found in religious traditions for supporting efforts for change for the better in the world?

NOTES

1. This instance resulted, however, in an intriguing and interesting dynamic of memory. There were those among the *"conversos,"* those Jews who were forces to convert to Christianity, who continued to practice Judaism, especially the rituals that were practiced in homes, such as lighting candles in observance of the Sabbath, in secret. These practices were passed down over generations, but often without a narrative attaching them to their Jewish origins. For example, women would light candles on Friday evenings because their mothers and grandmothers did, but did not know why. These actions then functioned as memorative practices attached to familial identity, but not explicitly Jewish identity.

2. Susan Brison, *Aftermath: Violence and the Remaking of a Self* (Princeton: Princeton University Press, 2003), 103.

3. Brison, 204.

4. Jenny Edkins, *Trauma and the Memory of Politics* (Cambridge, UK: Cambridge University Press, 2003), 16.

5. Edkins, 17.

6. See Johann Baptist Metz, *Faith in History and Society: Toward a Practical Fundamental Theology*. Trans. David Smith (New York: Seabury Press, 1980) and essays in *Love's Strategy: The Political Theology of Johann Baptist Metz*, ed. John K. Downey (Harrisburg, PA: Trinity Press International, 1999) for further reading of Metz's theology.

7. Jürgen Moltmann, *The Coming of God: Christian Eshatology*, trans. Margaret Kohl (Minneapolis: Fortress Press, 1996), 22.

8. Moltmann, 251.

9. Moltmann, 294.

10. Flora A. Keshgegian, *Time for Hope: Practices for Living in Today's World* (New York: Continuum, 2006). See especially chapter 4.

11. This paragraph and much of the next seven are taken or adapted from Flora A. Keshgegian, "Voices of Anguish: Listening to Victims of Violence," in *Ambassadors for God: Envisioning Reconciliation Rites for the 21st Century. Liturgical Studies Five*. Ed. Jennifer Phillips (New York: Church Publishing Incorporated, 2010).

12. See Nan Cobbey, "In worship, the Anglican spirit shows forth," *Episcopal Life* 9 (September 1998) 5 and Katie Sherrod, "Transfiguration Liturgy offers moment of blessing to Lambeth Conference," Lambeth Conference 1998. Archives at http://www.lambethconference.org/1998/news/lc113.cfm, accessed 10 March 2014 for accounts of the liturgy.

Chapter Four

"Hope Is Greater Than Memory" (*āśa vai smarād bhūyasī*) Chandogya Upanishad 7.14.2

Insights From the Hindu Tradition

Anantanand Rambachan

MEMORY AND SCRIPTURE

Memory (*smṛti*) is significant in multiple ways in the Hindu tradition. The four Vedas (Ṛg, Sāma, Yajur, and Atharva), regarded by Hindus as an authoritative revelation, were memorized and transmitted orally for centuries before these were preserved in writing. Students learned the Vedas by hearing the texts recited by a teacher and committing the verses to memory. Memorizing the texts made these easily accessible for ritual and study purposes and for use in daily life. The texts, in a profound sense, become embodied through memory. It was even believed that memory may be a better instrument for the accurate preservation of religious texts. One lives more intimately with a text that is memorized.

The learning of the Vedas through memorization continues to be an important feature in the life of Hindus. Young Hindu boys commonly undergo the sacrament of *upanayana*, at which time they are invested with the sacred thread, and commence memorization of the Vedas. The tradition of memorizing and reciting the Vedas has influenced similar practices with other texts. Portions of texts such as the Bhagavadgītā and the Rāmāyaṇa are memorized and repeated as part of domestic and public worship. Millions of Hindus across the world have memorized and recite daily the Hanumāncālīsā, a short poem attributed to Tulasidasa (ca.fifteenth century), in praise of Hanuman, a servant and devotee of God as Rama.

MEMORY AND PRAYER

Memory also plays an important role in a very common Hindu religious practice. This is the chanting of a single word or a verse from the scripture. This form of prayer or meditation is referred to as *japa* and is usually accompanied by the use of a *japa mālā* or rosary made up of 108 beads. Although the practice does not require a great feat of memory, as in the memorization of the Vedas, remembering and repeating God's name in this manner is highly valued since it fosters the unbroken loving remembrance of God. Remembering God throughout life and the time of death, according to the Bhagavadgītā (8:5), ensures that one attains God. *Smaraṇa* (remembering) is included as one of the nine expressions of worship that include listening, singing, ritual offerings, serving, praising, friendship, servanthood, and self-surrender. Hindus believe that remembering and reciting God's name, along with the expression of devotion, help us to develop mental and emotional control and heals mind and body.

MEMORY AND THE HINDU CALENDAR

The Hindu calendar could be described appropriately as a series of reminders about occasions that ought to be remembered. Each day of the week is associated with the worship of God in a specific form. Although there are geographical variations, Monday is significant for the worship of God as Shiva, Tuesday for the worship of Hanuman, the devotee and servant of Rama, Wednesday for Krishna, Thursday for Vishnu, Friday for Shakti, Saturday for Shani, and Sunday for Surya. Each form of God has a unique mode of worship, disciplines to be observed, and texts for recitation.

Birth anniversaries are special occasions for remembering. These include the birthdays of *avatāras* like Rama and Krishna that are celebrated with worship in Hindu temples and homes and with the recitation of texts that narrate the birth events.

The calendar also reminds us of the birth of great teachers in the tradition that include Shankara, Ramanuja, Madhva, and Chaitanya, but also more recent teachers such as Sri Ramakrishna, Swami Vivekananda, and Ramana Maharshi. Over the past year, Hindus throughout the world have been remembering and celebrating the great legacy of Swami Vivekananda, the first Hindu teacher to the western world, on the occasion of his 150th birth anniversary. The Hindu calendar, in fact, sets aside a special day each year, Guru Purnima, for remembering one's religious teacher. It is an occasion for visiting the teacher, expressing gratitude and honoring him with gifts. It is a time also for the renewal of one's commitment to the wisdom received from the guru. Guru Purnima, although holding special meaning for the religious teacher, is extended in meaning to include teachers of all subjects. Remembering our indebtedness to teachers is meant to awaken our own generosity to share knowledge with others and to support those who seek and impart wisdom. In a similar way, and for similar reasons, the Hindu calendar devotes a fortnight (Pitṛ Pakṣa) each year for remembering family departed ancestors. It is an occasion for the offering of prayer on their behalf but also for the expression of gratitude for their many gifts to us. We remind ourselves about the immense debt which we owe to those in our families who precede us and of the obligation to be generous in our own families. If we forget that we are receivers, we will not be generous givers.

MEMORY AND DAILY OBLIGATIONS

What a religious tradition asks us to remember offers great insight into what it values and holds dear. In the case of the Hindu tradition, these are identifiable easily in the five-fold daily obligations (Pañca Mahāyajña) required of all Hindus. Each memory obligation is referred to as a great *yajña* for a special reason. *Yajña* is a mode of existence born out of a deep awareness of interdependence and characterized by giving and receiving. It is commended as the way to flourishing and prosperity in the Bhagavadgītā 3:10:

> In the beginning, the Creator, having created beings together with *yajña* said,
> "By this may you prosper; may this be your wish-fulfilling cow."

The ancient *yajña* model is the Vedic fire ritual in which worshippers sat around the sacred fire-altar making offerings and reciting Vedic mantras. At the conclusion of the ritual, food, some of which would have been offered in the fire is distributed. Food is gratefully received, but only after it is given in worship. In the structure of Hindu worship, giving always precedes receiving. The five daily obligations ask us never to forget what we have received and to be generous as a consequence. Without the memory of our indebtedness, we are unlikely to share. Without this memory, we live, according to Bhagavadgītā 3:12 as thieves. We receive without ever giving.

The five daily memory obligations of the Hindu are as follows:

1. Deva Yajña: remembering the generosity of God through worship and service of others.
2. Brahma Yajña: remembering the generosity of teachers through sharing knowledge, study, and support for students.

3. Pitṛ Yajña: remembering the generosity of ancestors through prayer and the service of the elders in our families and communities.
4. Manuṣya Yajña: remembering the generosity of other human beings in our lives through lives of compassion and sharing.
5. Bhūta Yajña: remembering nature, the elements and other life forms, through an ecologically responsible life.

We are asked to remember that interdependence implies indebtedness (*ṛna*). Ingratitude is an expression of forgetfulness. Memory preserves the meaning and vitality of religious life.

THE DISCOURSE OF REMEMBERING AND FORGETTING IN RELATION TO LIFE'S ULTIMATE GOAL

The famous Advaita teacher, Shankara, uses the metaphor of forgetfulness to explain the fundamental human problem. In his commentary on the Brahmasūtra 2.1.20, Shankara tells the story of a prince who was given up at birth by his parents and raised in a family of fowlers or hunters of birds. The child forgot his identity as a prince and the inheritor of his father's throne. He believed that he was a fowler's son and learned to trap birds. A compassionate person (viz. the teacher) who knew of the boy's royal identity explained to him that he had forgotten himself. Soon, the boy remembered his princely state and gave up the thought of being the son of a fowler. In a similar way, the human self (*ātmā*), is non-different from the limitless (*brahman*). Under the condition of ignorance (*avidyā*), we are not aware of this truth of ourselves. We incorrectly identify ourselves entirely with the attributes of the body, senses, and mind and superimpose these upon the self. The self, intrinsically full, free, and identical with *brahman* is then regarded as a limited and finite entity, bound by time and space, and subject to birth, growth, change, decline, and death.

Liberation is not a change in the nature or state of the *ātmā*. It is understanding or remembering the true nature of the self that, in fact, is not affected by misunderstanding or forgetfulness. Many widely used examples underline this fact. Liberation is compared to searching for the necklace that one wears around one's neck but which one has forgotten. When one remembers it, one discovers that it was there all the time and never lost!

Analogies, like the one of recovering the necklace on one's neck, go only so far. Once recovered, one does not have to remember its presence constantly. Forgetfulness of the nature of the *ātmā*, however, is a deep-seated problem that conditions the way we think about ourselves, with far-reaching consequences. Since we are dealing with a long-established and habitual way of thinking, we are more than likely to become forgetful of a new understanding of ourselves and revert to old ways of thinking. In this case remembering the truth becomes a religious practice (*sādhana*). The consequence of self-forgetfulness may be, as Bhagavadgītā 2:67 reminds us, disastrous, and even the wise one may be swept away from wisdom. Self-understanding is a transformative process of replacing habitual ways of thinking with new ways of thinking and memory plays a vital role in this discipline. It is perhaps for this reason that Krishna in Bhagavadgītā 10:34 and 15:15 speaks of memory as a Divine gift. At the end of the Bhagavadgītā, Arjuna expresses his gratitude to his teacher, Krishna, for regaining memory (*smṛtirlabdhā*). In so many ways, taken too often for granted, memory makes possible and enriches our religious lives.

THE CHALLENGE OF MEMORY AS *RĀGA AND DVEṢA*

The Bhagavadgītā, one of the most influential of Hindu religious texts, speaks repeatedly about what it refers to in Sanskrit as *rāga* and *dveṣa* (2:64; 3:34; 18:51). These are presented in the text as a pair (*rāga-dveṣa*) and the teacher, Krishna, advises his student, Arjuna, that he should not allow himself to be controlled by these two. "May one not come under the influence of these two," says Krishna in 3:34, "because they are one's enemies." It is important to take note of the fact that the teacher does not ask for complete freedom from *rāga-dveṣa*, but for liberating oneself from being in the grip of their control.

The terms *rāga-dveṣa* have been translated differently as love-hate, like-dislike, or desire-aversion. Essentially, a *rāga* is a powerful like or attraction for a person, a group, an object or situation. Conversely, a *dveṣa* is a strong antipathy towards someone or something. In the teaching of the Bhagavadgītā, these twin attitudes are formed in the process of our socialization and identity formation in different cultural, social, religious, or national groups. We develop preferences for persons, groups, and situations that we consider to be sources of self-value and pleasure and despise those that we associate with unhappiness and pain. A pleasurable experience that is associated with a person, group, or situation leaves an impression on the mind, conscious and sub-conscious. Such an impression is referred to, in Sanskrit, as a *saṃskāra*. These impressions are stored as memories (*smṛti*). Such impressions and memories shape our characters and dispose us to seek out the persons and situations that we associate with pleasure. We return to these repeatedly and attachment grows stronger. The absence of these causes unhappiness and suffering. In a similar way, the experiences that we regard as negative and sources of pain also form memory impressions and dispose us to avoid specific groups, individuals, or situations and to regard these even with hate. These become associated in our consciousness with what is painful and to be spurned and rejected. The pairing of these is an important insight of the tradition since there is no strong like without some corresponding dislike and vice-versa.

Rāga and *dveṣa* shape our character in decisive ways and condition our responses to the world around us. The memories (*smṛti*) settle deep in us and control our reactions in a manner that seems almost natural. In time, we respond to persons and to situations without the knowledge that our responses are conditioned and shaped by particular historical events and circumstances. We give control over to these accumulated memories and become victims of our own past experiences. The Bhagavadgītā identifies anger (*krodha*) closely with being in the grip of these polarities. The impossibility of manipulating the world to conform to our own preferences and the inevitability of encountering that which we dislike and prefer to avoid result in anger and the possibility of violence towards those who are seen as frustrating the fulfillment of our likes. Memories can therefore be potent sources for a train of events leading to the destruction of self and others.

In its treatment of memories, and especially memories as expressing in *rāga* and *dveṣa*, the Bhagavadgītā and the Hindu tradition, broadly speaking, have given emphasis to the nature and implications of these for the individual and for individual relationships. There is no good reason, however why the Hindu insight about the nature of memory cannot be transferred to our understanding of groups and communities and their relationships. Although this would be a novel move, it is a very meaningful one. The fact is that many of memories that shape us and determine our disposition towards other communities are inherited from the groups to which we belong, whether these are religious, national, ethnic, or social in nature. *Rāga* and *dveṣa* are transmitted inter-generationally and persist even when the specific historical circumstances that caused these no longer obtain. These become the fuel for our prejudice, stereotyping, and demonizing of other groups and communities.

What are the religious therapies or techniques offered by the Hindu tradition, and especially the Bhagavadgītā, for dealing with the problem of *rāga-dveṣa* and especially those that lead to destructive behavior? Clearly, these are discussed in the sacred texts to help us understand their formation but also to help in their overcoming. The text (2:64) speaks of freedom from the grip of *rāga* and *dveṣa* (*rāgadveṣaviuyuktaistu*) and cautions (3:34) that one should not allow oneself to fall victim to these (*tayorna vaśam āgacchettau*). Although not underestimating the powerful hold of memories, the Bhagavadgītā holds out the possibility of our freedom. The process of attaining freedom from the control of memories, that are potential sources of pain and suffering, involves self-understanding and wisdom. The significance of the Bhagavadgītā's identification of *rāga-dveṣa* memories is to enable us to become aware of these and to understand the circumstances under which these are formed. We are blessed, in the vision of the text, with a self-reflective capacity in which may be found the seeds of our freedom. Without the exercise of this unique human gift, we are doomed to be victims of our past experiences. The exercise of this gift for self-inquiry is the source of our hope.

It is also clear that the process of seeking freedom from being controlled by memories occurs in the context of a search for a new way of being and a deeper wisdom about self and its relation to others. It is this wisdom, according to the teaching of the Hindu tradition that must inform our self-understanding and our way of being in the world, individually and collectively, and not unexamined memories.

The problem of memory as *rāga* and *dveṣa* must be seen in the context of the tradition's understanding of the fundamental human problem and its resolution.[1] As noted above, the Advaita tradition teaches the human self (*ātmā*), is identical in fundamental nature with the limitless (*brahman*). This teaching is presented most concisely in the four great sentences (*mahāvākyas*) of the Upaniṣads: "That Thou Art (*tat tvam asi*)" is taken from Chāndogya Upaniṣad 6.8.7 of the Sāma Veda; "This *ātmā* is *brahma* (*ayam ātmā brahma*)" is taken from the Māṇḍukya Upaniṣad 2 of the Atharva Veda; "Awareness is *brahma* (*prajñānaṁ brahma*)" is taken from the Aitareya Upaniṣad 5.3 of the Ṛg Veda; and "I am *brahma* (*ahaṁ brahmāsmi*)" is taken from Bṛhadāraṇyaka Upaniṣad 1.4.10 of the Yajur Veda. Each one of the great sentences point out an already obtaining identity between the self and the limitless.

Ignorant of the truth of the self as being of the nature of the limitless, full and complete, we cling to a constructed and historical self that is by nature limited and wanting and shaped by likes and dislikes. This constructed self seeks continuously to assert its own worth in relation to the diminished worth of others. The sense of inadequacy and incompleteness that results from ignorance about the unity of the self with *brahman* find expression in the multiplication of desires, positive and negative, in an effort to overcome this condition of lack. We exert ourselves for ends such as wealth, fame, and power, hoping that the gain of these will free us from self-inadequacy. We develop powerful culturally conditioned likes and dislikes, entrenched as memories, hoping that the fulfillment of one and avoidance of the other will bring us contentment and fullness of being. We discover, however, in the course of time and through analysis of our experiences, that every finite gain, provides only a short-lived sense of fullness and we are left wanting. As Shankara writes in his commentary on Chāndogya Upaniṣad 7.23.1, "the finite or the *small* always gives rise to longing for what is more than that; and all longing is a source of pain."

What wisdom does, most importantly, is to free us from the illusion that the gain or the avoidance of the finite will resolve our persistent sense of inadequacy. Bhagavadgītā 2:62–63, describes a ladder of descent to evil and self-destruction, identifying loss of memory (*smṛtivibhrmah*) as one of the steps of this process:

> In the person who dwells upon objects, an attachment is born with reference to them. From attachment is born desire, and from desire, anger is born.
> From anger comes delusion and delusion comes the loss of memory. Because of the loss of memory, the mind becomes incapacitated and when the mind is incapacitated, the person is destroyed.

This tragic state is contrasted with the condition of the person of wisdom:

> But the disciplined self, moving among objects with senses free from likes and dislikes, attains peace.
> In that peace there is the end of all suffering. The reasoning of one whose mind is calm becomes stable.

Wisdom enables us to become mindful of the memories and impressions that condition our response to the world. Wisdom enables to respond to the world, not from the dualism of like and dislike, love and hate, but from a vision of the unity of existence and the seeing of the limitless in all beings. Wisdom frees us from responding to the world on the basis of historically formed memories and enables us to do so on the basis of compassion. A wise person has no need to find self-value through the diminished worth or others or by asserting the superiority of a group identity. As Īśa Upaniṣad puts it, "One who sees the self alone in all beings, feels no hatred by virtue of that understanding. For the seer of oneness, who knows all beings to be the self, where is delusion and sorrow?" From a place of wisdom, we see how self-ignorance conditions our own responses to the world through ingrained memories. We understand also how the responses of others are similarly conditioned through their own memories. Our understanding of ignorance as the root human problem awakens a disposition of reconciliation and forgiveness since it orients us to look beyond behavior and to its underlying causes, both in ourselves and in others. We respond with hate when we believe that those who hurt us do so through intentional malevolence. If we see their actions, and our own, as rooted in self-ignorance and a false understanding of reality, we can be compassionate and understanding and liberated from the grip of memories that dispose us to have and to inflict vengeance. Wisdom does not obliterate memories but enables us to understand the sources of these and to respond in freedom from their constraints. Spiritual ignorance is perpetuated through memories; wisdom liberates us from the prison of memories.

Is there any place for such freedom, given the Hindu teaching about *karma* and the impact of the past on the present? How does teaching on *karma* help with liberation from the control of past memories? I offer a comment on this in the next section.

A REFLECTION ON HOPE AND KARMA

When we think of the meaning of *karma* in the Hindu tradition, there is one predominant interpretation that comes immediately to our minds. We think of *karma* as signifying the effects of past actions that we are experiencing in the present. We hear the word, *karma*, used most often in statements such as, "This is my *karma*," or "This is his *karma*." Expressions like these emphasize the meaning of *karma* as result (*phala*). *Karma* is thought of primarily as the consequence of actions done in the past, and more particularly in past lives, that are generating results for us in the present. We use *karma* to explain experiences and events in life for which we have no other rational explanations nor which we are unable to avert. It helps us to think that these events are not arbitrary and that we are not victims of random causes. *Karma* helps us to affirm an underlying meaning to our lives, even when we cannot see the whole picture.

What is the consequence of thinking about *karma* primarily or only as the result of past actions? What happens when we equate the meaning of *karma* with *karma phala*? The outcome is that the meaning and value of the Hindu teaching about *karma* becomes quite limited. *Karma* is reduced to a doctrine for explaining occurrences in life when we cannot see other causes. Even more importantly, *karma* as result encourages and inculcates an attitude of resignation and passivity. It does not make demands of us or encourage an active response, individually or on the part of the groups to which we may belong. Such an attitude becomes particularly problematic if *karma* is used, as it has been from time to time in the history of the Hindu tradition, to explain inequality, injustice, and suffering and to justify the power, privilege and oppression of one group over another. It results in blaming the victim for his or her suffering and provides no incentive for working for change. It does not promote self-examination; it justifies the status quo and not its transformation.

The question is whether the understanding of *karma* as result and the attitude of hopeless resignation that it encourages are the most important dimensions of this central Hindu teaching. Are hope, transformation, and *karma* compatible? Is there a possibility of freedom from the conditioning and grip of the past? To answer this question properly, we must examine the different meanings of the word *karma* and there are at least three that are important. First, is the literal meaning of the word. *Karma* means action (from *kr*—to do or to make). It includes mental, vocal, and bodily actions that have moral significance. Second, is the meaning of *karma* as law (*dhar-*

ma). Moral actions are consequential and produce effects for the doer of the action as well as the one who is the object of the action. The lie that I tell affects me as well as the person to whom it is spoken. The third meaning of *karma* is the one already cited above that speaks of *karma* as the result or fruit of action.

If we shift our focus from the emphasis on *karma* as result to the meaning of *karma* as moral action and as law of consequence, the significance and potential of the teaching become radically different. *Karma* becomes much more than just an explanation for those events in our life that cannot be otherwise explained and about which we are impotent. It changes the focus from the past to the present, from inaction and passivity to action and transformation, from powerlessness to empowerment, from hopelessness to hope.

Karma as action and consequence offers us a method of self-transformation in the present, including freedom from enslavement to memories. The core Hindu teaching about *karma* is that we are continuously making ourselves, constructing who we are now, individually and collectively, by the thoughts we entertain, the words we choose to speak and the actions that express our thoughts and words. The formation of character and culture is not mysterious or inexplicable; it is constructed by repeated and habitual thought, emotion, speech and action and relationship patterns.

This understanding of *karma* as self-creation or self-making is articulated clearly in Bṛhadāraṇyaka Upaniṣad 4.4.5.

> As one does and acts, so one becomes; by doing good one becomes good and by doing evil one becomes evil—one becomes virtuous through virtuous actions and evil through evil actions. As one desires, so does one will; as one wills so does one act and as one acts one achieves.

Just as our bodies are formed by what we consume, so also our character is made by our intentional thoughts, feelings, words, and action. We become (*bhavati*) what we think, speak, and do. To this we may add, the significance of memory. Our memories also shape who we are, informing thoughts, feeling, words, and action. Although the word *karma* as action includes mental, vocal, and bodily actions, this Upaniṣad verse wants to emphasize the primacy and importance of desire and intention in the formation of character. The nature of actions is determined by the quality of desires and intentions. Desire shapes will, will shapes action and action determines outcome (*yathākāmo bhavati tatkraturbhavati/yatkraturbhavati tat karma kurute/yatkarma kurute tadabhisaṁpadyate*). The significance of this insight is that the process of self-making or remaking begins with a transformation of the motivation underlying our actions. *Karma*, as action, is an affirmation of the freedom to become the kind of person we wish to be. It is, in the words of Swami Vivekananda, "the eternal assertion of human freedom."[2]

The kind of person the Hindu tradition wishes each one to become may be described in a threefold manner. First, is to grow in wisdom (*jñāna*). The essence of wisdom in Hinduism is a deeper understanding of the unity of all existence in God. Second, to grow in loving compassion (*dayā*) and third is to grow in generosity (*dāna*). Both flow from the vision of life's unity. *Jñāna, dayā and dāna* are the ideals that inspire our self-development and that can transform memory.

So far, we have spoken of *karma* as action and as a method of growth and self-transformation. This seems to be a very individual and personal way of speaking about *karma*. How about our relationships and our lives in our communities? How does *karma* as action and as law of consequence make a difference in our relationships with others and in bringing about change in our communities? When, through wisdom we transform ourselves, we begin to see and to experience the world differently. We come to a deeper appreciation of the presence of God in everyone and in everything. This leads to a deeper value and appreciation for the world and for all living beings. When we see the word differently, we respond to it differently. We respond on the basis of the values of wisdom (*jñāna*) loving compassion (*dayā*) and generosity (*dāna*) and not on the basis of ignorance, greed, hate, likes, and dislikes. When we respond differently to the world, the world responds differently to us. When we are motivated by ignorance, greed and hate, we see the world and people as existing to serve our own needs. People are instrumental to fulfilling our ambitions and we treat them in a manner that expresses our low value for them. Others see through our behavior and, because of fear of manipulation, become distrustful of us and grow distant from us emotionally. If, on the other hand, we treat others with wisdom, loving compassion, and generosity, they are likely to respond in a similar manner to us with trust and closeness. Our response to the world shapes the world's response to us. This is the fundamental insight of *karma*.

It is important that we focus on the potential in the Hindu teaching about *karma* for empowering us to transform ourselves, by transforming our motivations and by expressing a deeper generosity and loving compassion in our way of being. The hope for change in our families, communities and the world begins with us. Gandhi put all of these teachings beautifully when he asked us to "be the change you want to see in the world." *Karma* asks us to take responsibility for who we are, here and now. There is hope in the Hindu teaching on *karma*, but only if we change the focus from the past to the present, from passivity to responsibility and from powerlessness to empowerment. The Hindu teaching about *karma* has the potential to liberate us from the grip of the past and the memories associated with past events. This is only possible, however, if the teaching of *karma* helps us to self-critically understand how we have become the individuals and groups that we are.

CASE STUDY: REMEMBERING CONVERSION-CHRISTIAN AND HINDU

For the purpose of a case study, I have chosen to highlight the contrasting consciousness and memory about the historical and religious meanings of conversion to Christianity from the Christian and Hindu side. This does not imply that all Hindus and Christians think about conversion in the same ways; each tradition reflects a diversity of perspectives.[3]

Thomas Thangaraj, a Christian theologian, details the story of a group in the southern part of Tamil Nadu from a village named Chanpattu who converted to Christianity in 1804 and renamed their village, Nazareth. Members were Nadars, a lower caste community. As a low caste group, the Nadars were not allowed to read Hindu scriptures. Conversion to Christianity was a dramatic turn around for this group. As noted, they changed the name of their village. They adopted also Biblical and Western names. Debarred from reading the Vedas, Nazareth Christians received the Bible with great joy. According to Thangaraj, they saw "that as great privilege and took great pride in owning copies of the Bible. Interestingly, the Bible was called *Vedam* or *Vedagamam* and so they were now possessors of the Veda." For the first time, they joined a voluntary association that they owned and they were in control of its affairs. They were empowered by the fact that they built, owned, and used their own place of worship.

The descendants of the Nazareth Christians continue to have a negative view of the Hindu tradition, seek to emphasize differences with their Hindu neighbors and to affirm their distinctive Christian identity. For the Nazareth Christians, conversion to Christianity was an unprecedented opportunity for liberation and religious self-determination. Sathianathan Clarke describes its comprehensive meaning for Dalit Christians.

Religious conversion for Dalits thus includes a form of boundary smashing and boundary shaping that involves drastic erasure and thorough replacement of inherited but detrimental Word-visions and world-ways. It represents a decision away from intra-house options of minimalist tinkering with elements or maximalist transformations with structures of the Hindu vision of and way. Rather conversion represents a vociferous NO to the entire religious, social, political, and cultural system.[4]

Dalit Christians see conversion as offering freedom from the oppression of caste and for crossing over into a new religious community that affirms social dignity and worth.

Hindu activists and commentators, like Ashok Chowgule, have a diametrically opposed perspective. Chowgule sees conversion as the consequence of an obsession in the Christian tradition and its aggressive methods. After failing to convert *Brahmins*, according to Chowgule, the Church turned its attention to members of the lower caste.

> Only when they could not make a dent with the Brahmins that the missionaries turned to the lower castes. The conversions were obtained through inducements and not through any spiritual conviction. They were somewhat successful only when temporal power was with the invading Christians and the area was effectively a colony. The missionaries could project themselves to be benefactors of the lower castes, and ensure that governmental largesse would flow to them.[5]

The perspectives could not be more different. Chowgule denies the agency of the lower castes and sees conversion entirely as the outcome of the power the missionary and his material inducements.

Dalit Christians see their conversion to Christianity as an escape from the violence of caste, psychologically and physically. In the words of Clarke, they embraced "another religious and social framework that valued their own body in relationship to the rest of human society. Body crossings for Dalits was a search for religion to indeed function as a way of life, one that honors their own individual bodies but also gives them a new relationship model for a more elastic social body politic."[6]

Swami Dayananda Saraswati, on the other hand, a prominent Hindu leader and teacher, describes conversion as an act of violence and not as a quest for freedom from violence. In the words of Swami Dayananda,

> Religious conversion by missionary activity remains an act of violence. It is an act of violence because it hurts deeply, not only the other members of the family of the converted, but the entire community that comes to know of it. One is connected to various persons in one's world. The religious person in every individual is the innermost, inasmuch as he or she is connected to a force beyond the empirical. The religious person is connected only to the force beyond he has now accepted. That is the reason why the hurt caused by religion can turn into violence. That is why a religious belief can motivate a missionary to be a martyr. When the hurt of the religious becomes acute, it explodes into violence. Conversion is violence. It generates violence.[7]

These different perceptions of conversion are significant for both communities, since conversion has become the single most important source of tension, controversy, and violence between Hindus and Christians in India. It is a combustible issue that ignites passion on both sides, exploding easily into conflicts that lead to death and destruction. Such different memories cause deep suspicion and mistrust, underlying the need for deeper dialogue aiming for mutual understanding and trust.

HOPE FOR DIALOGUE ON CONVERSION

Dialogue on conversion between Hindus and Christians in India is difficult and challenging. This is one of the reasons why such dialogue is not occurring in any sustained and meaningful ways. If reconciliation, truth, mutual understanding, and peace are important concerns of religion and religious communities, then such dialogue is imperative and must be sought actively by both traditions. The following are some of what I regard as necessary for fruitful dialogue on this issue:

1. I think that the Hindu majority community should take the initiative for this dialogue. Religious traditions need to be especially attentive to the voices of those who claim to experience the tradition as oppressive and unjust and as denying them power and freedom. Causing suffering to others (*hiṃsā*) and indifference to such suffering are the antithesis of what the Hindu tradition advocates at its highest ethical ideal of non-violence (*ahiṃsā*). Radically different memories of the same event, when this event is a source of tension and conflict, must be an urgent incentive for deep dialogue. Dalit Christians, who feel alienated from the tradition and who think that the tradition does not accord them equality, are unlikely to be the initiators of this dialogue.

2. As noted above, there are radically divergent memories and narratives about conversion in both communities. The outcome of such different narratives is a deep mistrust. Dalit Christians, who see the tradition through the eyes of the oppressed, think that Hindu concerns about conversion are disguised efforts to preserve the privileges and power relationships inherent in the hierarchy of caste. Hindus, on the other hand, treat the convert as a child-like individual lured away from community by the seductive and unethical promises of Christian missionaries and who needs to be protected. There is a widespread Hindu suspicion of Christianity as a tradition that is concerned only with increasing its power through conversion and even suspicions about long-term political goals.

3. In these circumstances of mutual suspicion about motives, trust is a necessity for dialogue. Such trust will not be easy or immediate and religious leaders have a special responsibility for nurturing its birth and growth. Trust is the source of hope that memories can be shared and that each religious community can be mindfully attentive to the voices of the other. Trust allows painful memories to be shared, and difficult questions to be asked. Trust enables identification with the others' suffering, and makes possible self-criticism and transformation. The building of such trust is not a single event, but the nurturing of a relationship that cannot be rushed.

4. Our hope is that in the trustful sharing of memories, truth will emerge. Interreligious dialogue cannot be indifferent to truth. Our communities must be willing to receive these truths, however difficult and challenging. Hindu leaders and Hindus will be challenged by the memories of Dalit Christians to understand the many ways in which others experience the tradition as oppressive and as negating their human dignity and self-worth. This will not be easy since Hindu leaders still come primarily from males of the upper castes who have always experienced power and privilege within the tradition. Having never experienced religiously justified oppression and injustice, they may assume that the tradition that has been good to them is good for all born within it. On the side of Dalit Christians, Hindu memories could lead to consideration of methods and assumptions in some forms of Christian proselytization that are questionable and cause uneasiness and concern among Hindus. It is an opportunity for Dalits to ask questions about caste and an opportunity for Hindus to speak about those teachings in their tradition that proclaim the equal worth and dignity of all human beings.
5. The sharing of memories in this dialogue does not aim for consensus. The success of interreligious dialogue is not to be measured by consensus. It affords a space for mutual sharing and questioning that will hopefully lead to mutual respect, understanding, and the experience of our common humanity. Dalits must be allowed to articulate and explain the reasons for their embrace of another tradition; the integrity of such a choice has to be respected and be the basis for meaningful relationships with Hindus.
6. The Hindu teaching on *karma*, and the memory-formation process, discussed above, offer important resources and insights for this dialogue. Our memories about others and their memories about us are not mysterious. These are formed and shaped in specific historical contexts that are accessible to our understanding. The sharing of memories is an important process in the search for such understanding, and this becomes particularly important when one groups claims to be oppressed by another. We need to understand not only the historical origins of our memories, but the ways in which these memories determine our disposition towards other communities and the mechanisms through which these are transmitted inter-generationally fueling our prejudice, stereotyping and demonizing of other groups and communities. The participation of the other in this process is vital if we are to be honest and not fall into the trap of self-deception. Sharing of memories in a context like this facilitates our understanding of the other but, just as important, or even more important, our understanding of

ourselves. In the mirror of the others' memory, we see ourselves clearly and especially those features that we prefer not to see.
7. The teaching on *karma* not only helps us to understand the process or memory-formation, but offers us also the hope of having the freedom and the responsibility to transform our relationship with the other. We can liberate ourselves from the conditioning of the past and learn to see the other and ourselves anew. This is only possible when the teaching of *karma* helps us to understand how we have become the individuals and groups that we are.
8. On the Hindu side this dialogue must arise from and be sustained by its deepest spiritual wisdom about life's unity. It is from the perspective of life's unity that Hindus can question exploitative and unjust human relationships which foster conflict and divisiveness and it is the same perspective which urges us to seek and work for reconciliation and for the quality of human relationships which expresses this central truth of our existence. If our world is indeed a single family (*vasudhaiva kuṭumbakam*), both spiritually and biologically, the quality of our relationships should reflect the moral and ethical implications of this truth. Īśa Upaniṣad (6) reminds us that the wise person who beholds all beings in the self and the self in all beings does not hate anyone. From the profundity of the Hindu understanding of the nature of life's unity, estrangement from another is estrangement from one's own self and the hate of the other is the hate of one's self. To be in conflict with another is also to be in conflict with one's self. To inflict suffering on another is to violate one's own self.

This approach enables us to see the other, the one with whom we disagree and with whom we may be locked in struggle, as a fellow human being. We cannot dehumanize the one in whom we see ourselves or long for his or her humiliation. This approach was at the heart of the Gandhian philosophy and practice of non-violent resistance (*satyagraha*). Even in the midst of the strongest disagreements, Gandhi never sought to win support for his case by demonizing his opponent. He understood clearly that when a conflict is constructed sharply in terms of *we* and *they*, victory and defeat, the doors to reconciliation and a transformed community are shut. One is left with an enemy, a defeated enemy perhaps, and the next round of the conflict is only postponed.

THE PURIFICATION OF MEMORY

Although highlighted in various places on our discussion, it may be helpful to underline core elements of the wisdom offered in the Hindu tradition for the transformation and purification of memory. The most profound teaching is centered on the understanding of the unity and identity of self in all. It enables us to see oneself in all and all in oneself (*sarvabhūtastham ātmānaṁ sarvabhūtāni cātmani*). This wisdom enables us, according to the tradition, to respond to the world, not from the dualism of like and dislike, love and hate, but from a vision of the unity of existence and the seeing of self in all beings. Wisdom liberates us from responding to the world on the basis of historically formed memories and enables us to do so on the basis of compassion.

A wise person does not find self-value through asserting the diminished worth of others or by asserting the superiority of himself or his group. From a place of wisdom, we see how self-ignorance conditions our own responses to the world through ingrained memories. We understand also how the responses of others are similarly conditioned through their own memories. Our understanding of ignorance as the root human problem awakens a disposition of reconciliation and forgiveness since it orients us to look beyond behavior and to its underlying causes, both in ourselves and in others. We are more likely to respond with hate when we believe that those who hurt us do so through intentional malevolence. If we see their actions, and our own, as rooted in self-ignorance and a false understanding of reality, we can be compassionate and understanding. We may be liberated from the grip of memories that dispose us to inflict vengeance. Wisdom does not obliterate memories, but transforms these by enabling us to understand their sources and to respond in freedom. Spiritual ignorance is perpetuated also through memories; wisdom liberates us from the prison of memories. In spiritual wisdom is our hope for liberation for the transformation and even liberation from the grip of memories. As the title of my paper suggests, "hope is greater than memory."

LEARNING FROM OTHER TRADITIONS

Buddhism makes a very helpful distinction between forgetting and forgiving. The first is natural in contrast to the second that is intentional and involves making a distinction between doer and deed. It is a vision of the doer beyond the deed. Although this understanding coincides in important ways with the Hindu tradition, Buddhists offer many practices of mindfulness for its cultivation and internalization. There is much to learn from and share here especially in the ways in which spiritual practice "becomes a direct nurturing tool for political expediency." Are such practices and insights helpful for addressing tensions between Hindus and other religious communities?

This dimension of the Buddhist discussion was deepened for me by the probing Christian reflection on remembering as a "political action," and the corresponding observation that memories have to be evaluated on the basis of what they make and do not make possible. Memory, as the Christian discussion reminded us, is related to power and its uses and historically served the purpose of empire-building. How is memory and power related in our contemporary contexts? How does it inform Hindu relationships with other communities?

NOTES

1. My discussion here is with particular reference to the Hindu tradition of Advaita Vedānta.
2. Swami Vivekananda, *The Complete Works of Swami Vivekananda*, 8 vols., (Calcutta: Advaita Ashrama, 1964–1971), 5, 213.
3. For the Christian perspective, I rely particularly on two sources. The first is Thomas Thangaraj, "The Missiological Hermeneutics of a Convert," *Exchange*, vol.32, no.1, 37–41 and Sathianathan Clarke, "The Promise of Religious Conversion: Exploring Approaches, Exposing Myths, Exploring Modalities," in Christine Linemann-Perrin and Wolfgang Linemann eds., *Crossing Religious Borders: Studies on Conversion and Religious Belonging* (Weisbaden: Harrossowitz Verlag, 2012), 590–610. For the Hindu perspective I rely on Ashok V. Chowgule, *Christianity in India: The Hindutva Perspective* (Mumbai: Hindu Vivek Kendra, 1999). I am grateful to Thomas Thangaraj for his guidance and suggestions.
4. Sathianathan Clarke, "The Promise of Religious Conversion: Exploring Approaches, Exposing Myths, Exploring Modalities," 602.
5. Ashok Chowgule, *Christianity in the Hindutva Perspective*, 49–50.
6. Clarke, op. cit., 605.
7. See http://www.swamij.com/conversion-violence.htm. Accessed 9 December 2013.

Chapter Five

Memory as Benevolence

Toward a Sikh Ethics of Liberation

Rahuldeep Gill

PRAYERS FOR "US"

In his excellent memoir, *Acts of Faith*, Interfaith pioneer Eboo Patel remembers "growing up American" while "growing up other" in America: "I grew up," he writes, "with religious rituals. Morning and evening my family would gather for prayer, hands cupped to receive blessings, forehead and nose touching the ground in *sijda*, prayer beads sliding through our fingers as we chanted, 'Ya Allah, Ya Allah' (Oh God, Oh, God)." Eboo Patel was raised as an Ismaili Muslim.[1]

As Ismaili prayers did for Eboo Patel, Sikh prayers and practices rooted me in a centuries-old tradition that was foreign to my American neighbors and friends. Memories don't just sit in our brains, we feel them in our bodies. Sacred practices are a form of memory, reminding us about our sacred pasts and also teaching us how "we" are different from "them." For immigrant or minority communities, like mine and Eboo Patel's, these are some of the vehicles for our tradition to survive in strange lands. These are the ways "we" know who "we" are.

I recall hot, sweaty August days—the "dog days of summer," we called them in Massachusetts—memorizing Sikh prayers during my summer vacations. A one-week Sikh summer day-camp that, like so many events in our burgeoning disparate immigrant community, was held on an almost ad hoc basis in the Gurdwara (Sikh house of worship), where families from the suburbs of Boston would collect on Sundays. A leader of the community at the camp asked me to prepare and deliver a prayer called the *Ardas* in front of the whole camp, by the end of the week. He was bestowing on me a great honor; I was proud and nervous.

In Sikh tradition, the word *Ardas* has referred to a prayer of supplication, usually performed collectively. Today, it refers to a standardized prayer that Sikh community members perform in collectivity at the beginning of any occasion, during life cycle events, while enduring trials or tribulations, or at the end of a congregational service: be it a birth celebration, wedding, funeral, or daily congregational worship at a Sikh summer camp. The tradition of Ardas has developed over the five hundred years of Sikh history, but the standard text of the Ardas today was codified in the twentieth century. For members of a tiny suburban Sikh community in the American Northeast, the Ardas brings the members of the congregation together to recall their great tradition and offers them a lens to see their lives, as Sikhs, in the context of a grand Sikh experience in the context of the broader sociocultural landscape in which they live.

Ardas means "supplication." It begins by enjoining the deity, to whom the supplication is addressed and in whose holy presence the congregation makes this prayer. In Sikh thought, God is present wherever a handful of Sikhs gather to remember God. According to historian Gurinder Singh Mann, the Ardas holds a record of the community's historical memory from its founding to the contemporary period. Mann writes, "Through this prayer the Sikhs express gratitude to *Vahiguru* [a Sikh epithet for God] for guiding the community's destiny in the past, seek Divine blessings in dealing with current problems, and reaffirm their vision of establishing a state in which the Sikhs shall rule."[2]

Sikh tradition is a faith born around 1500 through a unique revelatory experience had by its founder, Nanak. Nanak became known by a title of adoration, *baba* ("father" or "leader"), and as a preceptor, or *guru,* of a message from the Divine realm. Guru Nanak was succeeded by nine other gurus, the last of whom died in 1708.

Sikhs sing the revelatory compositions of the gurus (*bani*) in a practice known as *kirtan*. Along with collective recitation of the Divine hymns, this singing forms the core of Sikh devotional life. Ethical uprightness and service, or *sewa*, has long been seen as a necessary extension of this devotional core.

Remembrance, and specifically communal remembrance, fuels the Sikh prayer. The Ardas remembers the ten gurus, or founders of Sikh tradition, who lived and worked to build the community, in succession from 1469 to 1708. The office of the guru since 1708 has not belonged to any human person but has been shared between the authority of the Sikh scripture (*granth*) and Sikh community (*panth*). After remembering the Lord, the ten living gurus, and the dual form of the guru in scripture and community, we then remember the members of the community throughout Sikh history who have contributed to the community's growth and success by laying down their lives for the Sikh tradition. Many Sikhs draw strength from these memories. The spirit of the Ardas helps us to surmount the tribulations we may face today.

The leader of the prayer, who can be any revered member of the community, man or woman, of great age or youth summer camp attendee, then calls on the community to repeat a name of God, *Vahiguru*: "Hail, Guru!" And the congregation responds,"Vahiguru!"

This call and response between the leader of the prayer and all those assembled in prayer continues as the text of the Ardas winds through memory of the community's history: through the tribulations of those men and women who have given their lives for the faith, bringing back to mind the circumstances of their violent deaths, the pain which they bore in steadfast silence for the sake of the community's persistence. The Ardas reminds its audience how these martyrs gave up their lives before they gave up their faith, renounced their breath before they renounced their beloved *kesh*, or hair—which is God's gift to all Sikhs and which they preserve in gratitude for His gifts, binding Sikhs to one another and to all reverent co-religionists who bare this gift of long hair.

> The prayer leader calls, "*Vahiguru*." The response comes, "*Vahiguru*."
> The Ardas recalls the temporal political centers of the Sikh tradition, the important historical Gurdwaras or houses of worship commemorating great events in Sikh history.
> The prayer leader calls, "*Vahiguru*." The response comes, "*Vahiguru*."
> The Ardas reminds us that this is a prayer of supplication of the entire Sikh community (or *Khalsa*) and asks that the Khalsa remember God at all times: "*Vahiguru, Vahiguru, Vahiguru!*" and from this remembrance, may the entire Khalsa find peace. And may it find comfort.
> The Ardas calls for the victory of the cauldron (*degh*) and the sword (*tegh*). Together the cauldron, which feeds the needy;and the sword, which seeks Divine justice—make up the emblem burned into the Sikh psyche and imprinted on the Sikh flag, reminding us just exactly for what we stand. Remembering these things, asking for the victory of these principles, we again chant. "*Vahiguru!Vahiguru!*"

God is supplicated to bestow the gifts of Sikh discipleship, hair, disciplined conduct, the ability to discern right from wrong, the gifts of faith, and the gift of all gifts: the ability to remember the Divine.

The supplication continues: may every Sikh be able to visit the center of the community in the city of Amritsar, which means "pool of immortal nectar."

Every holy site that has been split off from the Sikh community through the partition of the South Asian continent at the end of the colonial experience in 1947 is remembered, and God is asked to make sure that Sikhs continue to receive the ability to visit those sites and to serve them.

So much of the text of the Ardas calls to mind some of the most significant collective memories of the Sikh tradition. Indeed, this is how tradition is preserved in our religious communities, through practices that bring sacred recollections to our hearts, thereby re-collecting the disparate pieces of our traditions, and collecting us again together as a community. At the conclusion of the Ardas, the leader of the prayer asks the Almighty for forgiveness of all trespasses.

In the Ardas, Sikhs remember their gurus, their martyrs, and those who sacrificed for the faith. They recall their sacred spaces. The prayer itself reminds Sikhs why they bear the markers of their faith despite difficulty: to stand for the feeding of all that the cauldron provides, and for the justice that the sword promises. Collecting, gathering, assembling these memories we turn again and again to a community of believers. Re-membering, we again affirm and reaffirm our membership. For a young teenager learning the prayer, the end of the Ardas is like turning a corner: the end is near! Relief from standing in front of the community (and being on the spot and worrying about making a mistake) is about to arrive.

But there's another reason that the final phrases of this prayer mark a turning point: the prayer turns from specific, community-making memories in the direction of our common humanity with all the world's people. That is, the last three sentences take a somewhat unforeseen shift, moving from the specific memories, requirements, and supplications of the community addressing the Almighty to asking for the welfare of all people. The text enjoins the deity to fulfill the aspirations of all people, and asks, in the name of Guru Nanak, that all people should prosper according to the Divine will.

That the culmination of the most important Sikh collective prayer emphasizes a common humanity is what makes the Ardas exceptional for me. After remembering all of these great figures, painful events, specific historical circumstances, we are supposed to take the strength imbued in us through this prayer back into the world where non-Sikhs also live, and seek their benefit as well. This does not mean seeking their conversion or their realization that the Sikh path is the only path (which it is not) or the best path (which some may believe), but simply putting forth the unconditional request to God that all people fare well in God's mysterious, unfolding plan. The Ardas declares, "*Sarbat de kaarajraas*," "May the Lord be beneficent to all," and asks for *sarbatdaabhala*, the well-being of all.

Ardas is a modern way that Sikhs open up to the memories that make up our tradition and that make us Sikhs. Two basic issues about all of this are salient for our consideration in relation to our work in the Interfaith movement. The first is that memory, even in its communal form, is particular. We religious people remember particular moments in the histories of our traditions. In remembering these moments, we reaffirm our membership to a community. The very process of engaging in remembering these sacred events draws boundaries between our community and other communities. Memories of violence are particularly good at raising walls between us. In my spiritual life, I do not remember the Romans feeding my spiritual forebears to lions in the Coliseum. My Christian friends probably do not daily remember the Sikh victims of genocide.

But then there is the moment when the Ardas seeks blessings for all, a great universal moment repeated every time Sikhs fold their hands in prayer. And that is the second issue to consider: that we also belong to the universal we, the human we. We may be involved in working within and across faith boundaries because we have come to the conclusion that both the particular and the universal are necessary in continuing our existence. Placed in the realm of "our" particular communities, we also see ourselves as belonging to the "our" that is the possessive pronoun of the universal human "we."

Interfaith projects seem to require us to somehow belong to both of these communities. Interfaith asks of us to hold in tension the specific and the general, the "me" and the "we." Interfaith is not possible unless we come to these experiences as our best selves, and to do that we cannot compromise our most sacred beliefs. And so although some of our co-religionists cannot join us at the Interfaith table while affirming their specificity, we must respect that boundary even while we save them seats at the table. It is a challenge, and a tension, that we must affirm at every step. It is a challenge that all of us know is baked into the very thing to which we are committing ourselves when we gather at Interfaith events. This challenge is part and parcel of Interfaith: the tension between the particularities of our communities and our desire to stand for the universality of our common humanity.

It is heartening that this commonality-with-all gives Sikhs their zeal to be Sikhs—despite the difficulties, despite the hate crimes, and despite the unspeakably painful violence in situations such as in Oak Creek, Wisconsin, that shocked us all in August 2012. One way in which this *sarbat da bhalla* ("welfare for all") ideal was radically put into play was through the Ardas after that deadly attack on that Wisconsin Gurdwara. Members of the Oak Creek Gurdwara used the Ardas to pray for the soul of shooter, Wade Michael Page, that he may find his way back to God. I think it was a deep kind of love that got people in the Oak Creek community to commemorate Page's death. Where does that kind of forgiveness come from?

SIKH SCRIPTURE: THE LENS OF MEMORY

Memory provides lenses through which we see the world. Practices of memory, specific to each religious tradition, provide tools with which practitioners engage the world. Engaging the world in a holy way requires a different mindset than that of the profane. The depth that we bring to our practices, including practices of memory, determines the quality of what we bring to the world.

In Sikh spiritual practice, the remembrance of one's sure, guaranteed, impending death provides a horizon for the ethical life that one is to live on this side of the divide. Divine infinitude juxtaposed with human finitude requires that each of us remembers that he or she is a finite being. The implication is that death's ultimacy provides our lives with ethical limits. According to Sikh teachings, those who forget their death are haughty and arrogant, self-conceited, and self-possessed. Without practices that remember the Divine and our own death, we are caught up in untruth, and we are as good as dead.[3] Near the end of the morning hymn that Sikhs read daily (*Japji*), Guru Nanak implores his followers to wear the remembrance of death as if it were a hermit's cloak.[4] Elsewhere, and in a similar composition about cultivating a spiritual awareness, Guru Nanak implies that remembrance of one's certain, impending death functions to bring the mind under control in preparation for spiritual pursuits.[5] Guru Nanak portrays death as a wedding, and the soul has the opportunity to find union with the Divine groom:

> The day and date are fixed, we congregate to anoint the bride.
> Bless me, friends, that I may meet my Master!
> The invitation is sent to all the homes, and the call may come any day.
> Remember the one who calls us, the date grows ever near.[6]

That is, God sends daily reminders of our impending death, which we can celebrate as an opportunity to meet the Divine face to face.

For the finite human being, hope in this transient life is only available through remembrance of the Eternal, Omnipotent Being. Human existence is temporary, phenomenal. Guru Nanak teaches that the world's sweet pleasures lead to ruin if they cause us to forget the Divine; death is ultimate, and we should not waste the opportunity of life.[7] He reminds his followers that, when a loved one dies, others weep; but for the deceased opportunity for ethical reflection has passed. Guru Nanak continues on to say that even the mourners will die, implying that the funeral itself is an opportunity for ethical reflection on one's own life.[8]

Sikhs are called upon to transform their lives by remembering the Divine. Those who remember God are the saints, the pious ones, and their company must be sought. The process of remembrance, a practice known as *simran*, opens the possibility of living more fully. Being present in God requires remembering oneself, remembering the metaphysical root of one's existence, which is remembering that one is essentially connected to the Divine in one's inner being.

According to historian Gurinder Singh Mann, members of Guru Nanak's original community in the town of Kartarpur kept internal and external purity at the fore of their religious practice. Whereas the body was made clean by a morning bath, the mind was "sanctified with prayer, which included among other things singing and listening to Guru Nanak's compositions praising the Divine (*nam*). "Remembrance of the divine was supposed to continue during mundane activities: "While working hard, Sikhs were to remember the Creator in whose hands is the final outcome of their endeavor. They had to sow and weed the crops; the harvest, however, was a divine gift."[9]

According to the translators Arvind Mandair and Christopher Shackle, remembrance of God's essence, or the Name (*nam*), requires "attunement," which is a kind of "wordless communication, or rather a partaking of love between self and mind or soul." They continue that "the Name (*nam*) is not a particular word or mantra" but it is attained by the pious Sikh worshipper "through the practice of constantly holding in mind the Name (*namsimran*)."[10] There is no one "Name" of God chanted in all such practices and some think of the Name as a signifier for a totalizing experience of the Divine essence. Thus, for many Sikhs, "remembering the Name," or *namsimran*, is a series of practices that bring the practitioner closer to the Divine Being through reflection and meditation. As with Mann's statement about the early Sikh community, many Sikhs believe that service and world engagement is an extension of that reflective remembrance of God.

According to the compositions of the gurus, remembering God with one's whole being is an act of utmost piety. Sikh gurus write of this remembrance in terms of the deep and painful desire for reunion experienced by separated lovers. The human partner is a bride whose longing for the Divine Groom launches her attempt at reunion.[11] The pious constantly hold their Divine Beloved in their hearts.[12] The soul sings for union with God.[13]

Remembrance is a blissful act.[14] Remembrance is the path to liberation.[15] Remembrance is a healing practice.[16] It cultivates the human body, like a farmer cultivates crops, to live a life of contact with the Divine.[17] There is no other form of worship equivalent to remembering God.[18] Remembering God is a purifying act.[19]

Guru Nanak lays bare in his poetry the conversation of the devotee with his own mind, struggling to remember the Lord: *Why don't you remember The One, O foolish mind?*[20] And so we may be able to understand memory's tricky contours: the pleasures of the world we enjoy are quickly forgotten, and themselves cause us to forget our relationship with the Divine. Congregational worship is an act of collective remembrance that helps the individual come into contact with God.[21]

The gurus are quick to point out that rote memory alone cannot bring about the depth of experience necessary for religious devotion. The gurus demand that we remember God in our hearts and not just with our lips. Reciting sacred texts from rote memory has no efficacy and therefore is ultimately meaningless. The fifth guru, Arjan, compares the recitation of holy scripture from memory to other useless religious practices; he contrasts this with the real spiritual work of love and of loving God.[22] The enticements of the world cannot be overcome by merely reciting verses from memory.[23] Reciting sacred verses does not lead to a positive position in the afterlife; understanding God's message takes more work than that.[24] Superficial remembrance—a kind of passing allusion to the holy without intention, without one's fully present self—is useless.

One word for memory, *sammhal*, also connotes "care." So, in an interesting twist, God's Being is fully invested in the process of memory through God's care for creation.[25] God constantly cares for the world, and for humans to forget God is an act of ingratitude. The guru tries to put anxieties to rest by reminding the disciple that God can even make life grow in stone and takes care of migratory birds on their way to their resting spots.[26] It's not just us humans who remember God; God remembers, and cares for, creation as well.

God's care for the world is a model. Practitioners should seek higher spiritual states, become God-like, and find spiritual expression in remembering (and expressing gratitude) through caring for others (again, *sammhal*). This is also where the most universal Being, the Divine essence, provides support for each of us. Our relationship with God, and our witness to Divine care in the world, is the context we know and experience as care. Participating in God's Being simply means that we continue the cycle of care. Elsewhere Guru Nanak says that hard work and generosity (literally, "giving from one's own hands") are the marks of a truly spiritual person.[27] The cycle of remembrance goes both inward and outward.

Witnessing Divine care in the world might open us up to the possibility that sitting with, and learning from, people of other faiths can remind us of our common godly nature. It is hard work, and it can't be done superficially. But understanding people outside our faith traditions as God's own people, as beings receiving Divine care, should be able to expand our limited perspectives.

Moreover, if we are to act in a God-like way, then we should seek to care for others regardless of who they are. We should seek the benefit of others as the Divine bestows blessings on creation. In this way, the thematic shift at the conclusion of the Ardas makes sense: the Sikh "we" exists for the collective "we." The Sikh community even (or, especially) while experiencing its deepest trauma exists to enact God's care in the world, for the world.

CARING FOR THE OTHER, CARING FOR THE SELF

This spirit of care, and the use of care for others in time of trauma, is most clearly articulated in the works of Bhai Gurdas Bhalla, a very important Sikh writer from the 1600s. Bhai Gurdas responds to the extremely traumatic execution of the fifth Sikh guru (Guru Arjan) at the hands of the Mughal empire by referring to the practice of *parupkari*: care for the other. In Gurdas's philosophy, Guru Nanak was on a Divine mission to create a distinct religious path in the world because the world was suffering from the excesses of human egotism, and the other religions were not helping anymore. So God "revealed" Guru Nanak, whose great contribution to the world was the establishment of the Sikh community, through which God works in the world.

The metaphor of the tree is an image that one must pay attention to in Bhai Gurdas's works; this is one of his metaphors for the Sikh community. The kind of tree that Bhai Gurdas has in mind is the *borh*, or banyan tree. In the rural life of the Punjab region, from where Sikhism emerged, big trees like the banyan play a special role in hot summers. Trees with thick shade are natural, communal air conditioning. Villagers escape the oppressive, suffocating summer under the shade of a banyan tree. In a village one massive tree may offer refuge to dozens of people at a time.

So the banyan tree is a metaphor for cool shade, for caring about others, for making a better world, for providing space for people to thrive. It is also a metaphor for resilience. Trees bear a great deal of suffering. The tree absorbs the sun's heat and takes a beating from the hot solar rays while providing cool shade to all underneath it. The tree stands and bears heat and cold and rain and remains still and unperturbed.

Gurdas presents the Sikh suffering under Mughal tyranny as a means to future reward. From his own memoirs, we know Mughal emperor Jahangir assented to Guru Arjan's execution because he viewed the Sikh guru's mission as a threat to his imperial stability. Writing in that context, Bhai Gurdas said that, because they suffer, in the future Sikhs will have access to God's justice, which will vindicate the community and bestow upon it great success and joy. In the aftermath of Guru Arjan's execution, the tree was a metaphor for Gurdas to talk about how Sikhs should bear that trauma. Like the banyan tree, Sikhs should steadfastly bear the pain of the event. Like the banyan tree, Sikhs should continue to work for the care of others, through service to others.[28]

> For Bhai Gurdas, the tree is also a metaphor for Sikh growth:
> The Guru's form is revealed to the Sikh who contemplates his word
> From one fruit, a thousand Sikhs and congregations spread in God's way
> Seeing, hearing, believing—the Guru's own are rare in this world
> They merge with feet dust and the whole world seeks their feet
> The way of the Sikhs is established, trading in truth they transcend

Their wares are beyond appraisal, indescribable
The Guru's word is beloved in the saints' society. (v29.20)

Here we see Bhai Gurdas saying that the word, or text of Sikh scripture, contains the seed that results in the community's full bloom. Sikh scripture is conceived of as Divine revelation; Gurdas argues that the community continues that revelation by putting its teachings into practice. Elsewhere, he says that the guru is the manifestation of an invisible Divine seed (*nirankarekankar*) and the Sikhs are the fruits from the tree (kabitt 55). The banyan tree is unique because it has rootlike structures hanging off its branches, thus appearing that the tree's fruits are the same as its roots.

Again, these would have been salient metaphors to Sikhs who were in shock from the trauma of Guru Arjan's death; they were intended to help guide people through the hardships that the community faced at that time. Gurdas's often-repeated argument is that the community can transcend those hardships by taking on another characteristic of the tree—that is, benevolence (*parupkari,* "other helping"). This concept of benevolence appears in the compositions of several gurus, as well as being at play in basic Sikh institutions, like *langar*, the community meal. Today at Gurdwaras across the world, langars feed millions of people every day, none of whom is asked who they are or their ability to pay. As an outgrowth of Sikh philosophy, langar provides the community an opportunity to fulfill the Sikh mission by extending God's care into the world.

Other examples of benevolence in Sikh history include the water projects that the gurus initiated. To this day, original wells and pools are central features in several Sikh towns founded by the gurus: Goindval, Amritsar, and Tarn Taran.

The philanthropy projects of these gurus manifest the Sikh concern for the world.

CASE STUDY: PRABHJOT SINGH

After recently becoming the victim of a vicious hate crime in his home neighborhood of Harlem, Prabhjot Singh, a Sikh professor of global health and a physician, had to speak at a press conference because people wanted to know his response to the situation. He said that he had been the recipient of extreme kindness and compassion. Strangers on the street came to his aid. He was grateful to have received medical attention at the very hospital he practices as a physician. His friends rallied around him. He was grateful that the police department treated his case with extreme diligence.

Folks were shocked to hear that in his broadcast comments after the attack, Prabhjot issued an open invitation to his attackers to ask questions about the Sikh faith and to meet him at a Gurdwara to understand the Sikh religion.

He said that only if we welcome these misguided youths to engage with us can we really try to make sure they have an opportunity to learn from such injudicious acts. Merely holding them accountable through the criminal justice system, which we know is itself imperfect, would fall short of improving these youths so that they may become better people as a result of their mistake. Even though they attacked Prabhjot, in the true spirit of Sikhism he wanted them to become better people. They should take responsibility for their actions, he said, but also remedy their poor judgment and ignorance.

Prabhjot's gracious, and graceful, response was the Sikh response par excellence. He didn't have to respond as he did. Had he brandished a weapon that night to save his skin, hardly any Sikh would have objected. Attacked as he was, he could have suffered far worse injuries. He had a baby and wife at home, and a long life ahead of him. His attackers were many. He was with only one friend; he was defenseless; it was not by any means a fair fight. We might be able to draw elsewhere from Sikh ethical tradition that he would have been within his rights had he escalated the situation with a weapon. But he didn't do that—not at the moment with a weapon and not during the aftermath with his words.

Perhaps, as a Sikh, Prabhjot understands violence as an outcome of frustration. He doesn't condone it. He doesn't accept it. But he might be in a position to see that the violent have been victims of violence themselves. What good would it be to perpetuate anger, violence, and hatred? Isn't it so much better to try and end it with inclusion, education, and mutual engagement?

I believe that this was why Sikh survivors prayed for the soul of Wade Michael Page following his rampage at the Gurdwara in Wisconsin. The statement they made was that we may be lost souls, but we are all souls that belong to God.

For Prabhjot Singh, the Ardas's petition for the "welfare for all" was at work in those three people who helped Prabhjot off the sidewalk that night. They could have just kept walking, like sometimes happens in New York City. But they saw something was wrong and did what was right, beyond serving their own individual self-interest. That's the kind of community we need to build. That's benevolence. That's radical concern for the other.

How do we cultivate the kind of energy Prabhjot Singh has expressed? How do we express it and amplify it across society? The Sikh answer is that we do it through engagement, via a radical concern for others. The Sikh tradition teaches Sikhs to serve, to care, and to engage the world for the greater good. It's all about communities, Probhjot insists. The week after his attack, in spite of that attack and the healing he needed to do, he was already back at work for the greater good: teaching community health and attempting to increase positive long-term health outcomes for the community.

Interfaith cooperation is itself one form that benevolence can take. In this form of benevolence, religionists use their religious traditions to bridge divides through cooperation across boundaries. This does not require that anyone water down their religion, or indulge in either relativism or perennialism. This is something academics can encourage students to do in classrooms, on campus, and beyond the institutions of learning. It is something that religionists can encourage inside and outside of their places of worship. We can engage in service to the world, God's world, while engaging with our traditions *and* while engaging with each other.

Insofar as Interfaith work involves service to the world from the deepest Sikh values, Interfaith *is* inherently Sikh. Moreover, perhaps Sikh practice can be inherently Interfaith if we see that, in order to better serve the world in which we are blessed, we are required to work alongside our friends, neighbors, and community members who are not Sikh. Because we Sikhs find ourselves a minority tradition wherever we go, working across faith boundaries to make the world a better place is just a daily fact of life, and an absolute necessity. Active and intentional service work alongside members of other faith communities may also be the best way to educate people concerning Sikh principles and about Sikh identity. That is: work alongside them, enact the very best of our human heritage, and show them that our liberation is always bound up with theirs.[29]

LESSONS FROM 1984: THE SEARCH FOR JUSTICE

The interrelated issues of communal memories, trauma, and moving forward in a religiously sanctioned way are very clear to Sikhs in this thirtieth year after the traumatic "1984" in Punjabi history. In June of that year, the Indian army established martial law over the Punjab and, on the celebration day of Guru Arjan's 1606 martyrdom, invaded dozens of Gurdwaras in the Punjab. The operation, code-named "Blue Star," was nominally directed at driving militant separatists out of the Gurdwaras but led to the desecration of two of the holiest of Sikh shrines in the city of Amritsar.

Several months later, two Sikh bodyguards of the Indian prime minister shot her dead in revenge for the defilement inflicted on Sikh edifices and psyches. Without condoning this violence, we might understand the humiliation of a government's invasion and desecration on the scale inflicted in Operation Blue Star. We might also reflect on the juxtaposition of such humiliation with the power of communal memories of resistance. In late October of 1984, two young, well-armed bodyguards felt destined to exact revenge on behalf of millions of their co-religionists.

And yet, this revenge did not provide any final solution. By the time the spiral of violence ended, thousands of innocent Sikhs had been massacred by vengeful mobs in pogroms across India's cities, which some have remembered as genocidal acts of violence. It would be several years before the militancy was contained in the Punjab and only after brutal police action resulted in the death and torture of several more thousands of Sikhs. Sikh organizations in India and abroad, alongside non-Sikh justice seekers, continue to try to hold authorities to account for what they see as state-inflicted slaughter. But little has been achieved toward that end.

Our inability to achieve justice on behalf of those who have been wronged is extremely dispiriting and painful. For many Sikhs, the search for justice has rekindled their connection with a forgotten identity. Particularly in the diaspora, young Sikhs growing up in the West are drawn to connecting with Sikhism through stories of the wrongs experienced by Sikhs in the homeland. Memories of the past, rekindled trauma, draws us back into a community. It is really easy for identity to become the core religious issue, above and beyond all others. So there is a way in which "1984" is remembered in Sikh community as a very *Sikh* number, a very traumatic year for Sikhs. Those four digits hold specific meaning for Sikhs in a way that they do not hold for others.

And yet, as we've explored in this paper, the Ardas helps us to remember a particular history and then moves to a call for Divine intercession on behalf of the general—because the very reason the particular (Sikh tradition) exists is to serve the general (the whole world). The me exists *for* the we.

Mainstream Sikh spirituality has never tolerated world-denial; it has encouraged world upliftment. Sikh thought has not endorsed the status quo, but neither has it sanctioned escape from it. Purity of the body cannot be achieved by cleansing solely the body; it requires the full cleansing of the heart and mind. Guru Nanak says, "Impurity is not cleansed without wisdom"; and his fourth successor, Guru Arjan, teaches that we find deliverance in God's abode when we serve the Lord with a pure heart.[30]

And yet what good is purity of the heart in an impure world where justice is corrupted? The world as-it-is may not be ultimately just, or ultimately fulfilling. As a lotus rises above the muck of the pond in which it sits, Sikhs *need* to be distinct from the mess of the world in order to save it. Gurdas, for one, remembers that Guru Nanak came to the world for this truth and to save the world from itself by shedding the light of knowledge where there was the darkness of ignorance: "When Nanak, the True Guru, was revealed, the fog lifted and there was light in the world."[31] Sikh tradition remembers that the fifth and ninth gurus, Guru Arjan and Tegh Bahadur, respectively, gave their lives in testimony to this truth, having been executed as prisoners of the Mughal empire. They remember that the tenth guru, Guru Gobind Singh, lost his family and, indeed, eventually his life bestowing this mantle of truth upon the Khalsa, or Sikh community, as distinct from the world but working to improve it.

How do Sikhs proceed? In the general Sikh consciousness there may not necessarily be a corresponding opening up to the plights of others who also suffer injustice. It would be simplistic to tell a modern Sikh, traumatized by geopolitical events like the storming of the Darbar Sahib or the Delhi pogroms of 1984, that the way to use memory to overcome trauma is just to remember God. Neither can we just pretend that we are all world travelers who can forget the differences between us and the damage our communities have done to each other.

The very difficult question to answer is how do we create the *we* while living in the *me*? In other words, how do we live in our communities, peacefully, remembering that we are all part of the larger human community?

One way that we can purify the traumatic memory is to seek justice and work for justice, not just for ourselves but also for whoever needs it. I take hope from the Japanese-Americans after 9/11 who worked to protect Muslim rights. The memory of trauma borne by "our" people in the past sometimes activates us to stand up for others, so that no people should have to bear such pain in the future. Also inspiring to this end are images of Muslims, arm-in-arm and hand-in-hand, forming a human wall of protection around an Egyptian Coptic Church during recent troubles in Egypt. Engaging with others, and on behalf of others, offers more than just the opportunity for service; it offers the potential of radical transformation of the self.

I think this is where the focus for Sikhs must be. Guru Nanak provides guidance about this:

> The lowest of the low born, the utmost and very low
> Nanak is with those people! What need have I for the high?
> Wherever the low receive care, surely there are Your blessings.[32]

That is, Divine grace falls upon those in the lowest, and neediest, places. If we seek it, we should seek those who are in need. Further, more identification with the neediest in society leads us away from our needs to find the Divine in the opportunity to serve others. Certainly there are plenty of people within the community who could benefit from this. Some of these needy people are Sikhs—low caste, outcaste, and women—who still are made to feel like outsiders to their own tradition over five hundred years after Guru Nanak's revelation that led him to preach a radical equality.

So in the first Sikh hymn, on the first page of Guru Granth Sahib, Guru Nanak has left us all with a challenge. He asks a fundamental question for human life: "How do we get through falsehood? And how do we reach truth?" The answer, he says, is to understand God's will and command (*hukam*) and to overcome our own self-orientations (*haumai*) and the limiting beliefs that they entail.[33] The reason we forget, and are ungrateful for, Divine care is that we are caught up in our narrow perspectives. The hope is to live in a godlike way. We merge with God's command and order when we live in an orientation that is not just for ourselves, or just for our individual communities. This is where I believe the power of concern for others is most hopeful: in the struggle to get over ourselves.

CONCLUSION: TAKING UP GOD'S CHALLENGE

This paper began with a story told by an interfaith activist that demonstrates the importance of ritual action in inscribing collective memory—and thus meaning—into our bodies. Although collective memory designates "a people" versus "the world," and thus makes me an outsider to the Ismaili traditions of the *sijda*, I used this story to enter into my own memory of my own tradition.

In that tradition, collective memory is also used to demarcate religious identity in many ways, often through ritual. Communal memory makes and members the community. Communal ritual re-members the community. But the particularizing nature of communal memory (it is, after all, for *one* particular community) can be overcome; and that provides hope for future relationships between faith traditions. What responsibilities do all of our various religious traditions have to the world?

In Sikh scriptural tradition, the communal, particularizing trends can be trumped when we remember that we exist as a community for the betterment of the other. For the general, for the world.

Well, that's the ideal, anyway. In reality, Sikhs are people who live mundane lives alongside the world's seven billion other everyday lives. In the homeland of India, twenty million Sikhs may blend into the larger populace or may fight so hard for their recognition as a religious minority that they forget about concern for the other. Perhaps neither, perhaps something in between. In the Sikh diaspora, Sikh immigrants may be focused on the day-to-day questions of fitting into their new societies. Darshan Tatla, scholar of the Sikh diaspora, has argued that the traumatic events of 1984 were a transformative moment for Sikh identity all over the world.[34] Second- and third-generation Sikhs may be reconciling their adaptations to home societies and memories of tradition, whether they be distant or recent. Where they will go from here is unclear.

Sikhs should go far into the history and ethics of their tradition—but not to remember only that they are Sikhs: they should go so deep and so far that they remember what Sikhs were sent by God to do. As we have seen, sewn deep into the Sikh tradition are tensions within which the Sikh must live. God's command is in tension with our selfish tendencies. The Sikh community has a strong sense of communal identity, and yet its sources say that it must exist for the betterment of the whole world. Perhaps to live a good Sikh life is to balance these tensions, perhaps it is to do the impossible. Perhaps the only way to truly purify the self is to help purify the other.

We must affirm the communal and the universal even if they seem to challenge us in contradictory ways. God's challenge to the *community* is to improve the plight of the *world*. Here we are up against Divine possibility. It is a blessing and a curse, a set of limitations and inspirations. In the real world, we must seek justice for ourselves and celebrate justice for others as our own. There is no turning back. The only redemption for the dead is to ensure that communal violence never again grips us, for we—a worldwide community—should know better. We are here to make a world where our particularities don't obscure our general commonality.

That summer of my youth, I stood before the other campers. With the beginning of understanding, I led our ritual reciting of the Ardas. We traveled together, through devotion to God; through the remembrance of our martyrs, gurus, and community; through acknowledgment of death—all the way to the end, the meaning: service to the world. *Vahiguru.*

NOTES

1. E. Patel, *Acts of Faith*, (Boston, 2010) 19.
2. G. Mann. *Sikhism* (Upper Saddle River, 2004) 16.
3. *Seimuejincitinaavai.* Guru Granth Sahib (hereafter GG), page 1287.
4. *Khinthakalukuarikaiajugatidandapartiti.* GG, 6.
5. *Bissapataharobasrosangrahaitinikhorha nit kalusarai.* GG, 23.
6. GG,157.
7. *MithaKhadhacitinaavaikourhatanhudhai jai.* GG, 1243.
8. *Moiarohirondemarijahi.* GG, 1287.
9. Mann, 24–25.
10. A. Mandair and C. Shackle, *Teachings of the Sikh Gurus* (New York, 2005) xxx.
11. *Ghar hi mundhividesipiru nit jhuresammhale.* GG, 594.
12. *Nit nitridaisamalipritamuapnha.* GG, 752.
13. *Titugharigavahusohilasivarahusirjanhharo.* GG, 12.
14. *Nanak namusamalitujituseviaisukh hoi.* GG, 39.
15. *Jinitunsajisavariaharisimari hoi udharu.* GG, 51.
16. *Kiougobindumanahuvisariaijisusimaratdukhjahi.* GG, 218.*Kari isnanusimariprabhuapna man tan bayearoga.* GG, 611.
17. *Haluhalemihalicitucetavatarvakhatsanjog.* GG, 955.
18. *Harinamucetaavaruna puja.* GG, 1048.
19. *Pavannamujagatimaiharikosimarisimarikasmalsabhharu re.* GG, 220.
20. *Man ekunacetasimurhmana.* GG, 12.
21. *Satangiharisimaranhamalujanamjanamkikati.* GG, 48.
22. *Khatusasatbicaratmukhigiana.* GG, 98.
23. *Puja cakarbaratnemtapiauhagailinachori.* GG, 1216.
24. *Catur bed much bacaniucaraiagaimahalunapaiai.* GG, 216.
25. *Nerhahaidurinajanhiahu nit saresammhale.* GG, 489.
26. *Sail patharmahijantupae ta karijakuagaikaridharia.* GG, 495.
27. *Ghalikhaeikichuhathahudei.* GG, 1245.

28. The term for care for others is *parupkari*, service is *sewa*; this corresponds well with what in the Ardas, as above noted, is *Sarbat Da Bhala* (seeking "the welfare of all").
29. Indigenous Australian activist Lilla Watson is credited with saying, "If you have come here to help me, you are wasting our time. But if you have come because your liberation is bound up with mine, then let us work together."
30. GG, 472, 178.
31. Bhai Gurdas wrote an extensive treatment of Guru Nanak's mission in his Var 1.
32. GG, 19.
33. GG, 1.
34. D.Tatla. *The Sikh Diaspora: The Search for Statehood*, (London, 1999).

Chapter Six

Memory, Hope, and Systems of Repair in Islam

Muhammad Suheyl Umar

MEMORY

There are many forgotten truths that were considered self-evident in former times, in Islam as well as elsewhere. One of these truths is that we are defined by what we know. Muslims have always taken for granted that our humanity is inextricably bound up with our understanding. Life has a purpose, and we are here to achieve that purpose, but we cannot possibly achieve it if we do not understand. The first step in understanding our humanity is assimilating the guidance of the past. There is no simpler way to pass on this guidance than through rote memorization.[1] If we consign it only to written form instead of instilling it into our very bodies, we are abandoning the task of education.

We have forgotten how easy it is to memorize, especially when the techniques of memorization are embodied in the culture itself. It was always recognized that the most essential formal learning was memorization of the Divine Word, whether or not its meaning was understood. And the most essential parts of the Divine Word were those parts that have to be known in order to perform the basic rituals. The stress was always on bodily activity, the body being the indispensable support for everything human, not least the mind and heart.

The classical uses of memory, accentuated in the Islamic tradition, pertain to its logocentric nature. In the traditional Islamic context, education begins with memorization of the Qur'an, which is the highest possible wisdom. That becomes a source of never-ending inspiration for whatever fields of learning people undertake. The greatest and most sophisticated minds of Islamic civilization freely admit that what they know is merely a few trickles from the Qur'anic Ocean.

The Qur'an is first a recited book.[2] The Qur'an was recited to the Prophet by the angel Gabriel. The Prophet memorized it and then recited it to his followers, who also memorized it. Those who knew how to write sometimes wrote down what they heard. Those whose memories were still not weakened by dependence on writing learned the text by heart.[3]

Beyond the Qur'an, as the years and centuries passed, the living memory of Muhammad and his Sunna gradually weakened, and it became more and more necessary to record the details of his life and practice so that they would not be lost. At the same time, the areas within which Islam became established continued to go through the vicissitudes that mark human existence—the differences of opinion, the struggles for power, the loves and hates, the natural and man-made catastrophes. An Islamic reflection on memory therefore begins with the dual dimensions of memory—on the one hand, the centrality of memory as a means to gaining wisdom and on the other, the ways in which memory is recast and reshaped, in light of and in relation to historical processes. Herein lies a profound tension. On the one hand, the thrust of Islamic tradition is to capture memory faithfully, and it assumes such capturing is possible; on the other hand, we must recognize that memory itself has undergone changes in the course of history, complicating what has been learned and memorized.

This tension may be described also as the quest for truthful memory. If faithful memory is endangered by the vicissitudes of history, there is at the same time also a self-correcting potential for recovering authentic historical memory. The quest for faithful or truthful memory is a crucial component of the application of memory in a contemporary interreligious context. All too readily, truthful memory is sacrificed in the name of circumstances exterior to itself. It is the duty of the sages and scholars to uncover truthful memory, thereby upholding fundamental spiritual truths of the tradition.

The present paper explores this dynamic as they play out in relation to two historical situations—one between Islam and Judaism and the other within the internal Muslim divide of Sunni and Shia. In both cases, it is suggested that we have the possibility to recover truthful memory and that there is a religious mandate to engage in such recovery, regardless of how unpopular it is under given political circumstances. The paper is written from my own Muslim context, that of Pakistan, and draws heavily on conversations that have occurred within the Pakistani institutions of religious education and public system. I believe that the testimony of how issues of memory and truth have been worked out within one Muslim framework are of relevance to the broader Muslim community and to the interfaith community at large. I therefore offer the case studies below and the lessons they can teach us all as one way of tackling the challenges of memory and how it complicates interfaith relations. I believe that the method spells out below holds out the hope of recovery of truthful memory, thereby sending a message of hope to interfaith relations as such, suggesting that truth can prevail at the end of the day. The two case studies offer one particular strategy for addressing the challenge shared by participants in the present project. Purification or modifications of memory have the potential for bringing about healing between faith traditions. While the Pakistani context did not allow for such healing, given the absence of a Jewish community in Pakistan, the case study below offers hope that recovery of truthful historical memory could have such potential for Jewish-Muslim relations.

This paper suggests to start with looking at two initiatives that could be taken as case studies of "purification/modification" of memory from the perspective of healing memories with reference to relations between religions. The first is interreligious—between the two faith communities of Jews and Muslims—and the other intra-religious—between the two main divides within the Islamic collectivity, the Sunnis and the Shīites. Both cases presented below have spilled over into situations of violence and both extend to situations that involve national identity that is fed by religious identity. Both cases may be seen as instances of collective memories of different communities moving away from the norm of "truthfulness" and objectivity of memory and becoming enwrapped in modified and misplaced memories. These have affected discernment, influenced judgments and ultimately led to incorrect remembering. In short, incorrect remembering has resulted in acting unjustly or adopting certain positions that are not warranted or justified by Scripture and by the overall perspective of the tradition. The debates provide an occasion for framing behaviour in the light of the Qur'anic injunctions that emphatically reminded the Muslim community to be truthful and impartial and to uphold justice even in cases where a group or collectivity had wronged it or acted towards it in an unjust manner: *"You who believe, be unwavering towards God, as witnesses for fair play, and do not let ill-will toward any folk incriminate you so that you swerve from dealing justly. Be just: that is nearness to heedfulness; and heed God [Alone]. God is informed about anything you do."*[4]

According to this perspective, if an individual or a community allows itself to be overwhelmed by memories that had been modified in an incorrect or untruthful way it would not be fulfilling its moral obligations and the spiritual duty enjoined by Scripture. In both cases described below, the idea of moral and religious responsibility was invoked and eschatological vision played its part to help reframe these memories.

Let me begin by presenting the case relevant to an interreligious exchange—the status of the Temple Mount within the matrix of relations between Jews and Muslims.

CASE STUDY 1—AL-AQSA MOSQUE, JEWS, AND THE MUSLIM COMMUNITY

Perspective and Background

With regard to the religions that are, as it were, rooted in Abraham, the city of Jerusalem is of immense importance to all three of them, to each in its own particular way. A brief review of the history (see appendix B) of the Furthest Mosque (*Al-Aqsa Mosque*) reveals that both the Jewish and Muslim Communities have a feeling of religious and historical relationship to the Temple Mount and the holy places of Jerusalem. The nature of the relationship and its significance for the respective houses of faith are, however, different. For the Jews, this place of worship is their center and the site of their ritual orientation (*qiblah*)[5] and a reminder of their political power and past worldly glory. They face towards it for prayers and supplication and they have harboured the hope to revive the religious rites of worship in this precinct for centuries. Muslim respect and relationship to this place is also extraordinary. For Muslims it is one of the most important relics of their sacred history and the land of a large number of prophets of Israel. They honoured and rehabilitated this place of worship when it had become derelict as a result of the mutual conflicts of the Jews and Christians and they take pride in the service that they have rendered to the Holy Land over the centuries. The Muslim mind looks at this service as a blessed and laudable spiritual activity according to its religious, ethical, and intellectual standards.

This accepted and shared backdrop of historical and religious relationship and reverence to the same site also leads to what are seemingly conflicting claims of both the Muslim and Jewish houses of faith with regard to the Temple Mount. The question has several dimensions, legal, religious, historical, ethical, and ultimately involves a reading of Divine providence and its charge. From the perspective of the Qur'an and the Sunnah, it is the ethical, spiritual, and eschatological point of view that must be given precedence in cases of dispute. Nevertheless, in the wake of the emergence of the Palestinian problem, Muslim scholarship of the Indian subcontinent has undergone a conceptual shift, related to political positions taken by the Arab world. The core question on which this conceptual shift took place could be summarized as follows: Is it a demand of the Islamic Shari'a, a requirement of the Islamic law, that the Muslims should reject the Jewish claims of affiliation, feeling of relationship to and possibility of custodianship in relation to the Temple Mount? Alternatively, is the present situation merely an outcome of the workings of history and a consequence of contingent events that had created a situation in which the Muslim community had to shoulder the responsibility of the custodianship of the Holy Land and of looking after the places of worship situated there? In the Indian subcontinent a change of perspective occurred as a result of the Israeli-Arab conflict. The former view, that is, "a requirement of the Islamic Shari'a" dominated over the latter, which used to be the normative view until then. This conceptual shift emerged in the works of four leading religious authorities, who were outstanding scholars of their age—Amīn Ahsan Islāhī,[6] Sayyid Sulaymān Nadawī,[7] Abū al-A'lā Mawdūdī,[8] and Qāri Muhammad Tayyib.[9] Unprecedented in the entire history of Muslim scholarship on the issue, these views gradually dislodged the earlier views of Muslim scholarship about the Holy Land. The conceptual and doctrinal position that was an outcome of these formulations modified the collective memory to such an extent that it became the *de facto* standard of the Muslim narrative. According to this position, the Muslims had not become the custodians and caretakers of the Holy Land as a result of historical circumstances and political conditions of the times. Rather, it was divinely ordained that the right of custodianship of the two sacred Tabernacles of God should be taken away from both the lines of descendents of Abraham—the Children of Israel and the Children of Ishmael—for their deviation from the Covenant in the case of the former and for falling into idolatry in the case of the latter. As a result, at a certain phase of world history, the right of custodianship was conferred on the Muslim Community by a regular injunction of the Islamic Sharī'a which, as a consequence, abrogated the rights of custodianship held earlier by the Children of Israel.

Over the last decade a widespread debate emerged in the religious and political circles of Pakistan, with ramifications in the larger areas of Urdu speaking/reading regions of Muslim lands,[10] which challenged this religious/ doctrinal and intellectual/academic position and argued in favour of revisiting the issue in relation to the primary Islamic sources and the earlier practice of the Muslim community. Broadly entitled the *"Al-Aqsa Mosque, Jews and the Muslim Community,"*[11] this debate is a characteristic example of an attempt to modify/correct collective memories of a community that had moved away from the norm of "truthfulness" and objectivity. Different, often opposing, schools of thought participated in the debate.[12]

The doctrinal, historical, and circumstantial arguments that provided the intellectual and religious underpinnings for the conceptual shift mentioned above are detailed below.

Problem Statement

The region where Israel and Palestine are presently located is regarded as the Holy Land by both of the communities. A Large number of the prophets belonged to this area. *Al-Aqsa Mosque*, which is historically related to a large number of prophets of Israel, is also situated in the region. The issue of the custodianship or right of possession of *Al-Aqsa Mosque* vis-à-vis the Temple Mount is the bone of contention between the Jews and Muslims. The Jews claim that two Temples stood on this site. The first Temple was built under the direction of King Solomon in 961 BCE and was destroyed in 586 BCE by the armies of Babylon. The Second Temple was built under the direction of Ezra in 520 BCE on the same site and was destroyed in 70 CE by the legions of Rome. Despite the fact that there are internal differences among Jewish denominations and groups on the details, in principle, it is generally agreed that the site of the two Temples remains a place of great holiness and the reclamation and rebuilding of the Temple in the Messianic Era is an eschatological hope and essential principle of Jewish belief. For Jews, the Temple is a place for sacred service of God that bestows blessing on all humanity. While Jews do not wish to construct the temple, it is an important component of their eschatological vision. But even if building the Third Temple is part of eschatological hope, its memory is central to Jews. They wish to uphold its memory because it touches on core dimensions of identity and holiness, as these are channeled through memory.

The Arab position, that emerged in the wake of the Palestinian problem starting in the third decade of the twentieth century, eventually led to the assertion that the holy precinct which they call "*Al-Haram al-Sharif*" (the Noble Holy precinct)[13] has nothing to do with the Temples which prophets Solomon and Ezra had built. The debate discussed here apart from suggesting a practical solution,[14] (see appendix A) focused on revisiting the whole issue with a view to find out if the Muslim position had been influenced by untruthful memories and distorted images of the religious Other. The salient points of the debate have been summarized in the following.

- Along with the Muslim mosques, the Qur'an grants the status of "houses built for the remembrance of God" to the places of worship of other faiths and enjoins their respect and safeguard. *Al-Aqsa Mosque*, apart from the general sanctity, carries another distinction; it was built by a great prophet of Israel and throughout history it had been the center of the prophetic missions of scores of other prophets. Islam considers all the prophets as belonging to a single chain of Divine guidance, teaches to give equal respect and reverence to all the prophets and counsels to hold their relics and historical remains in honour. Therefore the Prophet of Islam described the *Al-Aqsa Mosque* as the third best mosque in the world that is ranked in excellence. After the takeover of Jerusalem in 638 the Muslims reclaimed and renovated this extremely holy place of worship that had fallen derelict for centuries. According to the principial teachings of the Qur'an and the prophetic Sunna, this action taken by the Muslim community was purely based on respect, reverence, and devotion. It was not driven by any idea of a "right of possession" or a claim for exclusive custodianship. *They had accepted the responsibility of being the custodians of the holy precinct as vicegerents or stewards in the absence of the Jews.*

- Respect and reverence towards centers of worship and places of spiritual orientation are foundational to religious life. From recognition of the sanctity of space arise deep religious feelings. These can be seen in the case of the Jewish people and its continuing attachment to the site of the former Temple. The deep sense of loss following its destruction and the enduring hope for the future rebuilding nurtured millions of souls over the centuries. These sentiments are lofty, blessed, and natural. The Qur'an not only mentions explicitly the fact that the Jews became deprived of their center of worship, due to falling short of their religious responsibilities and going against the Covenant, it also speaks of the possibility that if they repented this center could be given back to their possession once again. Since the time of the revelation of the Qur'an the religious conditions for rebuilding the Temple did not exist. Jews were not in a position, politically and collectively, to make a demand for it or to undertake any practical efforts to that effect. The custodianship of the precinct remained therefore with the Muslim community. *This extended period of almost thirteen centuries imperceptibly worked into the Muslim psyche a sense of belonging and an idea of a Divine right of possession which pushed the real issue and its true nature into the background. The true memory was overshadowed by untruthful memories. Muslims lost site of the expectation of Jews for the rebuilding of the Temple in the Messianic Era, failing to recognize it as an important part of the Jewish creed, distinct in quality from Islamic attitudes of devotion, respect, and reverence for the Holy Land.*
- In the last century when interest in the status of the Temple began to emerge in Jewish circles, such interest arose in relation or in the context of the Zionist movement. The moral responsibility of the Muslim community, undoubtedly, required that it should have treated the matter with objectivity, with a complete disregard for political conflicts, in the correct religious and legal Islamic perspective and in light of the principles of Islamic teachings, that is, with justice, impartiality, and fair play.[15] The cardinal teaching of Islam with regard to places of worship is of a divinely ordained tolerance and acceptance. Yet in the case of the *Al-Aqsa Mosque* the more one analyzes the attitudes and positions taken by the Muslim community it becomes clearer that it has been overcome by a mental state that could only be termed as "the psychology of the right of possession." As a result, a series of intellectual deviations came into play, leading to declarations that the custodianship of the *Al-Aqsa Mosque*, which had been "entrusted" to the Muslims by historical circumstances, was the permanent religious right of possession of the Muslims and the Jews had no claim over the holy precinct. These deviations were of different categories: One group of scholars categorically denied the continuous and uninterrupted Muslim view of the history of the *Al-Aqsa Mosque*. Another group adopted the position that the custodianship conferred on the Muslim

community was not given to it through the working of history and by contingent situations; it was a permanent and inalienable religious right. A third group showed complete disregard for religious ethics, their moral obligations and the principial teachings of the Qur'an and the prophetic Sunna and went as far as claiming that the actual situation of the last thirteen centuries was the decisive and ineluctable factor. These deviations have contributed to sentiments running high and tensions rising to the point that no one is prepared to undertake an objective and nonpartisan scholarly research and analysis of the problem.

- The upshot of all this is that the issue of the *Al-Aqsa Mosque* has become a moral dilemma and a test for making right ethical choices for the Muslim community. In its own way, this situation mirrors the test that the children of Israel have faced in the past. Unfortunately the Muslim community too has fallen short of the desired high moral ground, like their predecessors. In the present day geopolitical situation the question of custodianship and right of possession for the Palestinian lands is essentially a political issue. It is completely understandable that it gave rise to a negative response from the Arab nations and the Muslim community at large. Nevertheless, this reaction is far from justice. It is completely unbefitting of the Muslim community to characterize the Jewish religious sentiment as "a sacrilege of the *Al-Aqsa Mosque*," to turn it into a blameworthy attitude, to fall into a complete denial of the historical and religious roots of the Jewish view of the Temple Mount, to refuse to honor their ongoing feeling of relationship and—ultimately as the worst consequence—to deprive them of the right of worship in the precinct.
- The perspective of the contributors to the debate was informed by a set of basic perceptions that had emerged after sustained, serious deliberations on one of the core problems that had marred Jewish-Muslim relations over the years.
- The issue is very much alive today and directly related to our present day geo-political situation as it is not the case of a religious and ethical issue; it is deeply intertwined with the political dimension of the larger Palestinian problem. Having strong and decisive religious underpinnings, it could be rightly termed as the major and most crucial religious issue of the contemporary world.
- The unrealistic policies and attitudes that the Arab world has adopted with regard to Israel, if analyzed, could be traced back to the issue of the *Al-Aqsa Mosque* (called the furthest Mosque in the Qur'an)[16] and the psychological environment in which these strategies have emerged has been primarily nourished by the predominant idea of the exclusive right of possession of the holy precinct by the Muslim community.
- The question of affirming the historical roots of the Jews and honouring their ongoing feeling of relationship to the Temple Mount and the holy

places of Jerusalem—most often phrased as "custodianship and ownership/possession by the Jews" in the Muslim narrative—is the foremost and one of the most difficult problems that creates impediments for a sustainable peace in the region.
- The position and attitudes of the Muslim community, on the practical and political levels, have deviated from the high moral ground provided by Qur'anic perspective and Prophetic example. Swept away by historical expediencies and prevailed over by political opportuneness, having neglected self-criticism and soul searching, this attitude amounts to moral failure. The reason for this growing failure is that over the years the community's collective memory has become encrusted with layers of distorted memories, causing it to move away from "truthfulness" of memory and, consequently act in ways that could hardly be termed as just and fair.

Apart from suggesting a viable solution to the problem (detailed in appendix A) the impact of the debate was considerable. By revisiting the issue, analyzing collective memory for untruthful elements, and reframing memories with reference to the basic texts of the Tradition—the Divine perspective and eschatological vision were brought back into the picture. The Urdu and English Media, that was largely unaware of the classical and normative position of the Muslim community on the issue as well as of its narrative in the Qur'an, prophetic traditions and the classical works of Islamic scholarship, was able to present an informed discourse on the issue. The curricula, both of the religious centers of teaching and the public system of education, contrary to a widespread belief, did not actually contain any hate materials in the textbooks. That attitude had been originated and perpetuated through different channels and even that only in some of the institutions of religious learning. In these sectors where such a way of thinking had come to dominate, the counter narrative was introduced which made some inroads into the prevalent discourse.

Politicians were also among the beneficiaries in the sense that they now had access to an alternative view of the question that was so clearly grounded in the traditional sources hence providing them with a way out from the intimidating religious discourse that had engulfed them earlier and which had become laden with an atmosphere of emotional blackmail. Obviously this did not go to the extent of generating enough conviction within the political authorities in Pakistan to officially accept the State of Israel. Nevertheless, it went a long way to create among the educated a widespread awareness of the Jewish concern for the present and future status of the Temple, distinct from the Islamic attitude of respect and reverence for the Holy Land.

Perhaps even more importantly, it worked as holding a mirror to the Muslim community of the region wherein it could see that it had succumbed to the political exigencies and was losing its high moral ground by moving away from justice and harmony.

Salient Glimpses of the Debate

God never addresses the same message to two or more recipients of divergent character. Therefore, God's word enters history differently, according to Divine Wisdom, in relation to different receptacles. According to the Islamic lights, God sent his prophets and messengers to all human collectivities individually up to the Abrahamic age.[17] But after the times of Abraham, the Divine scheme chose Abraham and his descendants as the vehicles for the Divine message, to become a dazzling witness of the Divine message in themselves and to propagate the message to other nations of the world. This responsibility of the children of Abraham was divided into phases. The descendants of the Prophet Jacob were selected for undertaking the responsibility in the first phase, they were given the Holy Land, a law in the form of the Torah, a continuous chain of prophethood, as well as worldly glory and political power. The Temple of Solomon was built in Jerusalem which became the place of their orientation and a center of the religious and spiritual sentiments. The children of Israel, during the different periods of their history, would at times rise to the demands of their responsibility, while at others they fell short of it and went against the Covenant. After having been tested for a long time, when the children of Israel collectively relegated themselves, religiously and ethically, to such a low state that no hope was left, they were removed from their responsibility with the arrival of the Prophet Jesus. The responsibility was then devolved on the other branch of the children of Abraham, the children of Ishmael, where prophethood had been dormant for a long time.

The children of Ishmael were commanded by the Lord to inhabit an Arabian Peninsula, were given the essential doctrines, rituals, and code of worship of the house of Abraham, and were made the custodians of the outlying Tabernacle of God in Mecca. For most of their history the children of Ishmael were faithful to their original teachings but decline and deviation set in and, gradually, idolatry crept into their metaphysical concepts, rites and rituals, and social activities. Finally, six centuries after Prophet Jesus, the last prophet of the house of Abraham, the prophet of Islam, Muhammad, restored the Abrahamic faith in its pristine purity in Arabia and deposed the children of Ishmael from the custodianship of the House of God, the Tabernacle of Ka'bah at Mecca.

This apparent similarity that existed between the two lines of descent of the children of Abraham was the basis on which some of the twentieth century scholars of Islam had built their argument for the abrogation of the rights of custodianship of the children of Israel for the Holy Land and for the sacred places of Jerusalem.

To the extent of our knowledge, it was the first time in Muslim intellectual history that such a view was expressed. Throughout history, Islamic scholarship had seen this change as a punishment for going against the Covenant that could be reverted if the children of Israel repented and amended their ways.[18] In Islamic terminology it was an "Engendering Command or Providential Command (*amr takwīnī*),"[19] and not a "Law-giving Command" (*amr tashrī'ī*). The counter argument that emerged during the debate contested this view on two counts: Firstly this new discourse had obliterated the time honoured, standard distinction[20] between the two domains of *tashrī'* and *takwīn*. Secondly, the removal of the children of Israel from the custodianship of the Temple belonged to the category of a Providential Command that cannot be made a basis for a religious ruling. This second point was of primary importance since the Qur'an had categorically established this distinction with regard to the prophetic mission of Muhammad and had accorded completely different status to the two places of worship in this respect. Moreover the practical position that the Prophet of Islam had taken vis-à-vis these two places of worship was also totally distinct.

The counter argument points out that there are three aspects of the Law-giving Command for the banishment of the children of Ishmael that need to be kept in view with regard to the distinction established by the Qur'an between "The Inviolable Mosque" at Makkah and the *Al-Aqsa Mosque*.

- The rank and significance of the House of God, the Ka'bah, for the house of Abraham.
- The nature of the deviation of the children of Israel from the creed of Abraham that was different from that of the children of Ishmael.
- The punishment ordained by God for the children of Ishmael for their idolatry.

A secondary claim that has been advanced by Sayyid Sulaymān Nadawī in this regard pertained to the promise that had been mentioned in Deuteronomy[21] and argued that after the advent of Islam, this promise was made conditional upon the acceptance of Islam.[22] The counter statement of the debate pointed out the futility of the argument by saying that if according to the Islamic law the Jews were allowed to exist as a religious community and to practice their religion with freedom, and their religious places and rites of worship were respected, it was pointless to divest them from their site of orientation! Furthermore, the Prophet of Islam had made his conclusive and decisive argument against the Jews of the Arabian Peninsula who were only a small part of the children of Israel spread in different parts of the world. It would have been completely unjustified to apply the same decision to the entire Jewish community settled in Asia, Africa, and various parts of Europe who might not have even heard of the advent of Islam!

The upshot of argument is that parallels could not be drawn and the same conclusions cannot be applied to the Jews and the idolatrous Arabs on the one hand and "The Inviolable Mosque" and the *Al-Aqsa Mosque* on the other. That would be based on a false assumption that both communities were deposed of their status and responsibility for the same reasons. The children of Ishmael were banished from "The Inviolable Mosque" because the Lord had declared this house of worship to be a universal center of the religion of Abraham and the Arabs had fallen away from the essential message of the Unity of God by adopting *shirk* (associating with God/idolatry) as their religion. Therefore, by every religious and ethical principle, they forfeited their right to be the custodians of the house. Moreover, once the Prophet of Islam had given his decree against them through a revelation from God that they had no right to exist as a community anymore, there was no question of any kind of relationship with the House of God. None of these factors existed in the case of the Jews and the *Al-Aqsa Mosque*. Therefore the same religious ruling cannot be applied to them.

Arguments of a Partial and Secondary Nature (A Few Examples)

1. *Generalization of the prohibition for the idolatrous Arabs to take care of the houses of God.* An argument to that effect has been made by some of the scholars[23] on the basis of verses 17 and 18 of the Surah 9 of the Qur'an[24] which prohibit the idolaters to take care of the houses of God by generalizing the command given with regard to the polytheistic Arabs and claiming that the *Al-Aqsa Mosque* can no longer have any relation to a group that has deviated from the Divine message. The counter argument points out that it was a context-specific command which cannot be universalized in light of the evidence presented from the Qur'anic narrative.
2. *Parallel drawn with the idolaters.* An argument has also been advanced that even though the verses are directly and essentially related to the idolaters, using the principle of analogical reasoning (*qayās*) the ruling could be derived from these verses with regard to the abrogation of the right of custodianship of the Jews. The counter argument points out that each and every stage of the banishment of the idolaters was completed in the light of the Divine revelation and no step was taken by the Muslim community on its own discretion. The Qur'anic narrative gives all the details and categorically commands the Muslims with regard to the rulings that pertain to the idolaters there but it is completely silent on the issue of custodianship or of the ongoing

relationship of the Jews with the Temple. Therefore no valid parallel can be drawn with the idolaters.

3. *Argument from the Nocturnal Journey (Isrā) of the Prophet.* One of the most important events in the life of the Prophet of Islam is the nocturnal journey that he had miraculously undertaken from Makkah to Jerusalem and from there to the heavens and the Divine Presence. Described in the Qur'an,[25] with details in all traditional sources,[26] this event has been interpreted as foretelling the announcement for the abrogation[27] of the right of custodianship and belonging of the Jews, hence providing justification for it.[28] The counter argument points out that Islamic literature of the last fourteen centuries, both exegetical and historical, is completely silent on the issue. The Divine purpose understood from these verses by Islamic scholarship throughout the ages was that which is explicitly mentioned in the verses, that is, *"so We might show him some of Our signs!"* and no Qur'an commentator had ever derived this conclusion. On the contrary commentators, contemporary with the authors (cited above and in the endnotes) have made no mention of these views and have even recorded the opposite.[29] Moreover, the Qur'anic text, seven verses later, while describing the destruction of the Temple and the expulsion of the Jews, makes it categorically clear that it was a provisional and conditional punishment which could be changed with the change of heart of the children of Israel: *"Perhaps your Lord may show mercy to you. If you should turn back, We will go back too."*[30]

4. *The Change of Qiblah (center or place of ritual orientation).* Another argument that has been advanced with regard to the abrogation of the right of custodianship /relationship of the Jews pertains to the change of *Qiblah* which took place after the migration of the Prophet from Makkah to the city of Medina. When the Muslim community had settled in Medina, in order to test their faith and to generate a sense of intimacy with the Jewish community, God commanded the Muslims to pray facing towards the direction of Jerusalem and for seventeen months the Muslim community continued to make their ritual orientation during the canonical prayer towards the *Al-Aqsa Mosque*. Later on, revelation asked them to change it once more towards "The Inviolable Mosque."[31] Building his argument on this event, Sayyid Sulaymān Nadawī, wrote that "the holy house (the Temple) the second *Qiblah* of Islam and its custodianship is the right of the Muslim community."[32] The counter argument points out that the context completely denied any such interpretation. The change of *Qiblah* had a completely different significance and, moreover, the internal evidence of the text leads to a different conclusion. The change was a test of faith,[33] which the Prophet did not like[34] and which the Jews also were

unhappy about, as they would have preferred that the Muslims should keep praying towards their *Qiblah*. When one adds to this the views of the earlier Islamic scholarship, which had looked at the event as an act of reaching out to the Jews, to invite them to Islam and to make them think kindly of it,[35] one realizes that the entire event had nothing to do with the abrogation of custodianship. Moreover, if the Muslim right is supposed to have been established by the visit of the Prophet of Islam to the *Al-Aqsa Mosque* and by praying towards that direction for a brief period of time, then, by the same token, the Jews can claim a greater right because this place had been their *Qiblah* for three thousand years. A pilgrimage to this place is a part of their religious obligations and scores of their prophets and priests had been preaching and worshipping in this holy place.[36]

5. *Applying the word Masjid to the Temple.* Another argument has been made claiming that since the Jews named the place of worship built by the Prophet Solomon by the word temple and since God has mentioned it by the name of *masjid* in the Qur'an, it is a proof text that the Jews have no right over it because the word *masjid* can only be used for a Muslim place of worship.[37] The counter argument points out the inherent weakness of the thesis by referring to the Qur'anic text which uses the word *masjid* for the places of worship (churches and synagogues) of the People of the Book in many of its verses.[38] The Prophetic Hadīth also provides examples of the same usage.[39]

6. *Glad tidings of the conquest of the Holy Land.* The quotation given above with reference to the change of *Qiblah*[40] also mentions the prophecy for the conquest of the Holy Land as a proof for the abrogation of the right of relationship. According to the counter argument, the prophecy is completely unrelated to the question of custodianship. Moreover, according to Islamic law, since the city of Jerusalem was not conquered by the Caliph Umar and was surrendered as a result of a treaty, it cannot be treated as a conquered land hence the status of its places of worship.[41]

CASE STUDY 2—BETWEEN SUNNIS AND SHĪ'ITES: LESSONS FROM YEMEN AND IRAQ[42]

Perspective and Background

The second case study focuses on collective memory that is internal to the Islamic tradition as it pertains to the two main divisions: Sunnīs and the Shī'ites. Let us present it by means of the following formulation: the spiritual ancestors of the Shī'ites were those Companions of the Prophet who could not live without the presence of the Prophet and who had no choice but to attach themselves to what endured of him in the presence of his descendants; the Sunnis were those who could not accept any substitute whatever for this presence and who, thus, had no choice but to live only by his memory and in his *Sunnah* (practice, wont).

On the other hand the Shī'ites lived on another memory. There is a principle of fluctuation or adaptation,[43] the effects of which may be observed in diverse traditional climates and, not least, in primitive Islam, where the political regime which was finally viable did not correspond to the original ideal. The Sunnīs resigned themselves to this fatality, whereas the Shī'ites enwrapped themselves in the bitter memory of a lost purity. Combined with the recollection of the drama of Karbala[44] and considered on the level of mystical life, in relation to the noble sadness aroused by the awareness of our earthly exile. This exile has its expressions in injustice, oppression, and frustration in relation to basic virtue and Divine rights.

Problem Statement

The saving Manifestation of the Absolute is either Truth or Presence, without ever being exclusively either the one or the other—for Truth brings with it Presence, and Presence brings Truth. Herein lies the twofold nature of all the ophanies.[45] At the risk of oversimplification and expressing the matter schematically, it could be said that in Shī'ism,[46] the element Presence comes before the element Truth.[47] Sunnism anchored itself in the axiom that it is the absolute Truth that saves.[48] The element of exaggeration entered into the mix in both cases, and so the collective memories of the communities moved away from the norm of "truthfulness" of memory. Shī'ism's limitation came out as a consequence of the emphasis that only Presence saves, not Truth itself. From this it moved to the position that only one particular Presence saves. Sunnism on the contrary is founded on the axiom that it is only the absolute Truth that saves, and not the element Presence itself. From this it moved to the position that no Presence has any role in salvation.[49] It was precisely around these bitter memories that the theological and sentimental[50] fault lines between the two communities were drawn. Over the centuries, this resulted in situations of religious violence. Only through the healing of memory has it been possible in recent history to attempt a rapprochement between these two currents of the Islamic tradition.[51] This has been made possible by removing exaggerated or misplaced elements of memory, as these pertain to the Caliphate and the Imamate, representing the saving potential of Truth and Presence, respectively.

Impact Factor

As the claims of exclusivity of Presence were renounced on the Shī'ite side and the demand for the exclusivity of Truth was relinquished by the Sunnis through the removal of untruthful elements and the reframing of memories relating to the basic texts of the Tradition, conflicts were reduced and social harmony and mutual tolerance emerged and sustained for a long time. As in the first case study, the eschatological vision and the transcendent dimension of the Divine was the decisive factor.

What was achieved actually was that once the memory was corrected on the doctrinal plane there were positive consequences that flowed from it. The Shī'ite side, modifying the exclusivist claim of the saving power of Presence (read Imamte), by relocating it on a different level from the highest status of *usūl al-dīn* (principles of religion) which it had occupied earlier, allowed for a shift. The Sunni side, whose basic problem with the aforementioned theological stance was removed, reciprocated by modifying the exclusivist claim of the saving power of Truth by conceding to the working of the element Presence in salvation; hence the reconciliation. The reality today is thus different from what it was in earlier times with greater social coherence, mutual tolerance and increased level of acceptance for competing, dissident points of view.

Historically speaking, the initiative started with Allama Qāzi Shwakānī[52] in the Yemen, continued in the efforts of Ayatullah Muhsin al-Hakim[53] for purification of memories in Iraq with its larger area of influence in Iran and India through the initiatives of Ayatullah Gulpa'igāni[54] and, more recently, of Ayatullah Dr. Sādiqī.[55]

Looking at both cases, we note that hope for a better reality was generated and nourished by the resources offered by tradition. What, then, are the resources within the Islamic tradition for coping with the challenges facing us, for repairing/healing memory? Two points deserve mention, legal and spiritual. The legal mechanism facilitates reinterpretation, revisiting of the basic sources and opens the Canon to fresh insights, deeper levels of understanding and social reconstruction. This mechanism is called *Ijtihād* (analogical reasoning, literally: to exert one's utmost effort). It is the principle which allows Islamic civilization to cope with the inevitable change and evolution in human society and the problems that it brings in its wake.

The spiritual resources available for healing memory are related to the higher applications of memory. One central spiritual practice of Islam, certainly not unique to it, is the interiorization or reintegration of the soul in the Divine by means of rememberance of God, *dhikr* and internal conversion (*tawbah*). *Istighfār* (seeking refuge in God) expresses both regret for sin and hope of pardon. If sin brings about dispersion within the world by following one's passions, *Istighfār* ought to bring about a conversion from outwardness to inwardness. *Dhikr* (invocation, remembrance of God) may be seen as a fundamental expression of hope; the trusting desire for salvation. The desire to be saved or delivered is fundamental to the invocation of God's name, recognizing it manifests mercy and therefore has saving power. This spiritual path is central to the establishment of peace. To solve the "problem of Islam" that faces us in the Middle East today, we have to solve the "problem of the human race" that faces us wherever we look, especially inside our own hearts. Conversion of the heart and the memory of the higher reality of God are the keys to rising above our human weakness, a weakness made manifest in relation to various historical situations. Both the internal Muslim conflict and the conflict between Muslims and members of other religions have to ultimately be seen in light of a higher theory of integration of the human person in a higher reality and the subjugation of common human nature to higher spiritual reality. Therefore, we cannot achieve real peace, be it in the Middle East or elsewhere until such peace is found in ourselves. And we cannot find such peace, until we come to the higher recognition of God, the ultimate quest of our memory and the ultimate focal point of our hope.

APPENDIX A

Is there a Viable Solution to the Problem of the Temple Mount?

The debate mentioned in the text leads to the question of whether there is a viable solution to the problem of the Temple Mount that could be acceptable to both parties. Is there a way to negotiate a situation in which no one is deprived of the right of worship in this holy place and neither of the parties becomes a non-stakeholder? Is there a possibility that both parties could have the rights of custodianship and worship in the holy precinct? To the direct questions such as these, it is good to give an equally direct answer: Yes— unequivocally and unabashedly. This would, however, require revisiting the important aspects of the history of the problem.

The Temple Mount, currently known as *"Al-Haram al-Sharif"* (the Noble Holy precinct), is a rectangular area of approximately forty-five acres. Within this precinct Prophet Solomon (upon him be peace) had built the magnificent holy temple of worship which is historically known as Solomon's Temple. The location of the building, the description of its construction and the confines of the precinct were demarcated in the Bible. After its destruction in 586 BC at the hands of Nebūchadnez'zar,[56] (Nabukht Nasr), the second temple was built exactly on the same foundations and according to Jewish tradition the third construction of the Temple would also take place on these foundations. In a larger area around the original building of the Temple (i.e., the furthest Mosque) a boundary wall was also erected by King Herod of Judea in 19 BC. The boundary walls defined by Herod exists until today.

In AD 638 Jerusalem was conquered under the leadership of the Caliph Umar. The heaps of debris were cleared and after cleansing the holy precinct of the filth and garbage, a center of worship was selected near the southern wall of the precinct where, later on, a regular mosque was constructed. In the initial years this mosque was named the "Umar Mosque"[57] but as the Muslim community only consecrated this small area for their ritual worship, in Islamic parlance the expression "Al-Aqsa Mosque" gradually changed its connotation. Instead of its original meaning, that is, Solomon's Temple and the wall that surrounded the precinct, it was now used for this specific mosque. The caliph 'Abd al-Malik bin Marwān built a dome in the center of the precinct over the holy Rock. These are still the two dominant and important constructions within the confines of the precinct. Following in the footsteps of 'Abd al-Malik bin Marwān, Muslims built large and small domes in the same area over the years that were given different names.

Practically, this holy precinct is in the possession of the Muslim community for centuries and on the basis of this historical continuity the Muslim Endowment Committee of Jerusalem has taken the position that the Jews have no right whatsoever on any part of the precinct and that to give them a right of possession or custodianship over a portion of the precinct would go against the rulings of the Islamic law. The grand mufti of Palestine 'Ikrama Sabri formulated this position in the following words: "*all the buildings surrounding the Al-Aqsa Mosque have the status of an Islamic endowment. The doors, windows and passages of these buildings directly open out unto the Al-Aqsa Mosque and with regards to sanctity and holiness these carry the same status which is of the Al-Aqsa Mosque. Therefore according to the Islamic law, taking away any of these buildings and turning it into a place of worship of the Jews is an impossibility*" (http://www.la.utexas.edu/).

In our view the root of the conflict lies in this extremist standpoint of the Muslim Endowment Committee. It is necessary to revise this interpretation. It is a requirement not only of the basic Islamic texts of the Qur'an and the Sunnah but it is strongly supported by the attitude and practice that the Muslim community, while being in possession of the precinct of the Temple Mount, had adopted over the past centuries with regard to the construction of the Temple. In the light of the detailed discussion above it could be said with confidence that the entire precinct of the Temple Mount, including the Dome of the Rock, being a relic of the "Al-Aqsa Mosque" (the Mosque [Temple] of Prophet Solomon, upon him be peace) carries the general status of holiness and respect according to the Muslim lights. Nevertheless, religiously and historically, there is no justification or any necessity to put forward a claim for exclusive rights of possession or custodianship over the entire precinct of the Temple Mount. Such a claim must be limited to the confines of the present day Aqsa Mosque. According to our view this is the cardinal point that could provide us with a practical solution to the conflict. Looking at the issue from this angle would lead Muslims to approach the sanctity of this place of worship in a way that is completely different from that of the Jewish point of view, thereby avoiding conflict. As far as the Jews are concerned, their basic interest is in maintaining the sanctity of the Temple site and an eschatological hope for the eventual reconstruction, in the Messianic era, of the third Temple on the same foundations on which Prophet Solomon (upon him be peace) had built the first Temple and Ezra built the second Temple. Centuries have passed over the destruction of the Temple, its boundary wall had been extended and several constructions took place during the intervening period. Therefore it is not possible to determine the actual foundations of the Temple with any certainty without excavation and archaeological research. However on the basis of the details provided by the Bible and the Talmud the Jewish scholars have tried to find out these foundations. There are three views in this regard.

According to the first, called the traditional point of view, commonly supported by Jewish scholars and rabbis, Solomon's Temple was situated very near the place where the Dome of the Rock is situated today. Most Jewish archaeologists also uphold this view. Recent research has departed from the traditional view by suggesting that the Temple was situated slightly away from the Dome of the Rock. According to the view of the physicist Asher Kaufman of the Rakach Institute of Physics of the Hebrew University of Jerusalem, the most sacred part of the Temple, that is, the Holy of the Holies, was situated towards the north of the Dome of the Rock, at a place where the stone in the Dome of the Spirits is located.

According to the view of one of the eminent architects of Tel Aviv, Tuvia Sagiv, the Temple was located towards the south of the Dome of the Rock. This location falls at an equal distance between the Dome of the Rock and the present day Aqsa Mosque where nowadays Al-Ka's fountain is to be seen.[58]

The proper authentic religious motive of the (pre-politicized) Muslim community was not related to gaining the right of custodianship or possession, let alone to reconstruct the mosque on the actual foundations of the Temple. Their only demand is to retain the right of worship in this holy place. Therefore, whatever significance the specific location of the Temple described in the Bible or its stipulated parameters might have according to Jewish tradition, for Muslims the entire holy precinct is of an equal status with regard to holiness, spiritual excellence, and promise of greater reward of worship in it. Furthermore, even if the boundaries of the precinct were extended, no change would come about in its status of being meritorious and rewarding with regard to the acts of worship. That is precisely the reason why the place mentioned in the traditions as the location where the Prophet of Islam offered his ritual prayers on the occasion of his nocturnal journey to Jerusalem is situated within the precincts of the Temple but away from the actual building of the Temple. After the conquest of Jerusalem in AD 638 Muslims expressed no interest in finding the specific foundations of the Temple and, following the example of the Caliph Umar, started praying at the same location where the Prophet of Islam had offered his ritual prayers and later on built a regular mosque on the same place, initially named "'Umar Mosque."[59] This is the mosque which is now called the "Al-Aqsa Mosque." Whichever of the three locations suggested by the Jewish scholars be accepted as the real locale of the historical Temple, the present day "Al-Aqsa Mosque" is not affected by it.

The upshot is this: there is a viable solution to the problem of the Temple Mount, safeguarding the right of custodianship of the Muslims for the "Al-Aqsa Mosque." Obviously, this solution is readily acceptable by the Jewish religious circles, but the Muslim community would need to undergo a conceptual shift by distancing itself from erroneous ideas that have been devised in order to deny the right of custodianship of the entire place of worship for the Jews. In this regard they must keep in view the example set by the practice of the Caliph Umar as a guiding principle which limits the rights of the Muslim community to the place where, according to the traditions, the Prophet of Islam performed his ritual prayers and which the Caliph Umar demarcated for the Muslim place of worship.

APPENDIX B

Brief History of The Furthest Mosque (*Al-Aqsa Mosque*) — A Muslim Narrative

In order to provide more background material related to the issue and to situate it directly in the Muslim context, a brief history of the Furthest Mosque (*Al-Aqsa Mosque*), as found in the Muslim narrative, is presented here. Collected and edited from various sources it is a representative sampling of what the Muslim scholarship and religious stakeholders think about the issue and the historical data on which they base their views.

With regard to the religions which are as it were rooted in Abraham, the city of Jerusalem is of immense importance to all three of them, to each in its own particular way. The city of Medina on the other hand belongs to Islam alone; but this cannot be said of Mecca, even sacramentally speaking, for the Psalms are among the greatest treasures of both Judaism and Christianity, and Baca is extolled in the Psalms as one of the "Lovable Tabernacles" of God.[60]

Once the Jews came out of slavery from the Egyptians and Prophet Moses was given the Law in the desert of Sinai, he received commands from the Lord for the various forms of worship and sacrifices that were to be carried out in the Tent of Gathering. Details of the structure of the Tent and the objects that had to be placed in the Tent were given to Prophet Moses (upon him be peace).[61] This Tent has been mentioned in the Torah by different names. Prophet Moses was also commanded to prepare a box of a specific form and place the tablets of the Torah in it and to put the box permanently at a specified location in the Tent of Gathering.[62] The Torah calls it Ark of the Covenant. In 1450 BC Jerusalem was conquered following the Divine command under the leadership of Joshua b. Nūn and during the following four centuries the children of Israel were engaged in their struggle with the inhabitants of the region. Since their possession of the land of Palestine and their political domination was not yet firmly established, the Tent of Gathering remained their (mobile) center of worship. Finally during the times of Prophet David (upon him be peace) the children of Israel succeeded in laying the foundations for a permanent kingdom whereupon Prophet David received the command from the Lord to build a center of worship[63] for which he bought the land[64] and started the initial preparations[65] but as he could not complete the construction during his lifetime the task was bequeathed to Prophet Solomon (upon him be peace).[66] In 950 BC Prophet Solomon built the magnificent temple of worship which is historically known as Solomon's Temple.[67] Thus Solomon's Temple became the place of orientation for the worship and religious rites and the center of religious and social life of the children of Israel instead of the Tent of Gathering. An altar[68] was built for the burnt offerings and a special space was created for the Ark of the Covenant in the Temple.[69] The prayer which the Prophet Solomon had made[70] at the occasion of its completion clearly indicated that this place of worship had been made a spiritual center and gathering place for the children of Israel, a Tabernacle—*Mathābah*[71] in the words of the Qur'an—just like "The Inviolable Mosque" at Makkah was made the Tabernacle for the children of Ishmael.

Thus this place of worship became not only a center of religious and social life of the children of Israel but a symbol of their political power and worldly glory and magnificence. Words of warning and admonition had also arrived from the Lord on the tongue of Prophet Solomon,[72] a prophecy that finds its parallel account in the Qur'anic narrative.[73] The prophecy came to pass after 350 years after construction of Solomon's Temple during the times of the prophet Jeremiah as the children of Israel deviated from the Covenant. Nebūchadnez'zar[74] (Nabukht Nasr), the king of Babylon, prevailed upon them, destroyed the Temple and after a lot of loot, pillage, and bloodshed, carried the children of Israel with him to Babylon in 586 BC.[75] The children of Israel repented, mended their ways and as a result God once again gave back their freedom. Cyrus, the king of Persia, after conquering Babylon in 538 BC, allowed them to return to Jerusalem and once again build the Temple.[76]

The foundation of the building, map of its construction and the confines of the precinct were explicitly demarcated in the Mosaic Law. Nobody had the right to alter these conditions, therefore, in 515/520 BC, the second Temple was built under the direction of Ezra on the same site and exactly on the same foundations but this new building, for its modest construction, was no comparison to the original Temple of Solomon.[77] This Temple endured for another 350 years though it had to face the assaults of various invaders from time to time. In 169 BC the Greek emperor Antiochus Epiphanes the Fourth conquered the land, took over the Temple and plundered all its belongings and treasures,[78] which resulted in the revolt of the Maccabees who, under the leadership of Judas Maccabeus, succeeded in getting rid of the invaders, recovered the Temple and purified and cleansed it.[79] The Jewish annual feast of Hanukkah remembers the event. A large part of the second Temple (of Zerubbabel) was brought to ruins when the Roman army, led by General Pompey, conquered Palestine and the Temple though, later on the Romans conferred semi-political autonomy on the Jews. The king of Judaea, Herod the Great (37–4 BC), while reconstructing the Temple from 19 BC to the following forty-six years, increased the area of the precinct and built it on an elevated plinth. In a larger area around the original building of the Temple a boundary wall was also erected which underwent extensions in two stages; first by King Herod of Judea in 19 BC and then by the Roman Emperor Hadrian in AD 136. The boundary wall defined by Hadrian exists till today.

The second prophecy concerning the destruction of Solomon's Temple came to pass in AD 70. In AD 66 the Jews rose in rebellion against the Roman Empire and General Titus invaded Jerusalem to put an end to the insurgency in AD 70. There was a massacre of the Jews and the Temple was destroyed. Only the western wall of the Temple survived the catastrophe and gradually it became a gathering place of the Jews and the location of mourning, hence the name of "Wailing Wall."

Renovating the city, Emperor Hadrian named it Aelia Capitolina and erected a huge temple in the name of the Roman god Jupiter on the location where Solomon's Temple existed earlier and as Christianity became the state religion in the fourth century AD Constantine the Great converted the place into the Church of Resurrection.

In AD 638, when Jerusalem was conquered by the Muslim forces, Caliph Umar visited the city along with a few other Companions of the Prophet. The precinct of the Temple Mount was found to have become a "waste disposal site" and the holy site of the Rock was covered by heaps of filth and garbage. Umar showed great respect for the place and, aided by the other Companions, they cleared the site and after cleansing the holy precinct demarcated a location for Muslim worship area near the southern wall of the precinct where, later on, a rectangular wooden mosque was constructed. In the initial years this mosque was named as the "Umar Mosque."[80] In AD 688 the Ummayid Caliph 'Abd al-Malik bin Marwān built a majestic dome in the center of the precinct over the holy Rock which is known by the name of the

"Dome of the Rock." "Umar Mosque" was also rebuilt with extensions. This is the site and the specific mosque that has always been referred to as the "Al-Aqsa Mosque" in Islamic sources. These are still the two dominant and important constructions within the confines of the precinct. Following in the footsteps of 'Abd al-Malik b. Marwān, Muslims built large and small domes in the same area over the years that were given different names.

In AD 1078 the Seljuk Turks took control of Jerusalem. Christian pilgrims were made unwelcome in the Holy Land. During their reign of twenty years, Christian pilgrims were not treated well and facilitation was scant and their rights of visiting were not safeguarded giving rise to a wave of anger and resentment in Europe that culminated in the Crusades in AD 1096. Following the papal edict of Pope Urban the Second Christian warriors assailed the lands and took over "Al-Aqsa Mosque" and "Dome of the Rock" in AD 1099. "Dome of the Rock" was converted into a Church with a cross installed on top of the Dome and icons of the Christian Saints and martyrs installed. An altar was erected on the Rock entitled *Templum Domini* while the Al-Aqsa Mosque was named *Templum Solomonis*.

After a period of eighty-eight years Muslim forces, led by Salahuddin Ayyubi, captured Jerusalem in AD 1187 and the Islamic status of the "Al-Aqsa Mosque" was restored. During the intervening centuries the Holy Land was under the rule of various Muslim dynasties until the Arab Israel War of 1967 when Israel gained control of the Eastern part of Jerusalem where the "Al-Aqsa Mosque" is situated. Moshe Dayan, the defense minister of Israel, nevertheless, handed over the keys of the Mosque to the Hashemite ruling family of Jordan as a token of goodwill. Since then the control of the precinct and some of its adjacent buildings is in the hands of the Muslim Endowment Committee which looks after its affairs.

NOTES

1. In many other civilizations, children were fed the most sophisticated traditional literature from the earliest age, and they grew up knowing that they should model their lives on the greatest human examples of wisdom and compassion. The texts, woven into their flesh and blood, acted as an inexhaustible treasury from which to draw inspiration.

2. It is only a written book as a matter of convenience and as a concession to human weakness.

3. The Arabs of the time were so confident in their own memories and so accustomed to memorizing everything important that most of them never gave a thought to recording the text on paper. Only several years after the death of the Prophet did people recognize that the environment of Islam was changing so quickly that parts of the text might become lost or corrupted. Hence, the leader of the community ordered written copies prepared and sent to various places to serve as the official text.

4. Qur'an, 4:135; also repeated in another verse in a slightly different manner: "*You who believe, act steadfast before God as witnesses for fair play even though it is against yourselves, your own parents and near relatives; whether it concerns a rich or a poor man, God stands*

closer to them both. Do not follow any passion so that you may deal justly. If you swerve about or turn aside, God is still informed about whatever you do" Qur'an, 5:8.

5. And during the early Islamic history it had also served as the *qiblah* (center or place of ritual orientation) for the Islamic community.

6. Amīn Aḥsan Iṣlāḥī (d. 2000) was one of the most outstanding scholars of the early 20th century India. Founder of an influential school of Qur'anic exegesis, religious leader, prolific writer, public speaker, social activist Iṣlāḥī left an impressive legacy of books and students. His *Tafsīr Tadabbur-i Qur'ān* is regarded as one of the three best Qur'an commentaries of the 20th century.

7. Sayyid Sulaymān Nadawī (d. 1948) was the leading scholar, writer, historian, journalist, and religious leader of the school of Nadawa. His *Sīrat al-Nabī* (the life of the Prophet) and the philosophic and religious writings have influenced generations of Muslims in the 20th century.

8. The founder of the famous Islamic Party (Jama'at-i Islami), Abū al-A'lā Mawdūdī was also a religious leader, prolific writer, public speaker, and social activist whose followers are still active in the Pakistani society as well as in the Arab world.

9. Qāri Muhammad Tayyib was the rector of the biggest Muslim religious university of India, Deoband. A prolific writer, prestigious public speaker, Tayyib exerted a great influence on the masses and as well as the educated Muslim classes through his works as well as in his capacity as the head of the biggest institution in India.

10. With some spread out in the English readership through translations.

11. Spread over a period of several years, in the form of arguments and counter arguments, responses and counter responses that filled hundreds of pages of various scholarly religious journals, appearing in book form later on. See Muhammad 'Ammār Khan Nāsir, *Barāhīn*, Dār al-Kitāb, Lahore, 2011.

12. It deserves mention that the religious parties are significant stakeholders in Pakistani politics, the mainstream right wing political parties have their own religious affiliations and then become under influence from the religious parties when the issue has a religious bearing. Even the "secular" political parties cannot completely ignore the religious dimension of the problems.

13. A title which itself is a modern invention. The Prophet of Islam, when he described the *Al-Aqsa Mosque* as the third best mosque in the world, had actually referred to Solomon's Temple. *Haram* (Inviolable Precinct) is a technical legal term of the Islamic Shari'a and there is no proof with reference to the Qur'an and the prophetic Sunna the *Al-Aqsa Mosque* was ever given the status of a third *Haram* in Islamic history. The usage of *Al-Haram* for the *Al-Aqsa Mosque* has been denounced by the Islamic scholarship, both ancient and contemporary. See Ibn Taymiyya, *Majmū' al-Fatāwā*, 26/117; Ansāri, *Tahsīl al-Uns li Zāi'r al-Quds*, Cf. *Fazīlat-i Bayt al-Maqdas*, 43; Ruling No. 5387 of the Permanent Legal Committee of Saudi Arabia (*Ftāwā Lajnah al-Dā'imah*, 6/227).

14. On the question of a practical solution see appendix A.

15. Qur'an, 5:2, 8—(do not let ill will toward any folk incriminate you, just because they block your way to the hallowed mosque) (you who believe, act steadfast towards God, as witnesses for fair play, and so that you see swerve from dealing justly. Be just: that is nearest to heedfulness; and heed God alone.)

16. Qur'an, 17:1—"*Glory be to Him who took His slave by night from the inviolable Mosque unto the furthest Mosque whose precincts We have made blessed.*"

17. *For every community there is a Messenger* (10:47). *We have sent you as an announcer and a warner about the Truth. No nation exists unless some warner has passed among them.* (35:24). *And We never sent a messenger save with the language of his people, so that he might make [Our message] clear to them* (14:4). '*Unto each community We have given sacred rites (*mansakan*) which they are to perform; so let them not dispute with you about the matter, but summon them unto your Lord* (22:67). *And We never sent a messenger save with the language of his people, so that he might make [Our message] clear to them* (14:4).

18. *Perhaps your Lord may show mercy to you. If you should turn back, We will go back too.* (Qur'an, 17:8).

19. As if by Divine intervention.

20. That was rooted in the Qur'an and the normative practice of the Prophet.

21. Deuteronomy, 30:1–5.
22. Sayyid Sulaymān Nadawī, *Sīrat al-Nabī*, vol. 3, p. 254.
23. Sayyid Sulaymān Nadawī, *Maqālāt-i Sulaymān*, vol. 3, p. 68–69.
24. Qur'an, 9:17–18.
25. Qur'an, 17:1—"*Glory be to Him who took His slave by night from the inviolable Mosque unto the furthest Mosque whose precincts We have made blessed so We might show him some of Our signs! He is the Alert, the Observant!*"
26. See Ibn Kathīr, *Tafsīr al-Qur'ān al-'Aẓīm*, vol. 7, p. 34; *Al-Bidāya wa 'l-Nihāyah*, vol. 7, p. 109-111, in which has recorded the reports according to which, upon his arrival in Jerusalem, the Prophet of Islam led the prayers at the Temple of Solomon and the other prophets joined him in worship.
27. Amīn Ahsan Islāhī, *Tafsīr Tadabbur-i Qur'ān*, vol. 3, p. 470.
28. Sayyid Sulaymān Nadawī, *Sīrat al-Nabī*, vol. 3, p. 252–253.
29. Shabbīr A. 'Uthmānī, *Tafsīr 'Uthmānī*, p. 347; Mufti Muhammad Shafi', *Tafsīr Ma'ārif al-Qur'ān*, Karachi, 1984.
30. Qur'an, 17:8.
31. Qur'an, 2:142–145.
32. Sayyid Sulaymān Nadawī, *Sīrat al-Nabī*, vol. 3, p. 385.
33. Qur'an, 2:143.
34. Qur'an, 2:143.
35. Rāzī, *Tafsīr al-Kabīr*, vol. 4, p. 115; Ibn 'Arabī, *Aḥkām al-Qur'ān* vol. 1, p. 40.
36. (http://domino.un.unispal.nsf)
37. *Monthly Al-Sharīah*, December, 2003, p. 39.
38. Qur'an, 2:114; 18:21.
39. Bukhārī, hadīth No. 409.
40. Sayyid Sulaymān Nadawī, *Sīrat al-Nabī*, vol. 3, p. 385.
41. Ibn Quddāmah, *Al-Mughnī*, vol. 9, p. 284.
42. The initiative that worked in Yemen and Iraq and is gaining momentum in Iran.
43. Moses, upon seeing the Golden Calf, broke the Tablets of the Law and then, it is said, received others of a less rigorous nature.
44. Where the grandson of the Prophet was brutally murdered.
45. Thus, Christ is essentially a manifestation of Divine Presence, but is Truth by that very token; "I am the Way, the Truth and the Life." No one attains to the saving nearness of the Absolute except by a Manifestation of the Absolute, be it *a priori* Presence or Truth.
46. Which, in this respect at least, analogous to Christianity where the first element, as it were, absorbs the second, in the sense that Truth is identified with the phenomenon of Christ; Christian Truth is the notion that Christ is God. From this there arises the doctrine of the Trinity, which would be inexplicable if the starting point in Christianity were the element Truth, namely, a doctrine of the Absolute, as is the case in Islam, where God presents Himself as the one and only Real.
47. This reservation means that the theological viewpoint cannot escape a certain dualism, by the very fact of its devotional and voluntarist perspective.
48. In both cases it goes together, of course, with the consequence of this for the will.
49. The saving Truth "is the Truth"—not a "particular Truth"—because it concerns the Absolute, and not a phenomenon. It could be added here as a necessary digression that with Sunnism it is Truth that saves—since it is the Truth of the Absolute—means that all the consequences of Truth must be drawn and the Truth thus accepted totally, that is, with the will and the emotions as well as the intelligence. And to say with Shīism that it is Presence that saves—since this is the Presence of Divine Love—means that one must enter into the mold of this Presence, sacramentally and sacrificially, and let oneself be carried towards the Divine Love. One must start by loving, then come to desire and finally to know as the result of God's Love, whereas in Sunnism one must start by knowing, then come to desire and finally to love as the result of this knowledge of God.
50. One must never confuse sentiment, which is a natural fact with the excesses of sentimentality, that is to say the substitution of sentiment for intelligence and truth; the latter may determine sentiment but not inversely. Joy, for its part, is like an earthly trace of bliss; but

whereas bliss is an intrinsic felicity which is sufficient unto itself, the sentiment of joy, like all natural sentiments, has an external cause and expresses itself as an opposite. In the Scriptures the sentiments are like axes that go from the human to the Divine and thus do not exclude any level: "I will be glad and rejoice in Thee, I will sing praise to Thy Name, Thou most High," as the Psalmist said, and also "Be glad in the Lord and rejoice, ye righteous: and shout for joy, all ye that are upright in heart!" Same for the sentiment of sadness. "Blessed are they that mourn, for they shall he comforted," says the Gospel; and also "Blessed are ye that weep now, for ye shall laugh" [Matthew, 5:4; and Luke, 6:21]; and the Psalms: "They that sow in tears shall reap in joy" [Psalms, 126:5]. In order to fully understand scriptural passages of this nature one must take into consideration the gentleness and humility of sadness: it is opposed to pride and hatred and is close to love; it must also be appreciated that noble sentiments symbolize attitudes situated above and beyond the emotional plane. Seen thus, sadness, far from being opposed to the impassibility of the sages is an attitude of spiritual "gravity," an alchemical quality which brings our sub-stance into conformity with the contemplation of the Immutable; for gravity, and this is the important point, has the same virtue as tears, that is, it excludes, as they do, hardness, levity, and dissipation. If sadness is a weakness, we shall find no trace of it in the Divinity; but if it has a positive side, as it has, it is prefigured in God; now in God there is no suffering, but there is in him a sort of grave and merciful gentleness, which is not unconnected with the gift of tears in man.

51. Allama Qāzi Shwakānī's initiative in the Yemen, Ayatullah Muhsin al-Hakim's efforts of purification of memories in Iraq with its larger area of influence in Iran and India through the initiatives of Ayatullah Gulpa'igāni and, more recently of Ayatullah Dr. Sādiqī deserve special mention in this regard.

52. Shwakānī' was a great jurist, theologian, scholar of Islamic Sciences and one of the most celebrated and outstanding religious authorities of his times, equally respected by the Sunnis and Shī'ites for his erudition and insight.

53. Muhsin al-Hakim was the greatest *marja'* (the authoritative religious leader who has to be followed by the laity in accordance with Shī'ite perspective) of his times in Iraq with a very large following in Iran and other areas where Shī'ite communities existed.

54. Leading religious authority of Iran in the recent past.

55. Leading religious authority of contemporary Iran.

56. I have followed the spellings of the Catholic Bible (The New Revised Standard Version), Bangalore, India, 1993.

57. See Ibn Kathīr, *Al-Bidāya wa 'l-Nihāyah*, vol. 7, p. 56.

58. Lambert Dolphin and Michael Kollen, "On the Location of the First and Second Temples in Jerusalem," (http://dolphin.org/).

59. See Ibn Kathīr, *Al-Bidāya wa 'l-Nihāyah*, vol. 7, p. 56.

60. Psalm 84, which begins with the words: *How amiable are Thy tabernacles, O Lord of hosts,* there is a reference to Hagar and her son as well: *Blessed is the man whose strength is in Thee, in whose hearts are the ways of them who passing through the valley of Baca make it of a well* (5–6). However the vast majority of both Jews and Christians are unaware of the identity in question.

61. Exodus, 25–31; 36–38.

62. Exodus, 40:20.

63. Samuel, 5–7.

64. Chronicles I, 21: 25.

65. Chronicles II, 3: 1. According to the primary sources of Islam, in this case the prophetic traditions recorded in Bukhārī, the Prophet of Islam was asked by one of his companions as to which was the first mosque built on the face of the earth? The Prophet replied, "The Inviolable Mosque" (Arabic name of the Holy Mosque and Tabernacle at Makkah/Bakkah). "What next" he was asked, to which he replied "*Al-Aqsa Mosque* (the Furthest Mosque)" and when he was questioned about the period that had passed between the two constructions he replied "40 years" (Bukhārī, hadīth No. 3425). The apparent discrepancy in the text of the report with regard to the historical sequence has been resolved by the Hadīth scholarship by pointing towards the fact that, according to the Islamic tradition, and the actual location of the *Al-Aqsa Mosque* was specified by the prophet Jacob, to which the Prophet of Islam had alluded in his

reply, while the actual construction by Solomon was carried out after several centuries. Islamic scholarship is also aware of the fact that Biblical scholarship, especially after the "conquest" of the historical criticism, has often raised doubts about the authenticity of the Biblical narrative pertaining to the grandeur and magnificence of the temple of Solomon (see *Jewish Encyclopedia*, www.Jewishencyclopedia.com).

66. Chronicles I, B 22; 28, 11–21.

67. Details of the construction are recorded in Kings, I, 6–8 and Chronicles II, 3–5. According to the Qur'anic narrative the Jinn (unseen creatures of a fiery nature) were subjugated for Prophet Solomon to help him accomplish the task (Qur'an, 34: 12–14).

68. Chronicles I, 22:1.

69. Chronicles I, 22:19.

70. This extended prayer is saved in the Bible in Kings, I, 8: 22–53. Once again the Biblical account is corroborated by the primary sources of Islam, in this case the prophetic traditions recorded in Nassā'ī (No. 694) and Ibn Mājah (No. 1408) according to which the Prophet of Islam is reported to have said that, *"when the Prophet Solomon had finished the construction of the Al-Aqsa Mosque he prayed to the Lord that whoever visited this mosque for worship would return purified of his sins as if born of his mother's womb on the day."* He further added, *"I hope that the Lord must have listened to his prayer."*

71. Qur'an, 2: 125.

72. Chronicles I, 9:1–9.

73. See Qur'an, 17: 2–12.

74. I have followed the spellings of the Catholic Bible (The New Revised Standard Version), Bangalore, India, 1993.

75. Chronicles II, 36:11–21; Jeremiah, 52:12–14.

76. Ezra, 1

77. Haggai, 2: 3–9.

78. 1 Maccabees, 1: 20–24.

79. 1 Maccabees, 4: 36–48.

80. See Ibn Kathīr, *Al-Bidāya wa 'l-Nihāyah*, vol. 7, p. 56.

Chapter Seven

Memory in Buddhism

Michael von Brück with Maria Reis Habito

WHAT IS "MEMORY"?

In Buddhism, memory is not good or bad as such but is a necessary mental and social function to stabilize complex processes into a framework that makes sense. Memory as a stabilizing set of rules and procedures and the recognition of memory as an ever-changing construct needs to be in balance. This is to say, memory and breaking the fixation in memory are dialectical forces which work together. In Buddhism, memory and its functions are an integral part of mental formations, which are given and useful on the conventional level of life, but not valid in the perspective of an awakened consciousness: memory belongs to the realm of *samvṛti* (conventional reality), not *paramārtha* (ultimate reality). Only due to memory can humans practice the *dharma*, but *dharma* practice breaks through the constraints of memory into an open present.[1]

The following characteristics of memory inform a Buddhist view.

1. Memory has a collective and an individual dimension. Both are closely interlinked, because biographies develop in codependence, thus marking cultural processes: The individual memory reflects society and societies evolve in the interplay of individual memories and expectations. In both perspectives memory constitutes identity. This is to say that both in theories of cognition and theories of communication the interplay between the subjective and the intersubjective dimensions is essential for an act of cognition. In terms of cognition it is clear that I can identify something *as* something only by comparison with patterns stored in memory which are available as experiences on which any new recognition is based. Without being able to compare an

incoming stimulation at present with patterns of familiar structures any new experience does not make sense. So we depend on past patterns in order to identify, evaluate, and respond to present stimuli. Cognition, however, is not an individual process alone, for it depends on intersubjective exchange to pass as "valid." Thus, communication is necessary to establish a cognition which is experienced as valid. This is obvious concerning language. The individual does not invent language but inherits it. Formation and information go hand in hand, for the individual also contributes to change the language it inherits. It can change it only by intersubjective communication. Without language it cannot form concepts. By exchange the individual assures herself of the validity of a concept. Thus, the memory made available by language is formative for the stability of concepts informing the individual.

2. Memory establishes repetitive patterns of thinking, feeling, and acting. This is the precondition for stability and balance in a world of continuous change. Thus, memory is a delusion of stability, whereas in reality things change, and even memory changes individually and collectively. It is modified. Memory gives us the impression of stored events. However, both on the individual as well as the collective level memory is fluid and anything else than a "factual past" or "frozen time." On the individual level we know that memory is continuously adapted to expectations, interpretations, and evaluations in the present. When we compare an entry into our diary which we look up again after a certain time with what we remember of the circumstances concerning this given event right now, we would notice a significant difference. This is not only by forgetting details but also by regrouping and re-evaluating the details corresponding to the present life experience. However, humans strive for stability, for something to hold on. This seems to be a psychological necessity which, however, is a source for delusion: everything is change. Even the desire for no-change changes all the time.

3. Memory is enacted in rituals. These might be individual repetitive patterns in individual life and also in groups. Group identity is established in rituals that are based on specific experiences: those who share in the ritualistic memory are insiders; those who do not are outsiders. This mechanism is an unavoidable part of identification and self-identification. Colors, seals, flags, hymns, founding stories, other signs of demarcation form ritual identities due to collectively memorized signals. Thus, memory is the basis for rituals, legitimizes them and is being handed over to further generations in rituals. This constitutes identity of groups (nations, religions, parties, etc.) across time. Rituals are conservative. You cannot invent new rituals all the time.

They function because of the unchanging actions, forms and formulas, for this establishes the sought for connection over time with the ancestors, elders, and founders respectively. A present diversity of a discourse is being held together by reference to the commonly accepted rules and patterns of behavior of the past. Thus, ritually constructed stability is the precondition for allowing a variety of forms among different members of the community. Ritual memory sets the rules for the open game. This is to say, rituals tend to be conservative, their interpretation and justification, however, changes according to new environments. Otherwise, identities (individually and socially) could not be established.
4. Memory has an ambiguous quality: it stabilizes identities, but it also fixes identities and avoids change, hinders creativity and restricts people and peoples from further growth and development.

Ancient Buddhism[2]

The Buddha

During his meditation under the Bodhi tree the Buddha realizes his past lives. First, he recollects the imprints of the present life, second he becomes aware of all his past lives, third he becomes aware of all the imprints in all former lives of all sentient beings. Thus, memory is being expanded in a sense that all the imprints (events, experiences) of the whole universe are represented. This memory is a realization of the karmic connectivity. In other words, it is a realization of the interdependence of all that is.[3]

What is the importance of this insight into past lives? It is the insight into karmic interconnectivity: nothing exists independently. There is no Ego which would be independent of other Egos, but what appears as Ego is a temporal cluster of interconnected events. This happens not only in terms of space but also in terms of time. All events in past, present, and future are interwoven and influence each other. Thus, awareness of the karmic interconnectedness stimulates both: insight into the non-Ego and responsibility for one's actions. One's actions are conditioned by past imprints into consciousness. If they become aware (are brought into memory) they can be overcome by consciously evoked counteractions. Thus, hatred can be eradicated by a conscious turn of attention to thoughts of love. Responsibility is stimulated due to the realization that any present action of body, speech, and mind will have consequences for the whole system of living beings.

Monks and Memorizing

Monks memorize the rules, the enumerations of mental factors, and so on. The whole early Buddhist canon is formulated in such a way that it can be memorized easily. In fact, the canon comes into being by way of memorization: Ānanda recites what he remembers in front of the community, and these are the sayings of the Buddha in all details (each sutra starts with Ānanda's exclamation "Thus I have heard").

Memory evokes two different mental capabilities: it frames standards and norms and it shapes attention. Standards and norms are the sayings and recommendations of the Buddha, because he is remembered as the perfectly Enlightened Being, the teacher who himself is the model for one's own progress. In order to become a Buddha myself I need to be aware of what a Buddha is, that is to be aware of the standard. Memorization, however, is also a practice of focusing attention into mindfulness. Mindfulness practice is the central meditation practice of Buddhism: becoming aware of the processes of body, speech, and mind—in the past, present, and future.

Mantras as Memory

Mantras and *dhāraṇī* contain the condensed essence of the teachings; they are memorized and recited to activate the power of the teachings.[4]

Memory does not only put us in touch with semantic contexts that we have stored up in the past. It is also a link to the power contained in words (mantras). This is not so much the focus in early monastic Buddhism, but it has been and is widespread among lay people and also the monks in Mahāyāna contexts. *Dhāraṇī* are memorized and recited formulas that contain the essence of the dharma in condensed form. These are believed to have efficacy in warding off evil, unleashing healing power, as well as bringing about awakening. It is not the semantic content that matters here, but the vibrational quality of the sound. Those sounds need to be memorized and repeated in order to release their numinous power that would be beneficial both for the one who utters the sounds as well as the people whom the *mantra/dhāraṇī* is uttered for. (Certain *dhāraṇī* can be misused for black magic, of course, and therefore the practice of *dhāranī* requires proper initiation.) This concept is grounded in the belief that the whole world is basically vibration (*spanda*).[5] To enhance the vibrational patterns of the universe is a noble duty of the human being. It is to benefit all sentient beings.

Memory and Consciousness

According to the Vinaya, the monks and nuns are to search their conscience for wrongdoings and mental shortcoming in the *prātimoksha* (bestowing of the rules) ceremonies so as to make them conscious, confess them and avoid repeating them. Memory here has a cleansing effect.[6]

This is part of the practice of awareness. In order to improve one's mental system one needs to eradicate the *kleśa* (unwholesome mental patterns, the fundamental ones are: ignorance, greed, and hatred). This requires careful examination and study of one's own mental processes both at present and in the past. They need to be made conscious. The former mental imprints need to come into awareness. And this is a practice of memory.

Overcoming Memory

Yet, memory is to be overcome. It is a clinging to past mental events, and that is a clinging to karmic conditioning which needs to be overcome. Karmic conditioning creates an illusionary Self (*ātman*) that seems to be permanent. This Self wants to establish itself by discriminating Self from Other; it fails to realize the impermanence of everything. This has dramatic psychological consequences which are the basis for greed and hatred. This illusion is the result of false consequences drawn from the experience of memory.

To Buddhists, memory is an essential tool to go beyond memory, since we miss the present by clinging to the past. Surely, the present experience is conditioned by the past, but this is on only the relative level. The aim of Buddhism is to go o beyond that level. As we have seen, memory stabilizes mental frames, psychologically and socially. However, this makes us interpret the present with its new opportunities in patterns of the past. We do not see what is happening now, but misinterpret the now in terms of the memorized past. Memory is the projection of past patterns onto the wide horizon of the present. This makes the wide horizon shrink. This analysis holds true for both individual and social projections. The other is not seen as the other in her or his developing growth but in terms of my own stereotyped images. Thus I do not meet the other but just myself as mirrored in the memorized past. The result is that I miss new opportunities and creative new beginnings.

However, one of the basic methods to acquire concentration and insight is *satipatthana* (mindfulness).[7] The Pali term *sati* (in Sanskrit: *smṛti*) is derived from the root *smṛ*, and this has to do with memorizing or memory. Is there a distinction between useful and false memory? What is to be memorized in order to create *puṇya* or positive impressions in consciousness in difference to negative ones?

Indeed, memorizing which helps us to go beyond memorized patterns is wholesome (*kauśalya*), memory which keeps us imprisoned in our own perceptions of the past is unwholesome (*akauśalya*). How to make the distinction? By realizing one's own limited perception that recognizes the interpretation of all things only from the Ego-perspective, related to my own past, present, and future. And by realizing at the same time that this limited nature is not the ultimate reality—that there is something unconditioned, a nirvānic state of mind which "blows out" all of these limitations. This realization implies a wisdom-filled distance from one's own judgments and interests, a joyful and gentle letting go of the past and all memories attached to it.

Mahāyāna Buddhism[8]

Mahāyāna enlarges the narrative about the Buddha's past lives, using memory skilfully in order to enhance the present practice of spiritual progress. Thus the Jātaka tales especially describe the stages of the *bodhisattva* ("being on the path of awakening") in order to present the spiritual progress of the Buddha as a model for every human being.[9] The path is declared as open for everyone, and described in steps and stages which are to be remembered. Certain actions by the Buddha are upheld as exemplary, as models which are useful to everybody in different situations. The practitioner qualifies for spiritual practice by emulating and repeating those standard models.

This is a "skilful means" (*upāya*), one of the most central insights of Mahāyāna.[10] It recognizes that sentient beings are on different levels of insight and capability for practice, so that the *dharma* may be realized in many different ways and circumstances. This is an adaptive pedagogical programme. The narrative becomes important here, since it allows for emotional empathy and identification with the narrated story. In this way it generates motivation for practice and imitation of the narrated hero stories. The narrative, however, is based on memory. Even fictional stories make sense only in as much as they use images, symbols and action patterns which are known and memorized. Otherwise the listener would not be able to understand and integrate the stories.

In Mahāyāna, the power of the narrative and/or memorized events is therefore used in order to enhance the spiritual path. Furthermore, if we speak about steps on the path, like for example the ten *Bodhisattvabhūmi* (stages of the path to enlightenment) or the fifty-two different teachers in the Gandhavyūha part of the Avatamsaka Sūtra,[11] these steps can be appreciated and worked out only in relation to the other steps. The rhetoric of progress requires comparison. Comparison requires memory. Even though comparison again is dangerous to mental awareness, because it distracts from the focus on the here and now, it might be useful as an *upāya* to reach the stage of being in the present moment without comparing and projecting.

Memory as a Source of Confidence

In the Sukhāvatī (Land of Bliss, or Pure Land) tradition memory is decisive to implant confidence. Dharmākara, who becomes the celestial Buddha Amitābha, has sworn an oath to take care of everybody who memorizes his benevolence. That is to say: memory of the saving power of Amitābha is the basis for spiritual openness to let go of ambitions of the egocentric Self.[12]

Here the expression "the saving power of Amitābha" might be understood in a subjective or objective way or both together. First of all it is my duty to memorize Amitābha's deeds and trust his oath to save all sentient beings. Thus, memory is first of all my memory. But this memory depends on the objective memory of Amitābha himself who remembers his oath all the time. The saving memory of the Buddha himself is the basis for the meaningfulness of the believers' trusting memory in the power of this oath. Thus, only both dimensions taken together form a plausible basis for trust or faith. This is the understanding of faith and its centrality in Pure Land Buddhism, which is certainly the most common tradition in East Asian Buddhism.

Memory of the saving power of Buddha Amitābha and Bodhisattva Avalokiteśvara (Kuan-yin, or Kannon) is evoked through art—wall paintings and sculptures in temples and caves foster confidence in the "other-power" of salvific figures and rebirth in the Pure Land.

All media which reach the human heart are used to imprint this double memory just mentioned into the consciousness of the believer. Here it must be noted that in many East Asian languages (Chinese, Japanese) the term *hsin* encompasses both the meaning of heart and mind. That is to say: the power of knowing or epistemology and the power of feeling or the evaluating faculty are one single process which should not be split up. Therefore, images, chanting, all sense-impressions are made use of in order to help in transforming the ego-centred, doubting, and fear-projecting consciousness.

Pilgrimage and Memory

Pilgrimage to holy places associated with the life of the Buddha, with Bodhisattvas, holy hermits or founders of schools, foster memory of their presence while at the same time emptying the Self of its narrow concerns.

Like in other religions, pilgrimages and rituals re-present powerful spiritual presences of the past. Re-enacting these events is to make them available with their spiritual power right now. Ritual traditions encoded in pilgrimages and other rituals are wise enough to base their efficacy not just on cognitive or emotional insight but on bodily knowledge (Körperwissen). The body imprints insight into automated processes which are triggered and carried out without mental interference. Bodily knowledge is the result of experience in the past, and therefore it is itself a storage place for memory. It is the body which carries deeper and more lasting memory imprints than just the mind. This is the basis for many meditation traditions, especially for Zen. Therefore, spiritual practice in Zen is firstly and most decisively practice of the body (proper sitting and breathing).

The Issue of Time

The central concept of time takes a new shape in Mahāyāna. The present Buddha has predecessors in past worlds and successors in times to come (Maitreya). In the iconography and meditation (visualization) practice of Tantrayāna the future Buddha (Maitreya) needs to be remembered in order to assure human beings of their possible progress and help being given by the benevolent power of these Bodhisattvic realities. Memory here is a means to unite with graceful aspects of the Dharmakāya-reality of the Buddha. It is a means to become aware of one's own Buddha-Nature (*buddhatva* or *tathāgatagarbha*) by comparing it with past or future situations of Bodhisattvic reality, and this is an activity of memory. Though time is an illusion, it is a useful (skilful) means to get to an experience of an Absolute Present. And in that present memory is overcome by total Awareness.

In Mahāyāna this kind of memory (*upāya* memory as we could call it) is extended to all forms of life or to the whole cosmos. It is not just memory of the historical events. It includes the different worlds as presented in visions, dreams and all states of consciousness. All formations in the world are being represented in order to enhance the spiritual energy of the present moment. There is no limitation in space and time. Imagination can be a powerful tool to break through the limits of rational consciousness, which depends on three dimensions and is limited to our known space-time. In this visionary memory all possible worlds, all possible mental formations are used to realize the Oneness of Reality in and beyond space and time.

Yogācāra Teachings

The teaching of the Yogācāra school on the eight levels of consciousness, with the eighth consciousness (*ālayavijñāna*) as storehouse of all the impressions that create all mental and physical events has had deep influence on the Chan school. The eradication of all impressions leads to a state of freedom from rebirth.[13]

Here again we have the counterbalance to memory. All that is stored up as karmic impressions needs to be overcome. Consciousness works on patterns shaped by past formations of consciousness. Therefore, it is diluted. It needs to be cleaned from these fetters in order to allow a clear insight into its fundamental nature. Here, Buddhism goes beyond memory and this is certainly the final goal of all Buddhist spirituality.

Zen Teachings

In Chan/Zen consciousness cuts through the fetters of the past and memory is burnt up in an awareness of nothing else than total presence. This total presence in which no traces of ego-consciousness are left frees one to work for the liberation of all beings. However, in rituals of Koan practice and in incantations the chain of masters is invoked so as to set standards and to become assured of the quality of the present practice. Here again, memory is a means of assurance.[14]

Even Chan cannot do without memory. Its radical rhetoric ("burning the scriptures," "when you meet the Buddha, kill him") evokes a warning that all mental images are just images. When we meet the Buddha, we do not meet the Buddha, but our (memorized) image of the Buddha. The Buddha is beyond conceptualizations, it is a totally liberated mind. However, even Chan needs to set standards and does so by constructing lineages of authenticity which are celebrated with much self-congratulation and ritualistic glamour. Chan time and again tries to find the balance between beyondness over and against all cultural mental constructs and the need to use precisely those constructs to lead people on the right path. It is a matter of proper balance and the right means at the right time (upāya), depending on the situation of the person to be instructed or led on the path.

Consequences

There are a number of consequences from understanding memory through the lens of Buddhism.

1. Memory can be a useful spiritual means to become aware of one's own condition. This awareness is necessary to become free from the fetters of conditioning.
2. Memory has different aspects. Some are spiritually helpful (assuring), some are misleading (binding). Wise discrimination is necessary.
3. A strong distinction between forgetting and forgiving is to be made. Forgetting is a natural process and not a spiritual practice. However, "to forget" also means deliberately setting aside certain memories that lead to ill-will and animosity and focusing on the positive instead. Forgiving is a conscious act of placing mental impressions into a new context. It is a sign of spiritual advancement, because in forgiving a distinction is made between the actor (the doer) and the act (the deed). Forgiving is accepting the actor beyond his or her deed. It is to see the potential, the Buddha-nature in a being, even if this being in his or her deeds has not yet become aware of his or her true nature.

Hope

There is no equivalence in Buddhism for what is understood as a cardinal virtue in the Christian tradition. The traditional Sanskrit term for hope (āsha) is not important in Buddhism. The closest term perhaps would be śraddhā—trust or faith.

This is so because Buddhism puts all emphasis on the present, which has to be worked out by the individual. The individual decision to practice the *dharma* is not so much inspired by hope but by insight into the mechanism of suffering. Everybody can attain this insight, which grounds the motivation for spiritual practice on an attitude of self-responsibility.

Trust of faith in the compassionate vow of the Buddha Amitābha creates hope for the rebirth in the Pure Land; trust in the vows of the Bodhisattvas generates hope for the realization of certain promised results—both worldly and spiritual.

In the Pure Land tradition, hope is a category because the fulfilment of the spiritual goal is projected into a future life. Whereas Chan emphasizes the present (and future rebirths do not matter at all), Pure Land has an eschatological dimension—and in the case of the White Lotus Sects in China and the Kālacakra tradition in Tibet even a millennial dimension (the belief that a future Buddha will come to earth and set things straight). In the Pure Land tradition, Hope is grounded in faith (trust) into the power of the oath of Amitābha. In the Japanese Pure Land tradition, there has been a long debate on *jiriki* (self-power = Chan/Zen) versus *tariki* (other power = Pure Land) in terms of the power to attain Nirvāna. If the emphasis is on other-power, the assessment of one's own capabilities is weaker (as in Hōnen and especially Shinran, the founders of Japanese Pure Land). However, even in Ch'an, faith into the truthfulness of the teachings of the Buddha, the Patriarchs and the words of one's teacher is a prerequisite for practice. The tremendous hardship one needs to undergo in Ch'an is an investment into the (individual) future. The student sacrifices time and energy to master the practice, trusting the examples of those who have reached attainment, hoping that this trust will be justified. Chan/Zen practice requires surrender to the practice (and, sometimes, to the master). Surrender is possible only on the basis of trust.

The teaching of the three ages of the dharma in which people's capacity for enlightenment degenerates over time is the opposite of a hopeful reading of history. History is not progress, but degeneration.[15]

But not "all hope is lost," since the vows of Amitābha, and the coming of the future Buddha Maitreya (the coming Buddha for the next age) promise salvation.

Dynamics of memory at work—How it is addressed, how it is healed: Two case studies

One Classical Example

Buddhism's approach to memory can be illustrated by the story of Buddha's advice to Kisa Gautamī to help her overcome the death of her child. Kisa Gautamī grieves over the untimely death of her child and approaches the Buddha for help. He sends her away telling her that she should bring him a mustard seed from a house where no death had struck in the near past. She searches all the houses in the vicinity but cannot find one in which no death has occurred. So she returns to the Buddha who has helped her to realize that death is a human predicament which spares no one.[16]

All sentient beings are subject to suffering, but humans have the capability for the liberating insight of not identifying with the body. In this context, memory and comparison have the comforting capability to de-individualize one's own sadness, grief and shortcomings and see them as a general condition shared by all. Memory turns the focus on the Ego around, making insight into the general condition of life and human nature possible. Thus, memory turns episodic knowledge into structural knowledge.

One Contemporary Example: The Conflict between Tibet and China

In a conflict of interests, the memory of the conflicting parties who have a stake in interests and claims is different. In such a case, reference to memory may make conflicts visible or even aggravate conflicting claims. Memory depends not only on different perspectives and interpretations of (historical) data but also on selectivity concerning references to time and place.

The conflict between the Chinese government and the Tibetans (inside Tibet as well as in exile) is marked by differing historical memories and contemporary evaluations of the socio-political situation within Tibet today. In this conflict, memory is applied to the different times in the history of relations between China and Tibet. Whereas in the eighth century AD Tibet was strong and China weak, so that a certain dependency of China on the former can be remembered, the tables were turned after the eighteenth century, when China started to exert a strong influence over political affairs in Tibet. The situation changed again at the end of the nineteenth century, when the European powers England and Russia played key roles and complicated the relations between the two Asian powers through their interference and competing interests. We must be careful not to refer to "Tibet" and "China" in static or monolithic terms, because at different times in history, complicated political situations within those culturally defined territories influenced the overall picture within the whole huge territory concerned. Moreover, modern ideas of a national state and political sovereignty differ considerably from situations within the past that need to be described in their own terms. It is simply wrong to impose modern ideas and claims onto history and make political claims derived from selective reading of memories that are shaped into a one-sided narrative. Contemporary claims and standpoints related to this conflict may be sustainable or not, depending on the particular period(s) of history in mind.

In this respect we need to note that memory is always selective and cannot comprise the whole of history. Therefore, memory is used as an ideological tool to advance interests and certain arguments that sustain one's claims. However, a critical assessment of memory might show that the argument for claims based on historical memories is always relative and under question.

Therefore, Buddhism suggests that conflict resolution should be based on memory that is self-critical, taking both arguments deriving from the description of the complexity of historical processes as well as normative arguments of a balance of interests into consideration. A balance of interests is based on the insight that all parties involved are human beings who have the same human right to live in dignity, both individually and socially. A political solution, therefore, needs to be based on the acknowledgment of the rights and claims of the other side.

This requires a humanistic attitude towards the other who, as a human being, has the same basic human rights, even if he or she has differing claims. In Buddhism, such humanism is to be based on spiritual insight. In this way spiritual practice becomes a direct nurturing tool for political expediency. To give one example:

The fourteenth Dalai Lama emphasises not to hate the oppressors but to cultivate empathy and love for them. There are two reasons for this, which are both related to the power of memory. First, what the Dalai Lama expresses here is the old Buddhist insight that each enemy teaches me a lesson in forbearance, patience, and kindness. It is easy to be kind to those who do good to me. This is no spiritual achievement but a reaction based on interests of the Ego. However, to embrace the one who hurts me requires a deeper insight, and this is what the "enemy" teaches. So the spiritual progress is advanced by the enemy, and therefore I should be grateful to him. This is what Lang-ri-tang-ba (1054–1123) expresses in his Eight Verses of Training the Mind:

5: When others out of jealousy treat me badly

With abuse, slander, and so on,

I will learn to take all loss

And offer the victory to them.

6: When one whom I have benefitted with great hope

Unreasonably hurts me very badly,

I will learn to view that person

As an excellent spiritual guide.[17]

The Dalai Lama mentally goes through these stages every day in his meditation practice.

A second reason is a practical one: only a non-violent struggle will have lasting good results, since violence generates further violence. However, non-violence needs to be grounded in the right mental attitude towards the oppressor—otherwise it will not work. Therefore, the spiritual practice of remembering that, in the cycle of rebirths, all beings have been mothers and fathers to each other is crucial in cultivating a spirit of gratitude and compassion toward all those beings, even if they are my oppressors in this current life due to their ignorance.

NOTES

1. This introduction on Memory, Cognition, and Emotion is based on G. Rager, M. v.Brück (2012), *Grundzüge einer modernen Anthropologie*, Göttingen: Vandenhoeck & Ruprecht : 177ff
2. For this part on early Buddhism, see Michael von Brück (2007), Einführung in den Buddhismus, Frankfurt/Leipzig: Suhrkamp Verlag der Weltreligionen:103ff.
3. Lopez, Donald Jr., "Memories of the Buddha," in Janet Gyatso, ed. (1992). *In the Mirror of Memory, Reflections on Mindfulness and Remembrance in Indian and Tibetan Buddhism*, Suny Series in Buddhist Studies, Albany, State University of NY Press, Albany:21–47.
4. Braarvig, Jens (1985). "Dhāraṇī and Pratibhāna: Memory and Eloquence of the Bodhisattvas," Journal of the International Association of Buddhist Studies 8 (1), 17–30.
5. Dyczkowski, M. S. G. (1989), "The Doctrine of Vibration," Delhi: Motilal Banarsidass.
6. On Prātimokṣa see Prebish, Charles S. (1996). *Buddhist Monastic Discipline: The Sanskrit Prātimokṣa Sūtras of the Mahāsāmghikas and Mūlasarvāstivādins*. Delhi: Motilal Banarsidass.
7. Bhikkhu Anālayo (2006), *Satipatthāna: The Direct Path to Realization*. Birmingham: Windhorse Publications.
8. On Mahāyāna, see Michael von Brück (2007): 223.
9. Shaw, Sandra (2006). *The Jatakas—Birth Stories of the Bodhisatta*, Penguin Classics, Penguin Books India, New Delhi.
10. Pye, Michael (1978). *Skilful Means—A Concept in Mahayana Buddhism*. London: Gerald Duckworth & Co. Ltd.
11. Cleary, Thomas (1993). *The Flower Ornament Scripture: A Translation of the Avatamsaka Sutra*. Boston: Shambhala.
12. For the textual basis of the Pure Land tradition see Hisao Inagaki, Harold Stewart (transl 2003.): *The Three Pure Land Sutras*, Berkeley: Numata Center for Buddhist Translation and Research.
13. For Alāyavijñāna see Suzuki Daisetz Teitaro (1930), *Studies in the Lankavatara Sutra. One of the most important texts of Mahayana Buddhism (. . .) including the teaching of Zen*. London; and Kochumuttom, Thomas Augustine , *A Buddhist Dictionary of Experience. A New Translation and Interpretation of the works of Vasubandhu the Yogācārin*, Delhi.
14. On Chan see Michael von Brück (2007): 335–366.
15. Nattier, Jan (1999), *Once Upon a Future Time. Studies in Buddhist Prophecy of Decline*, Berkley: Asian Humanities Press.
16. See translation by Thanissaro Bhikku (1998), *Gotami Sutta: Sister Gotami*, http://www.accesstoinsight.org/tipitaka/sn/sn05/sn05.003.than.html.
17. The Fourteenth Dalai Lama. His Holiness Tenzin Gyatso (1984), *Kindness, Clarity and Insight*. Transl. and ed. by Jeffrey Hopkins, Ithaca:, NY: Snow Lion, p. 108.

Afterword

Toward a Collective Case Study — Hope for Jerusalem

Alon Goshen-Gottstein

A Jerusalem project informed one of the two thematic foci of this collection of essays—hope. As noted above, what started out as an acronym ended up in an invitation to reflect on the spiritual meaning of hope. Little did I realize when we set out on this project that Jerusalem and the Holy Land would figure so prominently in these theoretical exercises. As it turns out, all three authors speaking from within the Abrahamic tradition refer to the Holy Land and more particularly to Jerusalem in some way. Talk of memory and its impact on interreligious relations somehow leads to reference to the Crusades, to contemporary conflicting loves for the Holy Land and to reflection on Jerusalem and conflicting memories of its sanctity. While only half our authors have referenced the Holy Land or Jerusalem, I find it intriguing to consider how the testimony of our various traditions can address the situation of Jerusalem and the Holy Land. Jerusalem offers us the possibility of thinking along two lines of hope, suggested in our project. The most obvious sense of hope is eschatological hope. All three Abrahamic traditions associate their eschatological vision with Jerusalem. In that sense, Jerusalem channels the hope of the faithful of multiple traditions. However, it is a hope that rarely makes room for the other in the imagined future. Typically, the other is either removed from the vision of the future or somehow becomes identified to oneself, through a process of conversion, or recognition of the higher truth that will be known in the future. The hope one has for the other is therefore hope for the diminishing of otherness, perhaps even its complete removal.

I would therefore like to engage in the exercise of reflecting on what a *present* based approach to healing memory could bring to the reality of Jerusalem and the Holy Land. I would like to consider the different lessons that our authors have taught us as multiple perspectives, multiple tools, for addressing one particular situation that brings together multiple memories of injury and victimhood, suffering and painful memory. The multiplicity of memories refers both to the various partners whose memory has become intertwined with that of the city and to the multiple situations throughout the ages that have contributed to present day perceptions of Jerusalem as a conflicted spiritual center, where religions can at best exist alongside one another, but without true recognition, peace, or reconciliation. What are the accumulated lessons of our project that might allow us to offer a vision of peace and reconciliation for Jerusalem?

Perhaps the best place to begin is in the tension between the ultimate higher memories of a tradition and the historical memories of conflict between different religious groups. As noted, memory has two main expressions. The first is to recall the higher goals, ideals, and visions of the tradition. The second concerns concrete historical memories, which in situations of inter-group relations all too often focus on past injury, leading to present violence. In the initial project summary, I suggested that bringing these two dimensions of memory into rapport with one another is itself a basic strategy for dealing with the pain and poison of historical memory. Jerusalem affords us a possibility for exploring this strategy. What is Jerusalem? Surely it is more than a political center of successive kingdoms. There would be no point in fighting over it if all it did was to serve as a seat of temporal power. Each of the traditions that venerates Jerusalem looks at it as something other than the physical, temporal, and historical city. The city somehow translates, maybe even incarnates, higher ideals. It is these ideals, or that reality that informs the memory of believers. Von Brüeck has shown us that memory is not only historical. Memory is a recollection of ideals and spiritual realities, just as it is the calling to mind of historical facts of days gone by. If so, what is it that one remembers when one remembers Jerusalem? This is the beginning of a very important conversation, and one that I have never actually heard, certainly not in the fullness and depth that it deserves. We have spoken of the need for sharing memory. We can, of course, share the pain of successive conquests and the suffering they entailed for the population of Jerusalem, whatever it was during a given conquest. But that is not our deepest memory. Our deepest memory of Jerusalem relates to what it is we think of, what we aspire to and what vision we recall when we think of what Jerusalem truly means.

The resources here are enormous. To begin, there is probably no other city in the world, even holy city, that has as a fundamental part of its stock of associations and ideas, the view that the city has a celestial or heavenly counterpart, even if these cities are in some way considered gateways to heaven. We have never heard of a heavenly Rome or a celestial Benares, or even Amritsar. Significantly, this memory is shared, to greater or lesser extent, by all three Abrahamic faiths. The relative import of the idea of a heavenly Jerusalem in the overall economy of each of our traditions is itself a reflection of power relations and inter-group relations at crucial points in religious thought and history. But looking beyond these differences, one wonders what would it mean to share memories of the heavenly Jerusalem, as these are recorded in our respective traditions? How would integrating the idea of a heavenly Jerusalem in our view of the Holy City impact our day to day lives? How can it serve as a resource for peace, reconciliation, and harmony? And how can the vision of the heavenly Jerusalem of *another* religious tradition inspire us to recall something fundamental about a city whose memory is shared by three traditions?

One cannot dispute memories of a celestial world. Sharing visions of heaven is a relatively safe activity for interreligious exchange. But sharing memory may also be relevant to sharing what the city means to us and having space for the other to listen. On the whole, except for the broadest generalities, stated with almost total lack of feeling and empathy, almost no one in this city really appreciates what the city means, in terms of memory and its religious significance, for the believer of another faith. Our understanding has been reduced to repeating facts, but these facts are often not divorced from the recollection of how the memory of the other is also the source of my own injury. Sendor has made us aware of processes of sharing memory between Israeli Jews and Germans and the challenges of advancing on a meaningful Israeli-Palestinian exchange, along similar lines. What if the exchange focused not on hurt and victimization but on the meaning of what we consider most sacred in something we both hold dear? When Muslims deny Jewish presence on the Temple Mount, are they able to appreciate the depth of attachment to this site? And when Jews argue that Jerusalem is "only" the third holiest place for Muslims, are they able to integrate what the sanctity of Jerusalem has meant for Muslim pilgrims for centuries? If dialogue of memories is founded on trust, as Rambachan suggests, this might be a good way of building such trust.

Jerusalem's memory is inextricably linked with pain. Much of this pain does not relate to the groups that now inhabit the sacred city. For Jews, it is the pain of the destruction of the Temple by two kingdoms that have long passed away. If we speak of lament as an expression of memory, there are times when such lament is the order of the day, giving expression to deep seated memorialized pain. Christian memory is also laden with the pain of successive generations. It is a very selective memory that only focuses on the Holy Land and Jerusalem as sites of the incarnated Lord or as expressions of Christian former glory. And yet, I have never heard a Christian tourist guide addressing the notion of pain. If Keshgegian is correct and the Crucifixion is a trauma, not simply a glorified saving moment, what kind of experience should visiting Golgotha be? Simply looking at Jerusalem in view of the dynamics exposed by our conversations makes us realize how partial our approach to the depths of the city is, how limited the range of responses that are called forth from us really is.

One reason for this might be the complications arising from present power relations and the view of Israel as conqueror. This might be the case, though I doubt how far this explanation can go in accounting for the narrow range of sounds we are able to hear from Jerusalem. But let us assume this to be the case. We can acknowledge power dynamics in the ways Keshgegian urges us to do, even if our view is not as clear cut as the present day Christian removed from the ethos of empire and colonialism. Still, power issues are on the table, and certainly not beyond the realm of sharing and dialogue.

But sharing of memory involves more than willingness to discuss how Israeli sovereignty or conquest complicate the religious lives of other groups. Suheyl Umar has shown us how far-reaching the contestation of memory and its meaning is in the Holy Land itself. Perhaps we need to hear voices from other geographical centers that will allow us not only to share memory but to seek truthful memories. I do not believe that the search for truthful memories is the task of one religious community only. It may be glaring in the case of the Temple Mount/Haram al Sharif, as Umar shows us. But the dynamic is universally valid. If memory is a political act, as Keshgegian reminds us, and if memory serves social functions, as Halbwachs quoted in Sendor tells us, then we must be willing to consider memory truthfully on multiple fronts. Of course, this requires even greater trust than making room for the meanings that different religious communities attach to the Holy City and the Holy Land. But one can imagine that enough trust can be built to facilitate such an exchange.

Honest exchange and trust are developed in and fed by the present. Acceptance of the other is an *a priori* stance that is taken in relation to the other, validating her full humanity, including her full pain. These draw from the present, and here we return to a strategy that Sendor highlights for us—the importance of the fullness of the present. I submit that to a large degree we are locked into battles over memory because we do not know how to be in the present. Consequently, too much hinges on our presentation or reconstruction of memory. But the present has a commanding presence all of its own. No one is going away. No religion is going away. We are all here to stay, otherwise some of us would have gone away a long time ago. If anything, we have all come back in some form or another, in order to encounter one another and meet the challenge of how our multiple perspectives can give rise to some greater whole. Jerusalem is a symbol of this challenge, of this potential.

How then do we begin to live in the present and make the present a commanding presence of equal importance to our collective memories? One important beginning is the humanization of the other. Dialogue, as Rambachan has told us, is about humanizing the other. Transcending our harmful memories is transcending that in us which leads us to dehumanize the other. All our traditions have profound teachings that allow us to see the other in his full humanity, not in the shadow or impression of our own pained memory. As Sendor demonstrates, we have multiple voices in our tradition and so the fullness of memory requires recall of a broader range of teachings than we might be applying. As von Brück argues with reference to the Chinese/Tibetan conflict—ultimately it matters little whose memory is correct; we must find the way to recognize the full validity of the needs of all parties, grounded in their humanity.

There are other dimensions to the present that can be helpful. Our spiritual traditions allow us to recall a higher present, a higher presence. This is already implied in the appeal to remember the higher teachings of our tradition concerning Jerusalem. But some traditions make presence and especially presence to pain a focus of their teaching. Von Brück shares with us how memory is in fact awareness and mindfulness and how various Buddhist practices are geared at cultivating mindfulness and presence. There is by now accumulated experience of applying Buddhist techniques of mindfulness to situations of conflict, including to the Israeli-Palestinian conflict. Several groups have experimented with these techniques, which are in and of themselves religiously neutral, even if they are indebted to their Buddhist origins and theory. If we seek to make the present an important balance to the memory of the past, training in presence and awareness may provide a helpful tool.

But there are still other tools that our project offers. The Hindu and Sikh perspectives remind us of God and the union of all in God. Our highest memory is the memory of God and our task is to attain a wisdom that realizes the unity of all in God. All our traditions teach us unity, and yet unity is rarely practiced in the social realm, because of the conflicts between different groups and the burden of the memories they carry. The view of these wisdom traditions is helpful not only as an independent resource but also as a reminder, evoking in us the memory of a fundamental teaching we all have, that remains largely inoperative. In various ways, all our traditions affirm our ultimate unity, grounding it in God. Imagine how applying this insight to Jerusalem could look. Jerusalem already unites so many people in faith around one center. And these people all recognize the one God and affirm in some way the ultimate unity of humanity. What then prevents the wisdom perspective with its unitive vision from taking hold in this city?

The answer, I believe, is conflicting identities. As von Brück tells us, memory is necessary for identity construction. Our identities, informed and enforced by our memories, are so powerful, that they overpower the unitive drive, the regard of wisdom, the affirmation of unity that has its roots in our tradition, yet rarely gets a fair hearing. The tension between particular identity and universal vision is a central one. Living between the earthly and the heavenly Jerusalem might be an invitation, might require us to think through time and again what our identity means and how our particularity serves a greater goal. Abrahamic faiths are not in a position to simply transcend their identities. But there may nevertheless be a lesson learned from Buddhist communities of how to wear your identity with the kind of grace that does not lead to affirming one's identity at the expense of the other. Or differently put, we must learn how to reconcile different dimensions of identity. One may think of particular and universal dimensions of identity or one might also consider the tensions of identity, as noted above contrasting Hindu and Jewish views of identity. Is our deepest identity our social collective? If so, memory is indeed only about politics and social reality. Or is memory about recalling our higher spiritual nature, in which case it is a recollection of higher metaphysical reality. The resources for a universal higher awareness that does not do away with particular identity have not yet been fully mined, certainly in the case of Jerusalem. Jerusalem provides us with an invitation to discover these resources.

Sikh tradition too struggles with the tension between particular and universal. It resolves this through the notion of service. One's particularity is there in the service of the other. This is a striking notion through which to think of Jerusalem. Implicitly, we think of Jerusalem as a center of prayer, worship, and spiritual activity, evoking memories of millennia of spiritual life. But Jerusalem is also communities in need, deep social divides, profound estrangement, and endless opportunities for service. All religious communities serve, but they only, or primarily, serve their own. Combating negative memory, says von Brück, is by conscious introduction of an alternative force. Imagine service as a transformative force across religious diversity. Of course, interreligious collaboration is a global phenomenon and need not be limited to Jerusalem. But what would it do to Jerusalem if this insight could be practiced between members of its different religious communities? And how deeply and readily could we construct trust through service? And how speedily would memory, including memory of recent power imbalances, be redefined through acts of service, carried out in common? The faithful of this city, locked in their perspectives, fed by competing memories, have much to learn from a religious tradition that configures itself differently, yet affirms the same basic faith tenets. Affirmation of unity of God and His care for all translate into an ethos of service that can redefine social relations and memory.

Let me mention one more concept that appeared in several of our papers—ritual. Memory is closely related to ritual. Ritual keeps memory alive. Rituals construct identity. Rituals are also means of forgiveness and some of our authors have suggested we need to find new rituals that are inclusive of the other, rituals of reconcilliation. Jerusalem is certainly a city of ritual. If you don't just live there (and some do), then you engage in some kind of ritual or another. Let us consider how our rituals relate to our memories in this common city, shared and divided in reality and perception. Our rituals are practiced in isolation. Each group practices its rituals in the privacy of its institutional and religious spaces. One rarely enters the space of the other, even though most spaces are open to the presence of the other. With the exception of the Western Wall, there is no common space that is available for prayer to members of all faith. Rituals accentuate our identity and also our separateness, because they never allow the other into them. What would our rituals look like if they were witnessed by an other, as a matter of conscious intention? What degree of recognition would be afforded if we could intentionally practice our rituals alongside one another? In one way Jerusalem is already a haven for religious tolerance. All groups pray alongside one another in their respective spaces. But they do so unintentionally, and despite one another. What if ritual life could be an occasion for intentional coming together, while respecting the identity boundaries and ritual constraints of each group. I submit that opening up in ritual to the presence of the other (not shared ritual, but ritual that is welcoming and mindful of the other) is an important way of affirming positive memory and a gateway to the healing of negative memories associated with exclusion. It is also an important way of affirming common hope, whether such hope reminds us of our eschatological expectation or of our recognition of the power of the present. Ultimately, it is an affirmation of the depth of our common humanity, facing a common spiritual reality.

All this leads me back to what was the original impetus for our topic of memory and hope—the creation of a spiritual center in Jerusalem that would achieve precisely these goals. Considering what multiple religious voices have to say to the situation of Jerusalem provides us with a much richer spiritual tapestry than we had before we entered this exercise. Considering what such a spiritual center could bring to the life of Jerusalem, one realizes just how central sharing is in all its dimensions. Sharing of wisdom, complemented by sharing of friendship, builds trust to share memories, that find their validation as we share our rituals that affirm our deeper unity and our common presence before God in the holy center shared by all. Sharing wisdom also offers us some specific strategies that other religions practice, and that they might want to practice in Jerusalem with us, even as they encourage us to apply their wisdom to our local reality.

Jerusalem is, of course, only a test case. All that we have learned can be applied by us all whenever and wherever. Thinking of Jerusalem, I realize how much we have gained through opening up a conversation on memory and hope. We may have not reached a narrow agreement on something, but our shared mission of working through memory in the direction of hope has yielded a rich harvest that can be applied to many situations. Applying it is a matter of will. It is now up to us to consider what lessons we wish to apply either in our reading of our own tradition or in how we live our memories in relation to another tradition. Perhaps Jerusalem does have some special advantage though. Its pull is so constant and so present, that it might have the ability to drive our will to action in particular ways. If we have enough hope that some change can transpire, the accumulated force of generations of faithful of different religions sharing one sacred center might generate sufficient will to make Jerusalem not only a theoretical test case for an academic theological exercise. Jerusalem could become a model for how memory of the past can be reshaped in the present, with a will that draws from past, present, and future, from the resources of multiple traditions and above all from the unifying presence of the God that so many faithful have encountered in this Holy City.

Selected Bibliography

INTERRELIGIOUS—MULTI-RELIGIOUS

Brison, Susan. 2003. *Aftermath: Violence and the Remaking of a Self*, Princeton University Press.
Chowgule, Ashok V. 1999. *Christianity in India: The Hindutva Perspective*, Mumbai: Hindu Vivek Kendra.
Edkins, Jenny. 2003. *Trauma and the Memory of Politics*, Cambridge University Press.
Giliomee, H., and J. Gagiano, eds. 1990. *The Elusive Search for Peace: South Africa, Israel, Northern Ireland*, Cape Town: Oxford University Press.
Halbwachs, M. 1992. *On Collective Memory*, trans. L. A. Coser, Chicago: University of Chicago.
Jankelevitch, V. 2005. *Forgiveness*, trans. and intr. A. Kelley, Chicago: University of Chicago.
Linemann-Perrin, Christine, and Wolfgang Linemann, eds. 2012. *Crossing Religious Borders: Studies on Conversion and Religious Belonging*, Weisbaden: Harrossowitz Verlag.
Patel, E. 2010. *Acts of Faith*, Boston: Beacon.
Rager, G., and M. von Brück. 2012. *Grundzüge einer modernen Anthropologie*, Göttingen: Vandenhoeck & Ruprecht.
Ricouer, P. 2004. *Memory, History, Forgetting*, trans. K. Blamey and D. Pellauer, Chicago: Chicago University Press.
Yates, D. A., and J. E. Irby, ed. 1964. *Labyrinths*, New York: New Directions.

BUDDHISM

Anālayo, Bhikkhu. 2006. *Satipatthāna: The Direct Path to Realization*. Birmingham: Windhouse Publications.
Michael von Brück. 2007. *Einführung in den Buddhismus*, Frankfurt/Leipzig: Suhrkamp Verlag der Weltreligionen.
Cleary, Thomas. 1993. *The Flower Ornament Scripture: A Translation of the Avatamsaka Sutra*. Boston: Shambhala.
Gyatso, Janet, ed. 1992. *In the Mirror of Memory: Reflections on Mindfulness and Remembrance in Indian and Tibetan Buddhism, Suny Series in Buddhist Studies*, Albany: SUNY Press.
Hopkins, Jeffrey, ed. and trans. "The Fourteenth Dalai Lama. His Holiness Tenzin Gyatso," (1984) *Kindness, Clarity and Insight*. Ithaca: Shambhala.

Inagaki Hisao, Harold Stewart (transl 2003.) *The Three Pure Land Sutras*, Berkeley: Numata Center for Asian Research.
Kochumuttom, Thomas Augustine. *A Buddhist Dictionary of Experience: A New Translation and Interpretation of the works of Vasubandhu the Yogācārin*, Delhi: Motilal Banarsidass.
Nattier, Jan. 1999. *Once Upon a Future Time. Studies in Buddhist Prophecy of Decline*, Berkley: Asian Humanities Press.
Prebish, Charles S. 1996. *Buddhist Monastic Discipline: The Sanskrit Prātimokṣa Sūtras of the Mahāsāmghikas and Mūlasarvāstivādins*. Delhi: Motilal Banarsidass.
Pye, Michael. 1978. *Skilful Means—A Concept in Mahayana Buddhism*. London: Gerald Duckworth.
Shaw, Sandra. 2006. *The Jatakas—Birth Stories of the Bodhisatta*, New Delhi: Penguin.
Suzuki, Daisetz Teitaro. 1930. *Studies in the Lankavatara Sutra.* London: George Routledge.

CHRISTIANITY

Baptist Metz, Johann. 1980. *Faith in History and Society: Toward a Practical Fundamental Theology*. Trans. David Smith, New York: Seabury Press.
Downey, John K., ed. 1999. *Love's Strategy: The Political Theology of Johann Baptist Metz*, Harrisburg: Trinity.
Keshgegian, Flora A. 2006. *Time for Hope: Practices for Living in Today's World*, New York: Church Publishing.
Moltmann, Jürgen. 1996. *The Coming of God: Christian Eshatology*, trans. Margaret Kohl, Minneapolis: Fortress Press.
Phillips, Jennifer, ed. 2010. *Ambassadors for God: Envisioning Reconciliation Rites for the 21st Century. Liturgical Studies Five*. New York: Church Publishing.

HINDUISM

Dyczkowski, M. S. G. 1989. *The Doctrine of Vibration*, Delhi: Motilal Banarsidass.
Vivekananda, Swami. 1964–1971. *The Complete Works of Swami Vivekananda*, 8 vols., Calcutta: Advaita Ashrama.

ISLAM

'Ammār Khan Nāsir, Muhammad. 2011. *Barāhīn, Dār al-Kitāb*, (Arabic) Lahore.
Chittick, William C. 2003. *The Vision of Islam*, Lahore: Suhail Academy.
Hossein Nasr, Seyyed, and Huston Smith. 2007. *Islam—Religion, History and Civilization Islam—A Concise Introduction* (Two Books in one Volume), Lahore.
Hossein Nasr, Seyyed. 2003. *Ideals and Realities of Islam*, Lahore.
Mufti Muhammad, Shafi'. 1984. *Tafsīr Ma'ārif al-Qur'ān*, (Arabic) Karachi.
Schuon, Frithjof. 2008. *Understanding Islam,* Lahore: Bloomington.
Smith, Huston. 2011. *The World Religions—Our Great Wisdom Traditions,* Lahore: Sohail Academy.

JUDAISM

Avraham Yitzhak Ha-Kohen Kook, R. 1971. *Mussar Avikha u-Middot Ha-Re'iyah*, (Hebrew), Jerusalem: Mossad Harav Kook.
Bar-Siman-Tov, Y., ed. 2004. *From Conflict Resolution to Reconciliation*, Oxford: University Press.

Rogan, Eugene L., and Avi Shlaim, eds. 2001. *The War for Palestine: Rewriting the History of 1948*, Cambridge: Cambridge University Press.
Shavit, Ari. 2013. *My Promised Land,* New York: Spiegel and Grau.
Wolffsohn, M. 1993. *Eternal Guilt?* New York: Columbia University.

SIKHISM

Mann, G. 2004. *Sikhism*, New York: Upper Saddle River.
Mandair, A., and C. Shackle. 2005. *Teachings of the Sikh Gurus*, New York: Springer.
Tatla, Darshan. 1999. *The Sikh Diaspora: The Search for Statehood*, London: UCL Press.

JOURNAL ARTICLES

Monthly Al-Sharī'ah. December, 2003.
Al-Sharī'ah Monthly. December, 2003.
Braarvig, Jens. 1985. "Dhāraṇī and Pratibhāna: Memory and Eloquence of the Bodhisattvas," *Journal of the International Association of Buddhist Studies* 8 (1).
Cobbey, Nan. (1998). "In worship, the Anglican spirit shows forth," *Episcopal Life*.
Sherrod, Katie. "Transfiguration Liturgy offers moment of blessing to Lambeth Conference," Lambeth Conference 1998 Archives.
Thangaraj, Thomas. "The Missiological Hermeneutics of a Convert," *Exchange*, vol. 32, no. 1.
Treffert, Darold. (2010). "Hyperthymestic Syndrome: Extraordinary Memory for Daily Life Events. Do we all possess a continuous tape of our lives?" Wisconsin Medical Society.
Ovadiah Yosef, R., Yabia Omer, (Hebrew) vol. 8, H.M. 10.

WEBSITES

http://www.lambethconference.org
http://www.swamij.com
http://domino.un.unispal.nsf
http://www.accesstoinsight.org

Index

Abraham (biblical forefather), 110, 116–117, 149
Al-Aqsa Mosque, 117, 118, 119, 124–129
Amalek, 9, 29, 35, 36–37
Amitabha, 26, 140
authority, 2, 7, 12, 31, 50, 68, 90

Bhagavadgita, 76, 77
Bhalla, Bhai Gurdas, 97–98
Brison, Susan, 58
Buddha, 137–138, 144
Buddhism: Mahayana, 27, 140–142; Yogacara, 142; Zen, 26, 142

China, 27, 145
cognition, 27, 135–136
community, 29, 44, 51, 76, 81, 89, 92, 93, 98, 103, 109
conversion, missionary activity, 17, 55, 56, 82–84
crusades, 56, 129
crucifixion, 11, 13, 52, 59, 151

Dalai Lama, 146
dalits, 82–83, 84
dhimmi, 44
dialogue/interfaith dialogue, 3, 4, 17–18, 24, 68, 87, 92, 93, 100, 151, 152
doctrine, 51, 54, 60, 79, 116

education, 19, 23, 30, 107, 115

Egypt (Biblical), 8, 29, 37
eschatology, 4, 8, 52, 60, 109, 110–111, 122, 144, 149

forgetting, 7, 31, 33, 35, 40, 45, 68, 74, 87, 94, 96, 143
forgiveness, 9, 13, 32, 38, 40, 60, 64, 65, 78, 87, 92, 154

Greek philosophy, 12, 53
Guru Nanak, 20, 90, 95, 102

Halbwachs, Maurice, 7, 30–31, 35
Hellenism. *See* Greek philosophy
history, 21, 23, 55, 90, 108
holocaust (WWII), 9, 39–40

identity, 24, 42, 44, 57, 136–137
ijtihad, 122
Israeli-Palestinian conflict, 10, 41, 42–45, 151

Jerusalem, 22–23, 109, 110, 111–120, 123–129, 149–155
Jesus, 52, 54
John Paul II, 2
justice, 19, 52, 92, 101, 102

karma, 17, 78–80, 85–86
Kook, Rabbi Abraham Isaac, 36

language, 135
liberation, 5, 17, 20, 24, 74, 78, 95

Maimonides, Moses, 9, 38
Mandela, Nelson, 32
memorialisation, 11, 25, 51
messiah. *See* eschatology
Metz, Johann Baptist, 61–62
missionaries. *See* conversion
Moltmann, Jurgen, 62–63

nirvana , 144

Pakistan, 22, 108
Palestine, Palestinians, 23, 43, 111, 124, 126
pilgrimage, 141, 151
power, 11, 12, 22, 51, 87
Prabhjot Singh, 98–99
purification, 2, 16, 18, 20, 108

Quran, 109, 110

reconciliation, 9, 13, 16, 29, 32–33, 40, 42, 65–67, 78, 84, 122, 149
redemption, 13, 32, 35, 60–61, 62, 64
Ricoeur, Paul, 31, 32–33

ritual and prayer, 10, 14, 19, 25, 41, 44, 72, 73–74, 89–90, 91, 136, 154

Shi'ites, 120–121, 122
shoah. *See* Holocaust
sin, 13, 22, 44, 60, 64, 67
spirituality, spiritual awareness, 5, 15, 45, 94, 147, 155
suffering, pain, 63, 64–65, 79, 143, 151

Tibet, 27, 145–146
Talmud, 35, 36
Torah, Hebrew scriptures, 8, 53
tradition, 50, 54
transformation, 27, 59, 80
trauma, 1, 13, 40–41, 58–59
trust, 84, 140, 154
truth/truthfulness, 7, 21, 23, 51, 57, 74, 85, 107, 121, 122

Vedas, 71, 77
victim/victimhood, 6, 67
violence, 58, 101, 121

wisdom, 2, 9, 15, 16, 72, 76, 78, 81, 87, 101, 107, 116, 139, 153

About the Editor and Contributors

Alon Goshen-Gottstein is acknowledged as one of the world's leading figures in interreligious dialogue, specializing in bridging the theological and academic dimension with a variety of practical initiatives, especially involving world religious leadership. He is both a theoretician and activist, setting trends and precedents in the global interfaith arena. He is the founder and director of the Elijah Interfaith Institute (formerly the Elijah School for the Study of Wisdom in World Religions), and its rich website is testimony to his many and varied activities. A noted scholar of Jewish studies, he has held academic posts at Tel Aviv University and has served as director of the Center for the Study of Rabbinic Thought, Beit Morasha College, Jerusalem. Ordained a rabbi in 1977, he received his PhD from Hebrew University of Jerusalem in 1986 in the area of Rabbinic thought. From 1989 to 1999, he was a member of the Shalom Hartman Institute for Advanced Studies, Jerusalem, where he also served as director for interreligious affairs. Stanford University Press published his *The Sinner and the Amnesiac: The Rabbinic Invention of Elisha ben Abuya and Eleazar ben Arach* in 2000, and the Littman Library published his coedited volume *Jewish Theology and World Religions*. His *Beyond Idolatry—The Jewish Encounter with Hinduism* is to appear shortly. Several other collective research projects and edited volumes complement more than fifty articles, published in such scholarly journals as *Harvard Theological Review*, *Journal for the Study of Judaism*, *Journal of Literature and Theology*, *Journal of Jewish Thought and Philosophy*, *Ecumenism*, and *Studies in Interreligious Dialogue*.

* * *

Rahuldeep Singh Gill, PhD, writes and speaks about faith relations. He serves as Campus Interfaith Strategist at California Lutheran University where he is also a tenured professor in the Religion Department.

Maria Reis Habito is the international program director of the Museum of World Religions and the director of the Elijah Interfaith Institute USA. She studied Chinese language and culture at Taiwan Normal University in Taipei, and received her MA in Chinese studies, Japanese studies, and philosophy at the Ludwig-Maximilians-Universitaet in Munich. She was a research fellow at Kyoto University and completed her PhD at Ludwig-Maximilians-Universitaet. Dr. Reis Habito represents Dharma Master Hsin Tao on the steering committee.

Flora A. Keshgegian is a theologian and ordained Episcopal priest. Her book *Time for Hope* (Continuum) was awarded the 2005 Trinity Prize. She has taught at the Episcopal Theological Seminary of the Southwest in Austin, Texas, and Brown University in Providence, Rhode Island.

Anantanand Rambachan is professor of religion, philosophy, and Asian studies at Saint Olaf College, Minnesota. He received his PhD and MA degrees from the University of Leeds, in the United Kingdom and completed his undergraduate studies at the University of the West Indies, St. Augustine,Trinidad. He is the author of numerous books, chapters, and articles in scholarly journals and has been involved in the field of interreligious relations and dialogue for over twenty-five years as a Hindu participant and analyst. He has contributed to numerous consultations and discussions convened by national and international organizations concerned with interreligious issues.

Rabbi Dr. Meir Sendor received his ordination from Yeshiva University and his doctorate in medieval Jewish history from Harvard University, under the late Professor Isadore Twersky. He teaches and writes on Jewish philosophy, Kabbalah, Hasidism, the philosophy of Jewish law, Jewish history, and Jewish ethics, and is a member of the Think Tank of the Elijah Interfaith Institute.

Muhammad Suheyl Umar is the director of the Iqbal Academy Pakistan. Umar specializes in Sufism and in the intellectual history of the Indian subcontinent from Shah Waliullah to Iqbal. He is the editor of the journals *Iqbal Review*, *Al-Ma'arif*, and *Riyawat*, as well as *The Religious Other: Towards a Muslim Theology of Other Religions in a Post-Prophetic Age* (2008). Umar earned his BA and MA at Government College (Lahore), MPhil at Allama Iqbal Open University, and PhD at Punjab University in Lahore.

Michael von Brück is head of the Interfaculty Program of Religious Studies at the Ludwig Maximilians University of Munich, Germany. He studied theology, Indology, and comparative linguistics at Rostock University and Indian philosophy and religion at Madras University. He specializes in Advaita Vedânta and Mahâyâna-Buddhism. Besides, he received a four years training in Yoga at a Yoga Institute in Madras and studied Zen-Buddhism in theory and practice in Japan. After a visiting professorship at Gurukul Lutheran College in Madras 1980 until 1985, he became professor of comparative religion at the University of Regensburg in 1988. In 1991, he took over the chair of religious studies at the University of Munich.

www.ingramcontent.com/pod-product-compliance
Lightning Source LLC
Chambersburg PA
CBHW072137160426
43197CB00012B/2145